SCHOOL DEVELOPMENT SERIES
General Editors: David Hopkins and David Reynolds

TOWARDS SCHOOLING FOR THE TWENTY-FIRST CENTURY

OTHER TITLES IN THE SCHOOL DEVELOPMENT SERIES

TOWARDS SCHOOLING FOR THE TWENTY-FIRST CENTURY

Per Dalin
Val D. Rust

CASSELL

Cassell
Wellington House
125 Strand
London WC2R 0BB

215 Park Avenue South
New York
NY 10003, USA

First published 1996

British Library Cataloguing-in-Publication Data
A catalogue record for this book is available from the British Library

ISBN 0–304–33447–2 (hardback)
      0–304–33448–0 (paperback)

Typeset by Action Typesetting Ltd, Gloucester
Printed in Great Britain by Redwood Books, Trowbridge, Wiltshire

Contents

Series Editors' Foreword

It is now a truism to talk of educational change as endemic. In the past thirty years changes in education have moved from being the consideration of single, usually curriculum, innovation to a situation where schools today are the recipe for a series of often mandated external changes to which they are expected to respond. By and large the educational changes of thirty years ago were presented as a series of alternatives from which teachers and schools could select what was the most appropriate. Nowadays the luxury of choice is long gone, change is persistent, demanding and systemic.

This series, on school effectiveness and school improvement, is a child of its times. Put simply, its intellectual and practical purpose is to reflect on and make some sense of an educational system in turmoil, and to offer advice to schools on how to improve the achievement of students in times of change. Most books in the series take one or both of these purposes as their main theme. In so doing, our authors are presenting an image of schooling that, although positive and proactive in intent, is fundamentally a *reaction* to the reality of system-wide change.

In this book Per Dalin and Val Rust take a different and more radical view. Instead of responding to the current situation of systemic change, they look forward into the early decades of the twenty-first century and begin to sketch out a future vision for education. By drawing on the extensive range of both conceptual and practical examples derived from the IMEC SCHOOL YEAR 2020 project, Dalin and Rust undertake a fundamental analysis of the future purpose of education. Their scope is broad, the analysis trenchant, and they move beyond the western view of education to encompass the realities of developing systems as well.

The signal contribution of this book is that, despite the breadth of approach, the authors never fail to lose sight of the purpose of schooling – the educational development of the child. It is this commitment that gives the book its distinctive and humane flavour. It is one of the few educational books that has risen above the present and particular, that looks forward rather than back, that locates schooling within a broader societal context and, at the same time, is both analytic and visionary. As we progress towards the millennium, we hope that educational practitioners, policy-makers and researchers will meet the futuristic challenge that Dalin and Rust have given us in this timely and inspirational book.

David Hopkins
David Reynolds
October 1995

Acknowledgements

This book is largely an outgrowth of the deliberations and input of thousands of people, who have contributed both conceptual and practical examples of future education as a part of the *Schoolyear 2020* project. In 1987 IMTEC – The International Learning Cooperative initiated the *Schoolyear 2020* project, by inviting key resource persons to international meetings. The first meeting took place in Finland in 1987, where the group analysed the future relationship between the media and schools. In 1988 the Mid-Continental Regional Educational Laboratory participated with IMTEC in organizing the second international meeting in Colorado, USA, where the theme was comprehensive educational reform strategies. In 1990, the British authorities invited IMTEC to a third international conference, where the focus of attention was on education and work. Finally, in 1993, a fourth international meeting was held in Berlin, Germany and the theme was *The European Educational House*. We wish to thank those, who have been a part of these meetings and who have been a source of stimulation.

Chapter 1

Planning for the Coming Century

The year is 1894; the place, the first planning session of an international meeting with a charge: to determine the future of teacher education. The meeting takes place in Copenhagen, and the opening lecture begins as follows:

> We are confronted with an almost impossible task. There are some of us here today, who are just beginning their careers as instructors at the teacher training college, and at the end of their careers they will be teacher candidates, who will be instructing young children, who will still be active in their own chosen careers in society one century from now, in 1994. We know from past experience how fast our societies have been changing and we must assume that our societies will change just as rapidly in the coming century. It would be wonderful if we knew at least a little about the changes that will take place, so that we can prepare the new generations for the next century.

Few, in 1894, would have believed that the changes taking place in the next century would include the following:

- Then, the prevalent causes of death were tuberculosis, pneumonia and syphilis. By 1994, these diseases would have almost completely died out.
- Then, 70 per cent of the workforce was still working as farmers, 20 per cent in industry, and 10 per cent in the service sector. A century later, the last two sectors would be much larger and the number of people working on the land would have fallen to less than 5 per cent.
- At the beginning of this century, coal was the primary source of commercial energy but, in a brief thirty-year period, the primary source of energy shifted first to oil then to electricity.
- In the first half of this century, certain technological innovations – including X-rays (1897), automobiles (1900), telephones (1901), tractors (1907), radios (1922), commercial air travel (1936), penicillin (1939), and harvesting combines (1939) – would fundamentally change work and living styles.
- During this century, significant social changes would take place, including the first laws dealing with the industrial workplace, the Russian revolution (1917) and the social welfare laws of the 1920s and 1930s, culminating, in the 1950s and 1960s, with comprehensive social insurance throughout Western Europe. The most important social changes would include the growing role of women in the workplace and in leadership positions.

- This century would represent an unparalleled time of global and local conflicts and wars.

- This century would be characterized by social unrest and by mass migrations of people as refugees.

- This century would be characterized by unprecedented economic growth and industrialization (the economies of the Organisation for Economic Cooperation and Development (OECD) countries quadrupled from 1950 to 1980), which, combined with science and technology and new means of organizing the workplace, would lead to new and stressful demands on all people.

- This century would give people much free time and longer lives, resulting in leisure time and holidays previously enjoyed by only a small percentage of the world's population.

- After World War II, the youth would become a substantial and independent group with great buying power in the marketplace and a pervasive pop-culture with its own language and means of communication.

- During this century, the gap between the rich and the poor, between rich nations and poor nations, would widen. Poor nations would strive to develop themselves but most people in these countries would continue to live in unfortunate and demeaning circumstances.

- Toward the end of the century, the electronic media would begin to play an increasingly significant role in setting the agenda for social life, work life and the political process. A new, often centralized, media power would emerge that would become an important influence on the social system.

- Data technology would create new possibilities and define new relationships in social life and in the process place new competency demands on people.

- In 1894, approximately two billion people populated the earth. A century later, population growth would accelerate and more than 5.5 billion people would be on the earth.

Probably no one who participated in the 1894 seminar could have anticipated the future as it actually occurred. And, as the change process has accelerated, it has become more and more problematic to predict events and future conditions. If change is slow and moves in a clear direction, then prediction is rather simple and straightforward. But, when change accelerates, it becomes very difficult to anticipate what will occur. Some experts suggest that change has so accelerated that long-range planning is no longer possible. However, if we follow their conclusions, we would simply wait until the future was upon us, and only then react.

The great difference between today and 1894 is that then there was the general assumption that social progress would occur. There was a commitment to what some describe as an *enlightened dialectic* about the future (Adorno and Horkheimer, 1947). In contrast, Hans Küng describes the current situation so:

> The nature of rational enlightenment is the belief that reason, particularly scientific rationality, is more valid than irrationality. However, we have

discovered that not all science is dedicated to humanism. There is a growing abyss between the homogenizing world and the humanizing world. Natural science and technological boundaries, especially rationality, are no longer proving to be so completely and universally reasonable. Reasonable rationality does not appear to be so sane.

(Küng, 1990, p. 69)

One cannot read the daily news without realizing something is out of step with the assumptions of one hundred years ago, particularly with regard to the use of the world's resources:

- Every day, the world's population grows by 250,000.
- Every day, 35,000 babies and children die from hunger and malnutrition.
- Every day, several times as much money is spend on military armaments as is spent on foreign aid.
- Every day, 100 of the world's biological species die out.
- Every year, rainforests die out that would cover twice the land mass of the country of Denmark.
- Since 1950, one half of the cultivable land of the world has disappeared because of mismanagement, exploitation, or urban sprawl. The situation will become critical in the next thirty years because the cultivable land will be reduced from 0.7 acre to 0.4 acre of land per inhabitant.
- The growth in the world's food production can no longer be maintained in relation to the growth in the world's population. Even now, the resources in reserve could not sustain the world for more than six weeks.

The world cannot continue to move along the road it has taken in the recent past but stands before a fundamental choice. This choice will dictate the kind of life we will have in the future.

THE PARADIGM SHIFT

The world is presently going through a paradigm shift and there are certain consequences that follow, particularly for the educational community. Many believe the transformation process began as early as the end of World War I. For example, Hans Küng points to fundamental changes in world politics: the collapse of the European world order, the decline of the Habsburg dynasty, the Ottoman Empire, and of the Chinese Empire. These were epochal changes in the world's political relations (Küng, 1990).

The more general view is that the paradigm shift began in about the 1970s and 1980s and represents a movement from the modern to a so-called postmodern world. The *modern era*, which began around the middle of the seventeenth century with the philosopher Descartes, the natural scientist Galileo, and the introduction of secularizing laws, promised a peacefully transformed, evolving world order. That process was interrupted by National Socialism in Germany, Fascism in Italy, Communism in the Soviet Union, and militarism in Japan, and a century of war, confrontation, and repression.

3

Even at the beginning of this century, there was an active peace movement and a women's movement that offered energetic and timely criticism of civilization. The many developments of the past century formed a new foundation, and the possibility, now greater than at any previous time, to construct a qualitatively new future.

The world of today is in the middle of a dramatic transitional phase. Many institutions that contributed to stability and legitimacy appear to have lost authority. People react in different ways to the present instability. Some hold firmly to the hope that a cosmic force or greater power will rescue mankind from the anticipated catastrophe. Others remain detached in an apathetic way, believing they can simply live their lives here and now and not worry about future chaos. They have turned problems over to the next generation. Still others look at the chaos of today as necessary to a period of transition. They recognize the world is in the middle of a revolutionary process and that turbulence is a part of that process. They see dying and emergent forces at work in the world.

Each person can play a role in deciding the future. Each can help to define the story line, the myth that can guide future society. The choices made today are decisive and can contribute to a new and better world. It is unwise merely to wait for the future. Educators, particularly, must engage the institutions with which they work in framing the future, helping to define the norms and institutions of the coming era.

CONTEMPORARY PLANNING

Those who wish to participate in the future, must engage in the planning process. There must be points of departure, goals, and decisions about how to move toward those goals. In education, innovation and reform take place at a number of different levels, from the classroom to changes of the entire educational system. John Simmons (1974) and Rolland Paulston (1976) choose to reserve the term *educational reform* for changes involving normative national and broad structural changes. They reserve the term *educational innovation* for micro-level programmatic alterations in education. While the distinction drawn between the two is somewhat arbitrary, it is, nevertheless, useful to distinguish between local, institutional innovations and large-scale reform endeavours.

Conventional social planning processes, including educational planning at the level of national educational reform, encounter fundamental problems. In the educational sector of Europe, the planning process usually takes the following form:

1 Planning is based on data collected on specific educational practices and programmes of the proceeding two decades, through practical experiences, evaluation, and research, in an attempt to determine the weaknesses in the existing system.

2 An educational commission is established that sits for two or three years in order to decide what must be done in the next decade and makes recommendations.

3 These recommendations are debated in state or national parliaments and are translated into policy or laws that are also widely debated and discussed. This process takes one to three years.

4 An experimental and developmental process is usually initiated that involves planning and pilot programmes. This takes at least five years.

5 The implementation phase, intended to include most pupils in the new provisions, institutionalizes the plans. This process usually takes ten to fifteen years.

The time involved in the typical planning process varies a great deal. A national reform endeavour usually deals with problems that have been known for several years. It takes another two decades before the reform process is resolved at the state or national level. This time dimension alone presents a genuine planning dilemma. Politicians recognize that it takes considerable time to conceptualize a problem, establish policy, and implement a school reform and some politicians attempt to short-circuit the process by eliminating certain steps. While such a course of action may have a noble intention, an organization as complex and stable as the school will resist and subvert change that does not include the above steps. School people know that most ministers and ministries have a short life and a brief institutional memory, and they also distrust reforms which they have not helped to plan.

There are also many attempts to institute direct changes in the work world which have consequences on the educational processes. Such reform endeavours have proven to be subject to many methodological problems. Those in the work world often make limited and conservative projections of the consequences of their proposals, and underestimate the importance of engaging school people in the deliberation of intended reforms. As a result, they suggest changes that are unrealistic and uncharacteristic of educational institutions (Bailey, 1991).

This volume attempts to address issues related to educational reform by beginning to provide a new foundation for school development based on an interpretation of economic and social forces at work in contemporary society and by describing a tentative vision of future society. Of course, this is a very ambitious undertaking, perhaps too ambitious. It is impossible to go into great detail, here, with regard to individual problems presented. We are constrained to paint a picture with broad brush-strokes. And, almost every point brought into this discussion is subject to various interpretations and nuances. It may be argued that the arguments presented herein are misinterpretations of the best thinking that has gone into this or that aspect of the discussion. Such criticisms are to be greeted positively when they better inform discussion and dialogue. Discussion and dialogue must be the basis for orienting society in the direction that will lead to a more productive and satisfying future.

FUTURE SOCIETY

Any changes undertaken of a system as complex as the educational system must be relevant to tomorrow's world and require a sense of the kind of society we wish to have thirty to fifty years from now. If we hope to institute planned changes for the year 2020, we must begin to define those changes today. We have, at best, but a dim vision of what society will look like in thirty years. Those who experienced the oil crisis in 1973 or the collapse of socialism in 1989 know how quickly a single change can fundamentally alter how whole societies are organized and individual lives are led.

Revolutions are transforming social forces which can alter the way we understand the world and make choices in it. A revolution is what might be designated as a paradigm shift in social life. Given the multitude of deep social changes taking place today, it is almost impossible to predict exactly what the future will be. Nevertheless, changes do not just happen; people, organizations, resources, nations, can play some role in defining where humankind takes revolutionary forces. Visions of the future form the basis of any planning process. One possible vision will be outlined in this volume.

Visions do not appear in a vacuum, they reflect fundamental values and norms. And even though it is difficult to define a set of 'global standards' or norms, it is also irresponsible to avoid making tentative choices about the future.

YOUTH AND ADOLESCENTS

The life situation of children and adolescents is quickly changing. A growing number of young people no longer fit into the normal school framework and require alternative support and experiences. After leaving school, many young people are unemployed or under-employed. They are members of families that are dysfunctional and even destructive. The so-called *social capital* committed to school knowledge and available to the young, is diminishing in almost every industrialized country of the world.

The school is in increasing competition with many other institutions for the attention of the youth, particularly with the electronic media, data technology, and peer group influences, which challenge the norms and values that have hitherto defined a good life. Even though schools continue to be helpful to many students, they are increasingly on the margins for a growing number of students.

It is important to understand the changing nature of institutions that play an important role in the lives of children and adolescents. What relationship should the school maintain with these institutions? Can society rely on the relationships that existed in the 1980s and 1990s, or must endeavours be undertaken toward an alternative mobilization of these institutions?

We must better harmonize teaching, motivation, and engagement of energies so that there is a meeting between opportunity and interest.

LEARNING REQUIREMENTS

Future learning requirements must be defined in the context of the needs of youth in the next decades. Are the subject matters and competencies now considered fundamental going to be the same in the future? Can these subject matters and competencies be better learned in institutions other than the school? Can schools compete in some productive way with institutions such as the media and workplace? Should school be subject-oriented or problem-centred? To what degree should various subjects of study be dedicated to helping children and adolescents prepare for the largely ill-defined problems of the future?

Children and adolescents are presently being bombarded with impressions, isolated bits of information, and fragmented knowledge in a steady and disorienting stream. One of the main tasks of instruction may be to help to give some sense of order and meaning to the isolated and fragmentary information that bombards the young people. In order to do this, the young must learn to develop their own position, be able to argue their own views, move from mere information to true understanding. That is a difficult task.

The learning needs of children and adolescents should be defined in terms of a vision of the future. Today, most learning, for both the young as for adults, occurs outside the school. We must ask what role the school will play in helping the young to cope better with a new information-rich but conflict-filled future.

WHAT IS A GOOD SCHOOL?

What is knowledge? How does learning occur? What can the future school do to best exploit students' learning resources? These are questions that must be answered if a more meaningful school for the twenty-first century is to be defined.

In the past ten years, there has been much discussion about the kinds of factors that contribute to an *effective school*. While important, that discussion provides little help in the context of this book, mainly because the effective schools discussion too often has taken a backward look as it addresses fundamental questions about learning and education and how to prepare youth for future society. These are normative issues which define priorities in the setting of learning requirements. In setting those priorities, some vision of the future must be outlined in order to decide what kind of learning environment and experiences will most likely prepare the young for a shifting world. It is important to relate the life people will be leading to what they will do in school.

A good school is one which, itself, learns; it is a *learning school*, a living institution that changes in order to remain an institution that stimulates learning. One aim of this book is to show the place of a good school, a learning school, in the context of four perspectives:

1 a vision of future society, based on an understanding of the forces that are forming society today and will do so in the years to come;

2 an understanding of the world of the young, both today and in the future;

3 an explanation of the learning requirements of children and adolescents, who live in a complicated, information-rich and conflict-filled society; and

4 an analysis of what the school's special role is to be in the learning society we are approaching, and what is meant by a *good school*.

THEORIES OF SCHOOL DEVELOPMENT

The ongoing study of school development on the part of IMTEC has been oriented toward schools that are undergoing a change process, as well as more practical work with school development. IMTEC's studies have shown that a major factor in school development is participation in the conceptualization phase of an idea that will carry the school through the process of change. If there is no participation at the conceptual phase, an idea can be as good as it is possible to be, but it will likely not be transformed into practice. In a system as complicated as a school system, the idea will have little chance. Therefore, in order to improve schools, it is critical to have an understanding of the school as an organization, its leadership, and of school development theory. So far, most school-change programmes are undertaken with only a superficial knowledge of the process of institutional change. A Rand study of the 1970s concluded that 'implementation dominates outcomes', at least in the hundreds of federally funded school development projects in the US (Berman and MacLaughlin 1977). According to the Rand study authors, a very good and relevant idea is never implemented just because it is a good idea. And most ideas implemented rarely outlive their funded life. Most changes are adopted for the life of an experiment but fail to become a part of the core of the school's reality.

STRATEGIES OF SCHOOL DEVELOPMENT

What must happen if a school is to change its practices and actually improve itself? What must it do as an institution to become a better school in terms of future society? One strategy of school development has been to improve the competence of the individual teacher or leader. Schools have a long tradition of thinking that schools can be improved by working with individual teachers and leaders. There is evidence that individual improvement can be an effective strategy, at least in terms of classroom instruction in the subject-oriented school, though there are significant limitations. It is not yet clear if teacher-oriented programmes can be an effective strategy in schools that do not have a subject orientation or whether individual training of leaders can be an effective strategy for school improvement.

A somewhat less known strategy for school improvement, is to work with the individual school as a whole with the assumption that it can make productive improvement. This strategy builds on the assumption that the school is an organism, that its various parts hang together, that the school culture is open to change and improvement, that the school community can come to a common decision about aims and a vision of what is to be. There are ample examples that this strategy has some possibilities but it also has clear limitations.

The most typical strategy for school development is to consider the school as a system that agrees to change. System strategies are more or less carried out in every country. There is a solid foundation of research and of established practice that has emerged from the study of the strengths and weaknesses of this strategy.

In many countries, the idea is being explored, that greater freedom be granted the individual school, that the system be decentralized and community-based. This kind of change necessitates the development of quality control measures to ensure accountability. The problem is to find measures that allow different types of practice within the quality control criteria of school development.

THREE MAIN PERSPECTIVES

The main perspectives on school development discussed in this series may be summarized in the following way:

1 The *good school* of the coming century ought to be one based on a comprehensive analysis of the forces transforming society, a vision of the future society, and knowledge of the learning needs that schools can best satisfy.

2 *School development theory* ought to be based on an analysis of what characterizes different types of organization, especially schools, on what we know about leadership that contributes to school development, and what processes must be satisfied if a school's practice is to be renewed.

3 *Alternative practice*, in experimenting with the changing of the school, ought to be based on evaluations of projects of many countries.

Chapter 2

Children and Youth in Future Society

The conditions and environment in which young people grow up are changing and an understanding of this background is necessary if school development is to be appropriate to their interests and motivation for learning. Fortunately, the influence of the home, work world, of peer relationships, the church, and the media on the young have been the object of much study (Coleman, 1987; Coleman and Hoffer, 1987). In the coming years, this understanding will become even more crucial, because the role of the school must change dramatically if it is to maintain contact with the other rapidly changing social institutions that influence the young.

Schools must be able to respond to the pragmatic demands that are increasingly being placed on them. For example, new technology requires students with more education, but it is not reasonable to demand that the young receive more and more conventional schooling to prepare them for the work world, because there is less and less need for people to enter the work force. Schooling programmes must be based, in part, on projected needs of new industries and the changing requirements of the labor market. Youth must be prepared for the coming world of work through the development of appropriate knowledge, attitudes, and behaviours.

It is no longer certain what role schooling will play in the coming century. The notion of organizing a protected environment where children and youth develop educationally is a relatively new phenomenon in human history. As recently as the beginning of the twentieth century, schooling was still a privilege for those in the middle class, for those able to finance extended education of the young. Gradually, up through the 1950s and 1960s, the economies of Western societies geared themselves to the notion that all youth have the opportunity for an extended education and the state was required, by law, to finance major parts of that education (Hurrelmann, 1989).

After World War II, some Western countries moved quickly to institute a welfare state, which overcame some of the remaining difficulties youth faced in terms of education. For example, the Scandinavian countries experienced an economic development unparallelled in history, in that these countries became some of the wealthiest in the world. They chose to create a model of education that sought to combine private initiative and public control, so that the sharing of resources became the ideal. Scandinavian countries were among the first in the world to give youth the opportunity to live somewhat independently of family and church, due, in large part, to an extended schooling experience.

THE SOCIALIZATION OF CHILDREN AND YOUTH: A LOOK BACK

The responsibility for child rearing has undergone some fundamental changes in

Western society. In pre-industrial Europe, for example, child-rearing and education were mainly informal in nature. The responsibility for educating fell mainly on the shoulders of the family, though it must be understood that an organic environment existed at the time, where the household was bound together with community and church into an integral, seamless network. In the eyes of the youth, it was difficult to discern where family ceased and community began. Even so, the family and household carried the major responsibility for the youth, and the family and household were also the fundamental economic and social units. They were the focus of food production, manufacture of products and even religious life. In pre-industrial Europe, the major economic institutions were the family and guild, and apprenticeship was the major formalized mechanism for inducting the young into a special craft and occupation. In fact, at that time, the formal school was little more than a special guild dedicated to the preparation of clerics and school masters. Through the guild arrangement, the child was entrusted into the bonds of a guild master. Criteria for admission as an apprentice were generally settled on the basis of kinship, in that particular families maintained guild membership, so the guild was closely connected with the extended family and household. In other words, even occupational preparation and economic conduct were deeply embedded in family and household.

With the rise of industrial society in the nineteenth century, the socialization of children became increasingly differentiated and specialized. One major development was that various institutions lost their organic relationship with other institutions and became more autonomous and restricted. The family and household tended more and more toward narrowly defined units of husband, wife and their children, which we have come to identify as the nuclear family. While the nuclear family has remained the primary socializing unit of the very young, other institutions began to take over specific responsibilities for the youth. The school became responsible for general education, the workplace for vocational training, the church for religious training, etc. (Aries, 1975). According to the new socializing model, the family, church, school, and factory took responsibility for preparing youth for their proper sex, social class, and occupational role. In the process, education and socialization also became a public enterprise, diminishing the intimate, familial bonds of the past. The personality and skills development of youth became more and more a matter of public policy considerations. The situation stabilized over time, so that each of these institutions came to play its own specialized role in the overall socialization process.

However, in the past thirty or forty years, the system has begun to come unglued or at least somewhat off balance. This has been particularly evident with regard to schools, whose enrolments have tended to skyrocket and the length of school time has expanded until school has come to occupy enormous time in the lives of young people. In Central and Eastern Europe, for example, the socialist states did not entrust families with the important task of value formation, and systematically established formal educational and day-care institutions which were responsible for the business of child rearing from the time of birth until adulthood. The number of East German babies placed in crib-institutions rose from 9.1 per cent in 1955, to 50.8 per cent in 1975, to 68.1 per cent in 1987, while the number of children, aged 3 to 6, in kindergartens rose from 34.5 per cent in 1955, to 84.6 per cent in 1975, to 93.6 per cent in 1987 (Liegle, 1990, p. 162). Such dramatic changes might be dismissed as a peculiarity of the Soviet block, but a review of West German trends, which are akin to developments in the Western Europe, shows enrolments in kindergartens rose from 32.7 per cent in 1965 to 65.5 per cent in 1975, to 79.0 per cent in 1987 (Liegle, 1990, p. 162).

At the other end of the school spectrum, young people have been remaining in school for longer and longer periods of time. Compulsory attendance policies have moved from seven to eight to nine to ten years in most countries of Western Europe. The number of 15-year-olds in West Germany attending full-time schooling rose from 38.3 per cent in 1960 to 93.7 per cent in 1986, and the number of 19-year-olds doing the same between those years rose from 10.2 per cent to 23.2 per cent (Baethge *et al.*, 1989, p. 41). Such shifts in institutional arrangements, in concert with important economic and technological shifts, are having dramatic effects on the socialization processes of youth.

To understand how education will work in the future community, we must understand how the maturation and learning processes of children and teenagers have themselves changed. The communities of the past that engaged in optimistic development plans for education, were different than today's communities.

THE HOME AND FAMILY

The family as an institution has changed in character during the past century, with the extended family and broad household replaced by the nuclear family. What people usually have in mind when they think of the nuclear family is a husband-breadwinner, a wife-homemaker, and a number of small children living together in a separate apartment or house. This type of family became the standard, socially approved model, because its structure was well suited to the needs of an hierarchical, bureaucratic industrial society that required mobility and replaceable personnel. It also fitted well with the pervasive modern, specialization value system, that kept home-life and work-life in separate compartments.

The nuclear family of the industrial age remains the general ideal, and people tend to blame most of our social ills on the demise of that institution, claiming that the only way to correct these social ills is to restore the nuclear family. But, while people hold dearly to such an ideal, the nuclear family has already transcended itself. The home as an institution has changed character through this century, and we are just now beginning to understand certain lasting effects of that change:

- Families are smaller.

- Siblings are often closer in age.

- Parents are younger.

- Both mother and father work out of the home.

- Many homes are single-parent homes.

- Free time increases.

- Media and the consumer industry target products to different age groups.

- Adults and children spend less time together.

- Conflicts in the family are no longer solved as much by the families themselves, but increasingly by the society safety net.

The nuclear family functioned well in the industrial society. It was built on hierarchy and adapted quickly and created a private world, with its private standards and a work life that defined its own rules. However, the pervasiveness of the nuclear family has quickly declined, until it is now only one of many options in terms of lifestyles. What this means, is that the nuclear family remains today an important and viable option, but it is not the only option. It has been estimated that the standard nuclear family of breadwinner-husband, homemaker-wife and two children describes only seven per cent of contemporary American families. Even if the definition is expanded to include one or more children and a working wife, more than two-thirds of all adults do not belong to such a family and the number who do is shrinking rapidly (Toffler, 1980, pp. 211–12).

One of the major trends in the US is the so-called solo household, where a single person lives. The number of young, adult singles living alone tripled during the 1970s and continues to grow. Added to this are older adults, who are choosing the single lifestyle rather than seeking a partner. In addition, many of these singles are raising children. One child in seven in America is now being raised by a single parent. The figure in Great Britain is one child in ten. Another significant trend is that of families without children. Throughout the industrial age, it was uncommon for an adult woman to be without a child, but now almost one third of all adult, married women are childless, and great numbers of these are childless out of choice. In fact, married couples often decide that children would alter their lifestyles too much, so they choose not to have children.

Still, the family, weakened as it has been, remains central to the lives of children and youth. Other institutions could, theoretically, take over some of the family responsibilities. A growing number of families are joining together for one reason or another into a so-called poly-family. Single parents may form co-operatives so that one person, usually a mother, remains home with the children, while the others engage in a professional life outside the home (Mayeas, 1978). There is even discussion of legalizing polygamy in the US, because some women would prefer to have a wife at home taking care of the kids while they enjoy the benefits of a husband and a professional life.

Among the options emerging are homosexual marriages, contract marriages which define the length of time the couple is together, serial marriages, communes, extended family arrangements, expense sharing groups, etc. Probably the most significant generalization that could be made about the future is that no single family option will dominate. Life will be characterized by choice and variety of family arrangements.

There is a growing separation of the family from the work world and economic production, with a consequent downward movement in the labour force in terms of land use, once associated largely with the ties to the home, where the whole family was engaged in the production process. Everybody, including children, worked on the land, and the young had responsibility for specific work assignments and had clear role models. As the dynamics of the economy have shifted toward industrialization and the use of new technology, workers began to leave home to engage in gainful employment and factories and offices were separated from the home not only in geographic and economic terms, but corporate identity demanded psychological separation as well.

The industrialized economy and the current information economy created a completely new society. Home production has disappeared and the home has taken a back seat, quite cut off from economic life. Its effects have been compounded by the increasing entrance of women in the labour market, which has also taken them outside of the home. In Norway, for example, 46 per cent of the 1992 work force were women (980,000 of about 2.4 million). In that country, the modern welfare state, based on tax revenues from an improving economy, characterized the 1960s and 1970s. Not only was production moving outside of the homes, but the care of the old, the sick, and the young became increasingly assigned to society. Soon, none of the productive adults was home, and work life, ambition and desire to increase the standard of living led to a deep conflict between economic incentives and the welfare of the family. Consequently, social institutions eventually stepped into the void and began to take over some of the functions traditionally associated with the home.

In the 1980s, the economy experienced severe tests of its ability to maintain itself. Bankruptcy and a landslide of unemployment have been manifestations of the unsettled conditions. In social-welfare states, such as those in Scandinavia, particularly Sweden, the protected economy has been seriously affected in many areas by European bankruptcy. The poor economy has put increased pressure on the family unit, and the result has often been broken homes, with high personal costs and negative consequences for the social budget.

The impact on children is great. During this transition period, families appear to be somewhat dysfunctional in that they are not fulfilling their conventional role and many researchers suggest that the foundation on which today's families rest is less secure than that of earlier families. An increasing number of households with highly educated and financially secure adults remain without children (Coleman, 1987, pp. 4–5). All this is alarming, because the family and the personal relationships that exist there remain most important for the majority of children (Hurrelmann and Engel, 1989).

In large cities, the home and school are often so separated from work places that they constitute two separate worlds. The father and mother find adult friends connected with work and profession which may never intersect with the home and family. Gradually, they develop a friendship network away from the neighbourhood. Some (both young and old) have their friends in the electronic network! Thus the local environment, so important to the functioning of the family, is further weakened.

Parents spend less time with their children, and youth cultures thrive on the uncertainty of the adults. One consequence, is that the youth have taken on increasing power in the community. Even in a social welfare state such as Norway, over half of the teenagers now take jobs, even while they attend school (Bjørndal, 1988). The new economic market, relying on advertising expertise, targets the youth, who have their own resources and are able to choose what they wish in the shops and stores. The young usually have complete control over their resources, and they set their own standards for consuming. Youth with money and without adult supervision influence the music industry, a new role for youth in the community.

The Family and the Meaning of Social Capital

Studies have been conducted concerning the *home factor* in learning. These studies ask what meaning family history and the environment have in terms of the success rates of pupils in school, if the environment in which the child grows up has meaning, independent of inherited ability and construction. One important study in this area is *Public and Private Schools: The Impact of Communities*, where a number of concepts have been tested (Coleman and Hoffer, 1987).

Coleman and Hoffer claim the so-called *school contract* between home and society assigned the school certain responsibilities with regard to child care. These assignments evolved out of a mutual agreement between home and school, with positive results. Among others, the school's tasks were:

- to give students educational opportunities, through a defined curriculum, subjects, materials and qualified teachers;
- to require periodic homework, quizzes, and exams; and
- to give rewards and punishments to students, through daily reports, personal attention, grades and parent conferences.

The school tasks were taken for granted by parents, students and educational professionals. But if the school was to succeed in its tasks, the homes would have to shoulder another set of responsibilities, including:

- developing a positive environment to learn, by enforcing homework, supporting and encouraging the children in their school tasks;
- encouraging positive attitudes toward schools, to let children know work is so important, that they should be diligent in school, not give up when things are difficult, and finish what they start; and
- developing a sense of the children's self-worth, by stimulating them and supporting them in doing the things they like and enjoy.

Coleman and Hoffer were trying to understand what they call *social capital*, and about the implications of social capital for learning. In the first part of their study, they mapped out systematic differences in the achievement results in private and public schools of the US. If social policy had been effective, the differences would have been marginal with regard to grading standards and dropouts. The US has a large number of private schools of all kinds, especially at the secondary and technical school levels. It is theoretically possible to find private schools that are no different from the public schools, with the exception that private schools have pupils with parents who have a different standard of living and social status. Figure 2.1 shows the drop-out rates of different types of American high schools.

There is a difference between public school (14.3 per cent) and private school (11.9 per cent) drop-out rates, but it is not statistically significant when controlling for student background. However, a different picture emerges in terms of Catholic schools, where the drop-out rate is only 3.4 per cent. The better rate of success of Catholic schools is also confirmed by standardized tests. The findings of Coleman and Hoffer are particularly important, when the whole student spectrum is considered. They found that students from homes with distinct problems have less difficulty in the Catholic schools than in other schools. Those students somehow meet academic challenges more successfully and their performance is relatively high. Investigations were also conducted with regard to other types of private schools.

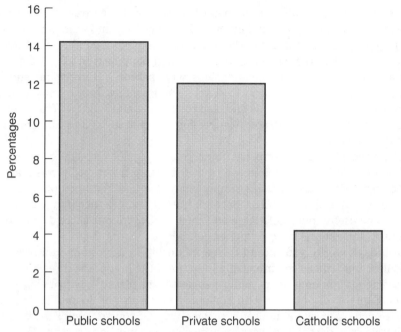

Figure 2.1 *Percentage of students dropping out of American secondary schools.*
Source: Coleman and Hoffer (1987)

The investigators found a parallel result in certain other religious schools (i.e. Jewish and Baptist schools). Corresponding results are also found in schools where the majority come from Japanese and Chinese homes.

Investigations found that these differences are, first and foremost, explained by different relationships between the school, the homes and the work environment. Especially important is the compensatory power of certain private schools for the social development of students from low-income families. The church also appears to exert a strong influence in the children's success rate.

Coleman points out that in the last twenty years in the US there has been a general 'erosion of social capital' (Coleman, 1987, p. 17). He notes that ego-centred activities, combined with less adult contact, increases the importance of the me-centred activities and reduces adult influence.

The school has problems, in large part, because the school contract no longer exists in any practical sense and there has been a decline in social capital. Consequently, if the weakest students are to be prevented from falling even further away, traditional parental responsibility related to the social development of children must be shared with other institutions in society,

THE PEER GROUP

When the family ceases to play a dominant role in their lives, children and youth begin to find role models among their peers, from the music industry, and from sports figures, etc. The result has been an increasingly horizontal society, where social development of children and youth is determined by the peer group. Social acceptance has an increased meaning in the Western culture in the last twenty years

(Allerbeck and Hoag, 1985), with dependence on parents decreasing. The youth create their own culture, based on their own ideas of what is important and acceptable.

Friendships are important to the social development of youth. Deep friendships can help people through crises, give balance and happiness in life, and serve as a necessary security in rivalry relationships with parents (Hurrelmann and Engel, 1989). Friendships require time to develop and solidify. In our unsettled times, friendships can easily be shallow and lead to mistrust and sadness. True friendships first develop when each person has freedom to choose, and is not pressed into forced dependencies.

The concept of friendship has undergone a significant shift in recent years. Bellah *et al.* (1985, p. 115) point out that friendship traditionally was made up of three components. First, friends simply enjoy one another's company. They take delight in being with each other. Second, friends assume that they will help each other and be useful in matters large and small. Third, friends share a common commitment to some moral good or higher ground.

In today's world, youth tend to see friendship in a more limited sense. Youth and adolescents usually see friendship in terms of the first of the three components; that is, friendships consist of young people taking pleasure with being with one another. Some level of the second component may also be found. That is, friends may see each other as being useful in some way. Of course, such a view can be as exploitative and destructive as it can be positive and constructive. What rarely exists in the way young people understand friendship today, is the notion that friends share a commitment to some higher good. In fact, it seems too often to be extraneous to the idea of friendship. Many feel that moral values and standards interfere with unconditional acceptance of the other and that it is necessary to eliminate any such standards if true friendship is to exist. In previous times, especially when relationships were tied closely to adults, virtues were indelibly associated with friendships, both public and private. Friends were seen as people who helped each other through hard times and tried to support the other in terms of behaviour and personal development. That appears all too often not to pertain to peer relationships of today.

One of the difficult developments in terms of peer influences appears to be gangs, particularly in urban settings. Gangs have a long history, but their number has escalated in recent years, and they have become increasingly associated with delinquency and crime. Many are highly organized and hold a tight grip on their members. A number of different types of gangs have been identified, including criminal gangs that engage in theft, extortion and burglary; gangs of violence, that provide a mechanism for young people to act out their frustrations and marginal place in society; and undercover business gangs, that engage in legitimate and illegitimate operations associated with drugs, stolen electronics equipment, betting, etc.

An alarming aspect of gangs, is their connection with schools. Gangs often use the school as a base of communication and membership recruitment. Members often have unhappy histories with school life and turn to gangs as a way to escape the press of schools or as a means of striking back at the school and the neighbourhood. Research also confirms that gang members usually come from troubled homes, where parents are probably alcoholic, out-of-work, and engage in abusive behaviour.

THE CHURCH AND THE PLURALISTIC SOCIETY

At one time, the church was one of the major institutions affecting the life of children and youth; prior to the industrial revolution and the advent of the industrial or modern age, the church was part of the tight network of institutions that formed the comprehensive and organic life of the people. The church maintained a virtual monopoly on knowledge in the Western world until the time of the industrial revolution and the advent of the industrial age. Even during the industrial age, the church continued to play a significant role, although it slowly took a back seat in terms of political importance and power, as secularizing forces were able to undermine the church's ability to dictate truth and morality. This was particularly so with regard to the role the church played in education, which became an important part of the agenda of each nation-state. In Norway, for example, the independent lay movement of the 1850s, which was religious in nature, argued that all public institutions were lifeless and overly bureaucratic. The reasoning was, the formal clergy was also part of this public school bureaucracy and the solution would be to separate the church from the state, including from the schools. The consequence of their activities, was that education moved toward a secular model (Rust, 1989, p. 74). Throughout most of Europe the detachment of the church from public schools was more direct and was related to secularizing motives of state bureaucracies, which demanded allegiance to the state rather than allegiance to God and the formal church.

The situation reached a point in many countries of Western Europe when the death of God and the church were almost taken for granted. The role of the church in the lives of people has shifted greatly to the negative:

- Most people do not attend church.
- Most of the youth do not take part in church; at the same time, a small number cultivate an individual relationship with their Christ, Buddha, etc.
- The church has lost its role in setting society's values – in concurrence with old and new ideals in an increasingly more pluralistic society.
- The church's control over people's morals is noticeably less than before.
- Sunday has become a play day rather than a day of worship.
- The busiest modern community leaves no room for meditating and reflecting over the purpose of life and questions of life and death – the primarily religious questions.

Gunleiksrud writes about the changes of the postmodern society (Gunleiksrud, 1990), and claims that traditions, values, and foundations of character existed in modern daily life in large part because of the influence of the church. This has been strongly challenged by attempts to do away with its authority and confining standards. She claims constraint and self-discipline have given way to an 'anything goes' belief system, and a 'decide-for-yourself' education. She feels the consequences for the future will be youth living in a world of chaotic standards, of changing and exchanging morals, where ethical values shift like the prices on petroleum.

At the time of the fall of the Soviet Union one of the Soviet's education chairmen, Dr Shadrikov, pointed out in the course of a conversation (Dalin, 1991b) that, with regard to knowledge in subjects such as mathematics and natural sciences,

Soviet students' minds were filled with the same material that fills the minds of students from Western countries. He was proud of this, but later added:

> Our problem is that we don't know what we should use our knowledge for. The glue (Marxism/Leninism) of our society has dried up. We no longer have something to believe in, some ideal to fight for. We have no course to follow, for our lives or for our society. A society can't exist without values. A school is meaningless without something to follow.

In spite of this negative assessment, a new perspective is beginning to emerge that suggests a religious reawakening. In the US, for example, two parallel movements took off in the late 1960s. On the one hand, fundamentalist Christians initiated an active assault on secular society, demanding that the so-called silent majority once again be heard. Evangelical churches provided the major organizational focus of this movement. Every five years the evangelical churches grow by eight per cent, while the mainline churches decline by five per cent, so that today approximately 20 per cent of the population of the US declares itself to be members of some evangelical group. This figure does not include traditionally conservative religions, such as the four million Mormons (Naisbitt and Aburdene, 1990, pp. 299–300).

In larger metropolitan areas, tiny storefront churches have emerged, which wage war on drugs, gangs, and failure. These churches are usually unconnected with any larger church and they survive by providing a sense of hope and an extended community to prostitutes, drug addicts, and an occasional working-class family. In the central city of Los Angeles, alone, 'several hundred tiny sanctuaries of God wedged into storefronts and low-rent cubbyholes' are to be found, sometimes four or five on a single block, running for mile upon mile through the blighted streets, having names such as 'I Am That I Am Church of Eternal Salvation', the 'Hosanna Community Church', or the 'Miracle Faith Apostolic House of Prayer' (Ferrell, 1993). Even though such fervour is not experienced everywhere, there are startling developments in countries such as Iran, where fundamentalism has come to dictate the nation-state. And in Central and Eastern Europe, there has been a flowering of religious revival since the collapse of socialism. In fact, evidence grows that more people in Central and Eastern Europe claim to profess a belief in God than those in many Western European countries. In Russia, for example, a recent survey found that two of every five people believe in life after death and in miracles. Since the collapse of the Soviet Union, membership in the Russian Orthodox Church has grown from 9 per cent to 29 per cent of the population (Stammer, 1993, p. B6). Everywhere in the region, private, religious schools are coming into existence and advocates are to be found, who maintain that religious instruction ought to be a core aspect of the school curriculum.

On the other hand, a general spiritual revival has been taking place outside organized churches. While membership in mainline churches declines, there appears to be a new awakening in religious faith and belief. In 1987, a Gallup poll found that 94 per cent of Americans claimed to believe in God and, in 1993, 69 per cent claimed angels exist and most think angels have special powers to act as guardians of mortal beings here on earth (Gibbs, 1993). Much of this new spiritual outlet comes in the form of so-called *new age* activities which build on non-European mystic and religious traditions, such as a belief in reincarnation, the practice of meditation and chants, reliance on crystals, aromatic oils, and spiritual gurus or people who claim to serve as channels for spiritual entities.

These developments suggest that religion continues to play a significant role in the life of the young. Up to half of the young people in America report that they participate in some kind of religious youth group, and approximately 80 per cent of the adults involved in youth-oriented religious organizations are volunteers, suggesting a continued sense of commitment and altruism (Carnegie Corporation, 1992, p. 52). God may not be dead in people's minds. Many polls show that over 85 per cent of people in Europe believe in God.

THE MEDIA – THE NEW TREND-SETTER

Another striking development is the growing importance of the role of the media as an institution. Of course, the media has always played some role, though this has taken different forms. One important finding of modernization studies conducted by social scientists in the 1950s and 1960s, was to confirm that one of the most important criteria for being modern was access to newspapers, radio, cinemas, etc. (Lerner, 1958). In fact, modernity has almost been defined as synonymous with media access (Inkles and Smith, 1974).

The mass-media has become an institution of powerful influence in the lives of children and youth. Those in modern mass-media know where and who its clients are and sell to an increasing number. The mass-media knowingly attempts to influence a wider variety of user-groups than any other institution.

Postmodern society is strongly influenced by the media – and by the music-culture society. Such a situation does not lend itself to the development of strong social qualities. The situation has become so accentuated, that the so-called *school crisis* may take a back seat to a more general *social crisis*, at least in the more developed countries. The media imposes itself on all groups, catering to base interests and attractions (Postman, 1987):

- The media has been a trend-setter and its influence has become a kind of clergy.
- The media's idols and the ideal images sometimes appear more credible than the adults in the home and neighbourhood.
- The media fills a major part of spare time spent in the home, time that once was exercised in activities related to sports, fresh air and culture.
- The media gives a wider range of information and knowledge than any other institution but, so far, its communication is jumbled; the media gives up-to-date but one-sided perspectives, and is guilty of *information overkill*.

Television is a hidden teacher, influencing young people as much as school does. By 18 years of age, the average West German youth has watched 13,000 hours of TV and has attended 12,000 hours of school (Opaschowski, 1983, p. 149). Of the hours spent watching television on the part of youth, movies and criminal films are most popular. Whereas 31.7 per cent of the waking hours of adolescents (aged 9–14) in America are spent in school, another 20.7 per cent of their time is spent watching television (Carnegie Corporation, 1992, p. 29). Through a nine-year period, Swedish students watched 6,300 hours of TV, the same amount of time spent in school. IMTEC's investigation shows that Norwegian students spend more than twice the time watching TV than doing homework.

In the more advanced countries of the world, it appears that adolescents are beginning to spend a substantial amount of time in front of the computer screen. Of course, much of this time may be engaged in useful activity, such as word processing, making graphics, etc. but it is more likely that most of the time youth are engaged with the computer is spent playing games, many of a violent and warlike nature.

The impact of the media is enormous. In a consumer-oriented society, television crams us full of needs. The 'use it and throw it away' society demands more and more sales and bargains. But, while neither standardization nor one-way communication is new and characteristic of the mass-media alone, TV and video idols exert their influence while hiding behind media techniques, and are supported by highly qualified market analysts and market executives. The priest or minister who gives a weekly one-hour sermon from the pulpit, is not really 'communicating' either! But, the priest is easier to respond to, is part of the local environment, one could meet and engage in conversation.

The young probably have a more accepting attitude toward the media than adults. Most of the media strategies are targetted at the subconscious; TV and video are ideal in that respect. But, young people are not taught to be critical about what they see on television and so take in this new teacher's suggestions and opinions and fail to use free time productively. The problem is, most viewers have no chance to adjust and come up with contradictory arguments before the programme has stimulated the subconscious. This leads to undeveloped pieces of knowledge and information, rarely allowing a chance for reflection and the development of real understanding (see Chapter 5).

The school has a dilemma. It recognizes the power of the media, but struggles to decide whether to attempt to be popular and go along with the media industry, or to challenge the media and attempt to be a 'server of the truth'. Neil Postman has identified the dilemma that hangs over the school and recognizes a global problem. The confrontation is between the *imaginary*, on the one side, and *sequential learning*, on the other side (Postman, 1987).

The media's effect is international. TV stations, such as CNN and BBC, are now located all over the world. There is scarcely a town in India where the television does not have centre stage. Western-oriented programmes project Western values, life-styles and products. Without a doubt, they have become a strong driving force, introducing the new age in these countries and, above all, forming the next generation. To an overwhelming degree, the media forms a picture of reality, one that is not very realistic, particularly in terms of economic expectations. The media, backed by the financiers of industry, goes with full strength into promising new markets (i.e. Vietnam and China) with the sole purpose of winning new market shares. This threatens not only traditions, values and culture, local life-styles and authority, but represents an ecological threat to life on our planet.

THE WORKPLACE

The role of the workplace in the lives of young people is taking on quite new forms. At one time, it was taken for granted that an adult male would devote his life to the workplace. Certain aspects of this tradition are being radically altered. For younger people in Germany, for example, who know nothing of the economic hardships of their parents following World War II, free time, rather than work, has become central to their lives. Until now, free time has been associated with vacation from work. Many young people are very active and use free time to do exciting and creative activities. Some are more concerned with their own free time than in school or work. Some are almost consumer-slaves, letting others determine what they do (Hurrelmann and Engel, 1989). This attitude about free time has developed gradually. Even as late as 1960, industriousness and accomplishment were values rated most highly in a survey among younger people; but in 1980, private thinking and feeling, enjoyment of life, fun, social contact, and self-realization were the most important values (Opaschowski, 1983, p. 30). As another example, those claiming that they were fully satisfied with work in 1967 was 64 per cent; only 39 per cent agreed in 1982 (Opaschowski, 1983, p. 31).

In spite of these attitude changes, the workplace promises to have an increasing impact on the youth of the postmodern world. The earliest signs are found in Japan and the US, where the large companies are becoming almost like autonomous societies themselves:

- Companies are increasingly aware of the importance of creating a company image that helps employees (and customers) to identify with basic company values and norms. Staff development and multiple career opportunities within the company help to develop ownership with the company culture.

- The companies consciously seek to create their own relationship with the company culture, including all of the members of the employee's family. Anything from a place in the company's kindergarten, to special rights to facilities (sport, vacation homes, etc.), to free clothing with the company's logo are examples of how modern companies also include the entire family in their culture.

- The rapid growth in living standards in the industrialized countries has been accompanied by a range of career choices, although not all are able to climb the traditional career ladder. Brooklyn Derr's work indicates a clear shift in career choices young people in developed countries are making.

(Derr, 1986)

The company attempts to fill the void many people feel in general life. People no longer look for a job, but a career. But, the number of necessary jobs in society will continue to shrink. The work world will be able to absorb fewer and fewer people. The 'Fortune 500' (1993, p. 174; 1992, p. 211) data confirm that job shedding by US corporations, that has been going on for several decades, continues in the 1990s. The number of employees in the 500 largest corporations fell by 3.4 per cent in 1992, and 1.8 per cent in 1991, and 1.2 per cent in 1990, and it is anticipated that it will continue to fall in coming decades, all while production has continued to increase dramatically. By 2010, the farming and industrial sectors will employ 5–10 per cent of all workers, though it will produce much more than today. In other words, job creation programmes represent, at best, a partial solution to unemployment.

Unemployment, because of the revolution in the workforce, is not only a difficult challenge to our democracy, but to young people's future. Postmodern sectors of economies will possess a very small blue-collar and farmer workforce. The decline of the blue-collar worker has been dramatic. In the US, for example, one third of all workers were in this category as recently as the 1970s. Today only 20 per cent of the workforce are blue-collar workers and by 2010 they will constitute a workforce as small as farmers, less than 5 per cent of the total workforce (Drucker, 1993, p. 132). If the definition of work is not changed, the situation will be catastrophic for young people and for society. The weakest among us will suffer the most. Obtaining an opportunity for employment, as it is presently defined, is a struggle in which all are engaged, and those with the weakest qualifications inevitably lose.

Unemployment is the product of a complicated economy, of technology, politics and international factors. There will probably be a period of greater trials, with hard readjustments and tragedies for people, before things get better. The world's economy is out of balance and the economic structure does not change without putting large numbers of people on unemployment. The imbalance in Europe and certainly in Eastern Europe is so serious that it is one of the deciding factors in a new Europe (see Chapter 3).

For the youth, unemployment is becoming an increasing tragedy. It is no longer possible for young adults quickly to find a job. Instead, calls are being made for young people to spend increasing periods of time in education, so they are not in the job market and are in a state of dependence for a longer period of time. For most people, this is the only alternative to give security for the future. For the weak, it often means they will not progress and so they will wander between part-time jobs, without hope for finding permanent work.

A number of other options may be available. One way to deal with unemployment might be to reduce the time people are in the workplace, so that more and more people can share in the limited worktime available. The hours of work for all age categories of people have gone down dramatically in the US since 1920. At that time, employed male workers aged 14–19 averaged 46.1 hours, and the average fell every five years until it reached 26.5 hours a week in 1977. Male workers aged 20–24 averaged 51.7 hours a week in 1920 and the average fell consistently until it reached 39.5 hours a week in 1977 (Owen, 1986, p. 13). The work week will continue to decline, at least with regard to certain types of work; however, the decline will clearly not be enough to offset the sharp decrease in necessary labour. An example about *time-sharing* is the decision within the Volkswagen firm (Germany) to reduce the workweek for all, blue- and white-collar workers, from five to four days, and at the same time reducing wages by 20 per cent. This policy was adopted to avoid a major cut-back in personnel and the company has regained its strength.

In spite of some other options, it is clear that the school is still being used as a holding institution. The school has long served the work world simply by taking large chunks of potential workers out of the employment pool. The prospects of full employment are bleak, and there is growing awareness that a major portion of workers do not even need special training. Even in the mid-1970s, German specialists were claiming that the economy would consist of 20–25 per cent unskilled workers, so an important consideration has been to keep young people out of the worker pool for as long as possible (Solmon, 1992). Within the *schooled society concept*, the young can expect to remain in school for longer and longer periods of time. This may be viable for part of the population, but the warehousing notion of schools has already contributed to alienation and violence on the part of a significant portion of youth.

In the next three decades, the time nations require major portions of the population to remain full-time in school will be dramatically reduced. School appears to remain a reasonable option for the very young, but other institutional arrangements will become necessary for growing numbers of youth. Justice will likely dictate that society will continue to ensure that every person has the right to, say, 12, 13, 14, or more years of schooling. However, a major shift will be, that it will not be necessary to obtain all of this schooling in consecutive years. After a minimum of schooling, which might be no more than eight years, young people would be allowed to engage in other kinds of activities, including travel, privately arranged personal development programmes, work, human service activity, etc. Naisbitt and Aburdene (1990, p. 244) even suggest that child labour laws are outdated. They were designed to stop exploitation of children in industrial settings, and these authors feel these laws ought to be adjusted to allow young people to participate productively, without exploitation, in postmodern societies.

Young people must have an opportunity to enter the work world at an earlier age than laws now allow, and it is unlikely that this will have a negative effect on the older labour force. Most of the activities youth participate in after they leave school will likely be unrelated to long-term jobs in which people engage.

It is becoming increasingly imperative that the notion of work will be redefined. It is possible that volunteer work and work in the home will need to be paid for. But, that will not solve the main question: How will our economy become balanced? How much should be imported and how much should be exported? There must be someone who will buy our services, not only at home, but abroad as well. This means a big readjustment of industry must be made and that is why unemployment cannot be solved by a simple handshake.

Most of us, including the youth, whose situation often seems hopeless, realize this. There are youth who do not have support from their homes or the industrial environment. They usually depend totally on social help. They are increasingly anxious and cannot find work. This has an effect on the students' motivation for learning. Without hope, many students will give up. Unemployment can be the beginning of a bad cycle, with great tragedies to follow.

The picture in Europe is rather discouraging. By way of contrast, however, the US has made quick adjustments in the 1980s and 1990s, though it continues to have unemployment problems. In Eastern Europe, the situation is near catastrophe. One serious concern, is that many with good educations are not able to use their intellectual skills. The question is again being raised: 'Does extended education pay for itself?' This question holds true even in countries such as Germany, where tens of thousands academically qualified individuals are not employed. Germans expect unemployment for the educated to reach over 500,000 by the year 2000 (*Der Spiegel*, 1993).

The situation in underdeveloped countries is even more difficult, though in some newly industrialized countries (i.e. Southeast Asia) the wheels are turning full speed. Big industrial countries, for example Japan, establish firms in those countries which are showing a steady growth. Here the cheap ticket exists; the timing is right and the price is cheap and flexible. Consequently, the young people are able to find work. But these countries also follow the Western consumer growth.

The other issue related to the workplace closely connected with the first issue of unemployment, is the capacity for relevant and fast adaptation and change. Our workplaces are undergoing dramatic changes, transformations which require a competent workforce. The problem is, that changes in the education system often take more time than changes in industries. The educational system not only needs to follow the developments in the workplace, it needs to be ahead. And that is not possible with the present planning and development process.

There are countries that have accomplished change and that keep unemployment at an acceptable level (under 5 per cent). Compare the three largest economic regions: Southeast Asia, North America and Europe. There is no doubt that in the past twenty years Southeast Asia has mastered the development process in the market place. North America has been engaged in a serious readjustment period and is now on the offensive, while Europe has similar problems. An additional challenge exists in Eastern Europe.

For the individual student, the selection process is complicated. Norway is a case in point. Increasing competition in the world market means changing the dimensions of Norway's workplace. It means the creation of totally new professions, the lay-off of many employees, extensive staff development and alternative careers for others. It is very hard to predict what careers will be in demand in the year 2020. The best advice is for young people to obtain the best education in the field that interests them most, and they must be prepared for change!

For countries such as Norway, this means mass enrolments are to occur in higher education. This is difficult for policy makers to comprehend, because there already appear to be too many students. Students usually spend their childhood on things that represent a poor investment in the future and they must begin, as adults, in preparation for a more suitable career and life. Norwegians have attempted to anticipate how to cope with such problems, and we see some promise in the so-called *Reform 94*. The school system is not prepared for the turbulence that exists in the workplace and the only clear advice that can be given is for students to obtain the best available education.

In OECD countries, training programmes in industry become more important as a change strategy, and the budgets for human resource development (HRD) are growing fast. In addition, companies are starting to play an important role in developing the school system. Such action is not entirely because of altruism. Of the approximately 40 billion dollars used each year for company training in the US, eight billion goes to teaching basic reading and writing skills (Shanker, 1987).

Today's students, in the long run, will have to undergo training as a natural part of their work situation throughout their entire career. It will be a positive opportunity for many, yet a great challenge for others. Work life will be a lot more competitive in the future than today. If contemporary societies continue to wish for a life that now exists in the Western industrial countries, they must conquer the issue of change and turbulence. This means that educational qualifications will be even more important in the future, and it also means that the weaker student has even less chance than today. This again brings up the difficulty motivating school-tired youth to do school work.

The four institutions in our society – family and the community, the church, the media, and the work place – have the most powerful influence over youth. At the same time, these institutions are themselves changing, and developing and their destiny is not at all clear. No doubt that such change is a result of comprehensive changes in the economy, technology and other forces in society. The developed world is experiencing a paradigm shift. Some people have the means and talents to make quick changes for positive learning, while others meet more problems with a passive or doubtful attitude and have fewer resources to meet changes.

In the next chapter, we will look to the future. One thing is certain: today's teachers have a different kind of student than teachers had twenty years ago. Changes have come quickly, especially in the large European cities and in North America. We are only at the beginning of a comprehensive, world-wide change process. We now turn to that future.

Chapter 3

The Paradigm Shift

In the early 1970s, a European institute made a study about the future of schools. It was produced prior to the oil crisis, an event so dramatic in its consequences that the study was subsequently considered useless. A 'future study' made in mid-1989, just before the fall of the Berlin Wall, an event of such significant and transforming consequences, would have faced similar problems.

Projects such as these certainly do not represent the first time people have tried, unsuccessfully, to look into the future. In connection with the 1893 Chicago World's Fair, 74 commentators from the American Press Association were asked: Could you look 100 years in the future? They made some of the following predictions:

- Prisons and poor houses will not exist, and divorce will not be necessary.
- Women will be able to ask a man to marry her instead of waiting for him to ask her.
- At the end of the twentieth century, taxes will be almost nothing and the entire world will be open for international trade.
- There will no longer be a need for armies.
- People will live to be 150 years old.
- In 1993, the public sector will have decreased to a small and simple system, because in reality large size works against simplicity (*US News and World Report*, 1993).

Those who are still working on futures research have learned it is dangerous to use the words 'never' and 'always'. Who would have believed, in 1945, that Europe, in a generation's time, would be working toward a unified economic organization? Or who would have believed that forty years after the bombing of Japan, that country would be a world power. Five years ago, would anyone have thought that Communism in Eastern Europe would collapse within a period of two years, resulting, in part, in major border disputes among Central and Eastern European nations. Is it possible today to think the market economy will soon be functioning with an ecological consciousness?

In 1798, Thomas Robert Malthus predicted in his famous study, *Essay on the Principles of Population*, that England would soon experience a continuous condition of famine and starvation. He had calculated a doubling of the English population every 25 years. That led to an intense debate. Optimists thought that knowledge and technology would solve the impending food crisis and pessimists thought there would be a catastrophic famine (Malthus, 1798).

Optimists did not dispute Malthus' data, but gave three reasons why famine would not occur.

- There would be great out-migration of people. Twenty million British immigrated to North America in the period 1815–1914.

- At the same time a dramatic increase in British productivity and land use occurred.

- England was at the forefront of the first industrial revolution, which increased national productivity by a factor of 14, while the population doubled four times.

In this instance, the optimists in Great Britain were correct; however, over the past 200 years, the world has gone through a string of crises where the pessimists were more correct. Since Malthus, we have learned a great deal, and technology breakthroughs have solved some of our biggest material problems. But, we did not become better at predicting the future. Take the case of Mercedes motor car manufacturers.

In 1934 Mercedes, the automotive manufacturer, conducted a study anticipating the next fifty years. Mercedes planned for a considerable increase in production, from under 2000 cars per year to 40,000 in 1984. This was evaluated to be a technical possibility even while upholding the high quality of its automobile. At the same time this forecast was rejected by many economists, 'because they doubted the school system could train 40,000 qualified drivers a year!' In 1934, it was thought that though a Mercedes would be driven by the owners themselves, the automobile was so complicated that all drivers would have to be auto mechanics. Mercedes, on the other hand, predicted that the educational system could provide for such educational and technological growth for society.

People make judgments on the basis of their own mental picture, or hypothetical assessment, of what is possible or what is desirable. This can best be illustrated by a simple, every-day example: Let us suppose Jim Williams has decided to buy a car. He wants to make an informed decision and listens to a number of arguments back and forth but finally decides on a two-year-old Volvo 460. The car is safe, nice looking and every indication is that it is reasonably reliable. Jim Williams buys the car, and in the next few weeks he begins to notice more Volvo 460s on the road than he had noticed before. The fact that many other people own this car model confirms his conviction that the Volvo 460 is a good car. He also begins to pay more attention to advertisements for Volvo. He finds that most ads comment on safety features and environmental advantages. Jim's neighbour has a Japanese car and he asks his neighbour about the safety and reliability of the Japanese car but continues to remain satisfied that his choice has been a good one. Soon Jim is an expert on the Volvo 460; he knows all the model choices and colours. He can cite the features highlighted by the manufacturer He is on the 'Volvo wave-length'. At the same time, there are many signals about problems and difficulties with the Volvo 460, but because they do not agree with Jim's mental picture of his car, he tends not to register them in his mind. He simply tends to disregard images that contradict his informed and reasoned personal opinion of his car.

Most people behave as Jim Williams does. They filter images and are selective in what they allow into their consciousness. This is particularly so for those who try to plan for the future. They become caught up with their own hypothetical projections of the present and have difficulty evaluating alternatives. Consequently, projections into the future must be tempered with great caution; though it is becoming more and more crucial that we engage in such projections.

TOWARDS A NEW HISTORICAL ERA

Europeans and North Americans are experiencing the most important period of change in this century. The collapse of the Soviet empire has contributed to a collapse of ideologies supporting that empire. These ideologies are in a state of total breakdown. At the same time, the old ethnic and national resistances existing prior to the emergence of the Soviet Union, have returned and have devastated a continent that behaved as if these animosities had been swept away. A new era is being created before our eyes; we see on daily TV a veritable revolution occurring in that region of the world.

Western Europe is also going through a quick transformation, moving towards the creation of a common inner market that is expanding until it will probably incorporate all of Western European countries and some associated countries from Central Europe. This future is difficult to see clearly, because an enduring characteristic of Europe is change. It will be exciting to see Western Europe in ten years. In that time, it is likely that the personality of its basic structure will be decided for many generations to come.

These changes are only examples of the turbulence connected with the changing of times. We find ourselves at a point in history when all the fundamental ideologies, politics, economics, structural and social traditions, are changing at the same time. We will have a new pattern. We need another blueprint to write and understand what is happening.

Today, there are indisputable signs of social disintegration and evidence that institutions are no longer as capable of performing their basic functions as in the past. We in the Western world have reached a stage in which institutions struggle to survive as much as they struggle to govern. The social forces are like an engine out of phase, working against itself, using up enormous energy while accomplishing little.

It can be predicted that the disorientations of the present will continue until the new emerging age begins to take form. Only then will we gain a new sense of continuity and stability. George B. Leonard reminds us that productive human action is always guided by a positive vision, which takes shape in the form of a myth or story. The myths of the modern age are dying but they will eventually be replaced by another 'bold positive vision of destiny appropriate to the times' (Leonard, 1974, p. 15).

When the new age begins to take shape, the meanings of the new world will be quite different from those of the old world. Information, vocabulary and institutions may be much the same, but they will be reorganized into new relations and placed in such a framework that, in the postmodern world, they will assume quite different meanings and take on quite a different Gestalt. For example, we may assume that the term family and the family as an institution will exist, but we also anticipate that, in many cultures, it will have quite a different meaning and probably a different function than it now has.

Never has it been more difficult to anticipate and predict. There is no one, who can, with any authority, predict the future. There are instances where some have tried to find a way out of the chaos, such as the Club of Rome, which entitled its findings *Limits of Growth* (Meadows, 1972); or the *Forum Zukunst* in Germany (Hesse and Zopel, 1987); or the study group in the US which published *Global 2000: A Report to the President*; or Paul Kennedy's investigative study, *Preparing for the Twenty-first Century* (Kennedy, 1993). Several major international groups have their own future study circles that are developing alternative scenarios. But, few can come up with a valid hypothetical situation about the future, because we live in a time of great change. This means, among other things, change in society's simplest institutions. We must develop the ability to be creative and adapt to increasingly rapid change. Education will play an active role in society's capacity to adjust. How can educators plan anything when it is not certain what kind of adjustments will be needed?

TO PLAN THE FUTURE SCHOOL

The dilemma for educational planners is how to develop a productive future plan without relying on outdated notions of education. Educators are hesitant to formulate goals before they know what kind of society there is going to be. Yesterday's problems shape the present school. The future school which prepares the young for the future society will have to be very different from today's school! There is one possibility: as adults and responsible citizens and in light of the fundamental challenges we know we have ahead of us, to propose the kind of society in which we want our children to grow up.

Any sound proposals must be based on a firm empirical foundation. For example, we must operate with the knowledge of the type of population growth we will experience in the next twenty years. However, any sound analysis must also have a clear normative foundation. We must have a clear vision of the world we want to create in the future.

This raises a major question. How much choice does any individual person, group, or nation have? If, as a nation, we want to maintain the consumption level we have today, or our material standard of living, do we really have such a choice? Do we have choices with regard to the use of technology? Do we have the freedom of choice with regard to the environment?

What we know is choices go together. When we take a position on a main question, then we must also accept the consequences for the smaller questions. A better school in the future depends on the choices we make right now. We have no alternative but to begin the process now.

As authors, we have gone through the long assessment period and have asked ourselves if it is possible to give a brief picture of the factors that will influence our future. The landscape of the future is broad and would require experts in many of the areas being debated, and every point of view needs further expansion and discussion. Our hope is that this book has a sound enough empirical and normative foundation that certain insights into the future can be provided. The intention of this book is to give some notion of the kinds of choices that lie ahead.

The future is, in other words, a matter of choice. It is a question of what we want, as individuals, as a group, and as a nation. Many of our assumptions are tied up in complicated politics, economics and the structural relationships on which we build our everyday life, but choices determine our future course. Nobody can absolutely predict the future. Even speculation is very tentative. We must, nevertheless, exercise our individual right and duty to form a better future.

TEN REVOLUTIONS

The word 'revolution' in this volume means a major change in the way realities are thought about and explained, in attitudes, in power relations and structures that have a major influence on the future of societies. In the world, today, many revolutions are occurring, simultaneously. Some insight into the future can be drawn from what has happened in the transformations toward the modern, industrial world on the part of Third-World cultures. Karl Deutsch, (1961, pp. 493–514) coined a phase, *social mobilization*, to describe that process. He claims that a number of specific processes are bracketed together as a culture moves from a traditional orientation to a modern orientation. And a number of social scientists confirmed such relationships as they found a high correlation between GNP, population growth, radio audiences, newspaper readers, educational levels, workforce in agriculture, urbanization, political development, etc.

Today, the world is moving from the modern, industrial era to a new era, the postmodern. The world is in the middle of a social, political, economic and intellectual revolution. Education will likely undergo a radical change in the near future. Education is the central theme of this volume, because education promises to play a significant role the world of the future. What will the educational role of the school be, in future society?

A great deal of the discussion in this volume will be familiar to the reader. It might have been advisable to have gone into greater detail with regard to most issues being discussed, but the purpose has been to outline a basic orientation, a helicopter perspective of postmodern society, to sketch primary changes in this transition period and to suggest certain aspects of the era to come.

Many readers may feel dissatisfied with the level of treatment of certain issues. If so, one of the aims of this book will have been accomplished, in that the readers will be moved to pursue these issues further, to engage in their own study of the future. The ten revolutions are outlined in this chapter:

1 *The knowledge and information revolution*
   This revolution emerges out of a new basic understanding of science, out of a large knowledge industry in numerous fields, and out of the development of an electronics and global infrastructure leading to the rapid expansion of knowledge and information.

2 *The population revolution*
   Also called a population explosion, population growth is covering the whole planet at exponential speed.

3 *The globalizing and localizing revolution*
   A new world political picture is being formed, resulting in new alliances, a globalization of trade, and major population movements accompanied by ethnic and political crises that are transforming and changing cultures.

4 *The social relationships revolution*
   Minority groups and women are taking on new roles, creating new ways of living in a multicultural and pluralistic society.

5 *The economic revolution*
Economic growth is reaching new countries at faster speed, creating new competition, development toward a global economy featuring enormous multinational companies and new goods and services.

6 *The technological revolution*
New perspectives and possibilities, as well as new products and services promise to solve an expanding array of problems and also create unanticipated problems.

7 *The ecological revolution*
A whole new meaning for life on earth and boundaries for our future development are being created.

8 *The aesthetics revolution*
A complex artistic transformation is renewing people's history and bringing artistic and creative interests back into people's lives.

9 *The political revolution*
Fundamental questions about democracy and minority rights are being raised.

10 *The values revolution*
Fundamental questions about the pluralistic society are being raised which may contribute to a set of global values.

These ten revolutions are part of a larger process of change. Other forces are at work, but these ten are fundamental and of special importance for the future of education and schooling. It must be understood that these revolutions are interlinked and constitute an integrated phenomenon. Even though they must be seen as an complex whole, it is conceptually necessary to treat them here as individual revolutions. However, it is crucial to understand that these forces function in combination and the synergy effect of various revolutions will have significant consequences that cannot be anticipated.

THE KNOWLEDGE AND INFORMATION REVOLUTION

In the early 1970s, Daniel Bell declared that the industrial era was over and that a new social order was emerging, where knowledge and information was replacing industrial commodity production as the axial principle of social organization (Bell, 1973). Bell claimed society was becoming characterized by processes in which 'telecommunications and computers are strategic for the exchange of information and knowledge'. If modern society was characterized by a focus on a more effective use of mechanical labour, then postmodern society can be characterized by increasing reliance on technical knowledge.

Bell's predictions of two decades ago have not only been exceeded but have resulted in what Charles Jencks (1987) calls an 'instantaneous, 24-hour information world'. As early as 1962, Fritz Machlup had given solid evidence that almost half the work world in the US was engaged in information production and distribution. By 1980, the estimate had grown to 60 per cent (Jencks, 1987, p. 45) and, by 1990, the figure had grown again to an astounding 75 per cent (Toffler, 1990, p. 71). This development has profound implications for the entire world.

In all areas of life, the expansion of knowledge is occurring with astonishing intensity and speed. Analysts of the workplace in Germany claim that 50 per cent of the knowledge necessary to operate new machinery is obsolete in five years time. In certain other vocations, knowledge doubles every two years (SCANS, 1992). Although it is not critical to specify exactly how rapidly the knowledge explosion is occurring, it is critical to understand what the implications are for education, training, research, and work.

Knowledge production has never been so intense and diverse as today. All countries see the importance of research and development, and large resources – public and private – are invested. The world is now at a turning point or engaged in a fundamental paradigm shift in terms of knowledge production. That shift is equivalent to a shift from the Newtonian to a quantum physics scientific order (Capra, 1983; Herbert, 1987). Major discoveries in physics, in biology, in chemistry and other sciences have implications for the development of social science fields of study, e.g. *self organization theory* (Nonaka, 1988), *chaos theory* (Briggs and Peat, 1989) and alternative medicine. Research in almost any major field is undergoing change and contributing to a basic understanding of nature and humankind.

Knowledge is one of the most important competitive factors in the future of any society. The more the physical and social world is understood, the more lasting change will be. It is uncertain whether the knowledge of humankind represents progress, but it is fruitless to try to stop the knowledge explosion. Most mature, modern nations have already decided to invest in the continued production of knowledge. Japan and Germany are examples, in that these nations invest heavily in the development of their primary resource: people. The consequence has been the development of a strong educational system, a powerful research base, and unprecedented economic growth.

Alvin Toffler, well-known analyst of the future, in an interview, said about knowledge as a competitive factor:

> Knowledge has always been closely related to power. But what I call in the *third society wave*, is knowledge directly connected to the economic system in a way we never thought possible . . . . If one has the right knowledge and information at the right time and place, that person is in a position to reduce the meaning of the length of the work day, energy, raw materials, capital, and more important, time. What is conclusive is that manual labor is being replaced by intellectual work. We are moving from manpower to brainpower.
>
> (*Aftenposten*, 1994)

In the same interview, the well-known French sociologist, Edgar Morin, said, regarding knowledge:

> . . . the knowledge of words has many meanings. The first is enlightenment. It is obvious that people who are educated, have a jump on those who are not educated. The second meaning is knowledge that can screen enlightenment. The third has to do with intelligence, consciousness, and wisdom. Intelligence is the art to put knowledge together in a relevant useful way . . . . One must understand the parts in order to understand the whole. One must also understand the whole in order to understand the parts. We

33

live in a time when all specialties receive meaning by putting them in a global relationship . . . .

(*Aftenposten*, 1994).

Knowledge has functions beyond the competitive factor. It contributes in many ways to life's choices; it provides a base for a good life, for new directions and insights, for a valuable life. It can also be used as a servant for brutality and harm. Knowledge, in itself, is neutral. It is up to individuals to decide how they will use their knowledge. Utilization of knowledge is based on a conscious or unconscious choice of values – by the individual, by groups and by society's political organizations.

Half a century ago, researchers were viewed as possessors of special knowledge, and it took decades before that knowledge came into the public domain. The present situation is quite different. Communications has come to the point that new knowledge, often in a popularized form, is almost immediately available to the public world and disseminated over the entire world. Knowledge is made visible, often because of TV, in the furthermost country town and the poorest developing nations.

Discoveries are easily thought of as magic, promising many in smaller, developing countries, that they will soon be delivered from their miserable situation. Through TV the world confronts daily the images of what is seen as the good life, creating a demand for satisfaction. The developing world has gambled on educational investments, giving an enormous share of their resources to the enterprise, with unimpressive results. There appear to be few shortcuts to knowledge. The way is long and concrete; the consequences of these investments for a country's standard of living remain unsure (Lockhead and Verspoor, 1991).

Therefore, the continuing flood of information often serves to create feelings of discouragement, envy and aggression. The good life remains all too often reserved for the few. This is often the same reaction in industrialized societies. There are those lucky few who have been admitted to the kingdom of knowledge and there are increasing numbers of adults who fall behind and become functionally illiterate (Shanker, 1987).

The knowledge and information society has the tendency to layer-down society by accentuating social classes. Knowledge increases the distance between those who succeed and the others, either those who are at the lower end of the North–South axis or at the lower level of the social strata. These divisions appear to be sharpening.

Because the brain will be increasingly more important, the transition is made from blue-collar, to white-collar workers, businesses have begun to work seriously on methods to manipulate the biological processes that can make our mental processes more effective. Medication is being developed that influences different sides of our brain, that influences our personalities. Drugs exist that promise to decrease anxiety, to increase the ability to remember and concentrate, to enhance learning ability. Prozac is one of the most commonly used such drugs. The new behavioral drugs of the 1990s promise to revolutionize treatment of many personality problems, not the least, our ability to learn (Kagen, 1994).

The ethical side of knowledge development will continue to be an important concern to all those who have access to new knowledge. The ethics of knowledge will have a natural place in the future school (see Chapter 7).

THE POPULATION REVOLUTION

Growth in the world's population is one of the most serious problems our children will face in the future. As Figure 3.1 shows, approximately one billion people lived on the earth around 1800, a total that took thousands of years to reach. During the 1800s, in just one hundred years, the population doubled. It took another 50 years to reach the third billion, and from about 1960 to today, in just thirty years, the world's population has increased by two billion. In the past ten years, another 900 million have been added, and the world's population will double by the year 2025, when there will be between 8.4 and 9.4 billion people on the earth (World Population Prospects, 1988).

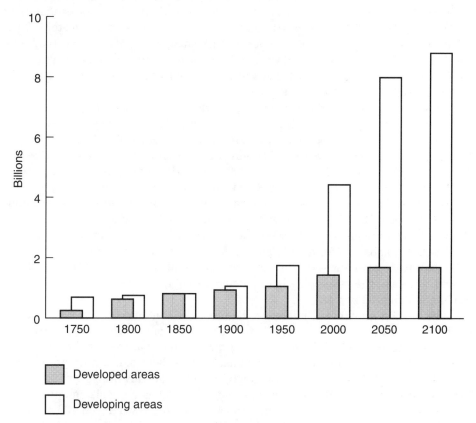

Figure 3.1 *World population increase, 1750–2100, in billions*
Source: Kennedy, 1993, p. 23

It would represent a major accomplishment to break this development, but it would be like trying to stop a supertanker. Quite a few nautical miles would be covered by that supertanker from the time the order, 'full speed toward the rear', was given and the time it finally stopped. The World Bank believes the world's population will stabilize at about 10 or 11 billion people around the year 2100 while others believe it may climb to 14 to 15 billion (Kennedy, 1993, p. 23).

While growth figures are fairly speculative, it is certain that the most growth in the population will take place in the so-called developing countries that have the fewest resources to meet the anticipated growth. In fact, approximately 95 per cent of all growth in the next three decades will occur in the developing world. Africa is an illustration of what has happened and what will happen. Its population was half the population of Europe in 1950. In 1985, these two continents had about the same population (480 million), and it is estimated that in 2025, in just thirty years, Africa's population will be three times as great as Europe's (1.58 billion compared to 512 million) (Southeimer, 1990). The main reasons population growth has accelerated are the advances in medicine and in the health system.

Some will say that population growth will begin to regulate itself and they point especially to the coming of AIDS in Africa; a variety of analysts have made major projections. The World Health Organization has recently adjusted the total estimates for those dying from AIDS from 25–30 million to 40 million, with approximately 90 per cent of these living in developing countries (Altman, 1991). The World Bank predicts the birthrate in Africa will drop to 2.75 per cent in the next hundred years, but this change in estimated growth rates will not significantly affect the prognosis for the next decades (*Economist*, 1989).

The serious part of this prognosis is that the economic situation will be almost hopeless for a major share of the world's population, who live on the hunger boundaries. It is estimated that approximately 500 million people live in such a condition and, in twenty years, this figure will rise to between 1–2 billion people. The gap between the rich, Western world and the developing nations will increase dramatically, and the tension in the world will inevitably increase.

It is not a question of just producing more food. The biotechnology revolution that has already been developed, will make it possible to produce enough food. The question is both a matter of distribution and who will and can pay for the food. Of course, it is impossible for a large part of the world's population to participation in the abundance of the world. With increased dependence on biotechnological production of food, the developing world would probably be even more dependent on the rich, industrial countries.

Population growth will influence the direction of all areas of politics and economics in the next hundred years. It will have direct and indirect influences on all people on earth. The most pessimistic interpretation is that there will be an uncontrollable hunger catastrophe, ethical and national conflicts, and large migrations (for example, from Africa to Europe). Such migrations are already bringing difficulties to the US, where the current population stands at 255 million people and projections are that, because of immigration, the population of the US will reach 400 million by 2050 (Bouvier and Grant, 1994). These population shifts promise to affect the lifestyles of those living in the first world and will contribute to a different type of dialogue between North and South.

THE GLOBALIZING AND LOCALIZING REVOLUTION

Many of the changes taking place in this revolutionary period are transnational in nature. That is, they transcend national boundaries and impact on the entire globe. While one of the primary characteristics of modernity has been its focus on the nation-state as a rather autonomous, independent entity, globalizing tendencies are beginning to overshadow the role of the nation-state and require that it take a back seat to other social, political, economic and cultural forces. These forces are moving in two directions. On the one hand, there are localizing activities that focus on ethnic and cultural identity. On the other hand, there are more global activities that dictate nation-state programmes and policies. While the international revolution is related to a full range of issues, including the business of narcotics, people's rights, hunger, communication, control of international companies, and war and peace, we shall focus here on one major internationalizing issue that, to a large degree, will influence the order of the day in the next ten years: the intermixing of ethnic and national bodies.

Western Europe and the US are moving from homogeneous to more heterogeneous societies, from societies dominated by a single ethnic group with a definite culture foundation, to societies into which many ethnic and cultural groups have immigrated. The world has always been extremely diverse. In the past, this diversity was manageable because most cultures of the world remained in isolated cells and relatively few people interacted with other cultures. This has quickly changed in the last part of this century, and there is every reason to believe that the so-called developed world will move steadily to more heterogeneous societies both in terms of permanent residents and temporary encounters between people. In 1989, 450 million passengers travelled within the US, while more than a billion passengers travelled by air somewhere in the world. By the year 2000, it is estimated that more than two billion air passengers will be served (Naisbitt and Aburdene, 1990, p. 119).

In 1987, the twelve member nations of the European Community passed the Single European Act, which aimed to formalize the creation of a Europe without internal frontiers by 31 December 1992. The four basic freedoms to be realized through the Single European Act are directly related to various forms of free movement: free movement of capital, service commodity exchange, the freedom for any inhabitants to live where they wish, and the freedom to work where they desire (Schmidt, 1992). This is not insignificant, because there are impressive indications that these agreements will result in increased jobs, accelerated economic development, more stable prices, and greater trading power outside the European Community. The Single European Act formalizes a dual globalizing and localizing process that has been under way for years. Social forces in European nations have already broken down most national barriers. A growing number of people were already moving from one nation to another, and those internal minorities were gaining a voice in public affairs that had long been suppressed. Today, more than 15 per cent of all residents of the European Community could be classified as people who do not represent the dominant group in the nation-state where they live. For example, fully one quarter of the residents of Luxembourg are not Luxembourger, 7.5 per cent of the residents of Germany are not German. Almost everyone living in Belgium professes a greater allegiance to their ethnic (Flemish or Walloon) group than to being Belgian. In addition, more than ninety different mother-tongue languages are found in Belgian schools (van Daele, 1991). National identity has, in many instances, given way to some other identity, including a European identity.

Social development in a balanced, heterogeneous society where no ethnic group has the majority, finds few models. Certain areas of the globe are moving toward an open and exciting development, especially North America, but similar developments are also beginning in most continental countries of Europe. Regionalization represents the largest social experiment in our present times, though it may soon be overshadowed by an increasing tendency towards attempts for ethnic groups and nationalities to establish enclaves of ethnic and national purity.

Throughout the modern age, the US has been thought of as a leader in diversity issues due to the heritage of many diverse groups founding that country. In the past, Americans have spoken positively about assimilation of all groups, but this has recently been challenged and even condemned. Even though the rate of legal immigration increased sharply in the 1980s, it never reached the rates of the turn of the last century. One reason for this attitude change has been the unbridled illegal entrance of aliens, mainly from Mexico and Central America. Since 1980, it has been estimated, as many as five million illegal aliens have entered the country each year. Even though more than one of three is apprehended, that still leaves several million who remain each year (Crane *et al.*, 1990, p. 10).

> Attitudes are also changing because the notion that the intense and unprecedented mixture of ethnic and religious groups in American life was soon to blend into a homogenous end product has outlived its usefulness, and also its credibility . . . . The point about the melting pot . . . is that it did not happen.
>
> (Sills and Merton, 1991).

Throughout the 1990s people of colour, white women, and immigrants will account for 85 per cent of the net population growth in the US. By the year 2010, caucasian men will account for less than 40 per cent of the total American labour force. In that time, the population is expected to grow by 42 million. Hispanics will account for 47 per cent of the growth, Blacks 22 per cent, Asians and other people of colour will make up 18 per cent. Whites will account for only 13 per cent of the growth (Johnston and Packard, 1991).

The fall of the Berlin Wall and the breakdown of communism and the economy of Eastern Europe has only exacerbated old ethnic and national opposition that has already been awakened in Europe. In an unusually short period of time, the old tensions and oppositions have been revealed to all. One of the major disintegrative forces in the Russian Republic today is the insistence of local groups that they have autonomy. Even though the USSR was formally based on a federative principle, it behaved as a centralized, unified people, with the Communist Party acting as the unifying element of power and decision-making. In the early days following the revolution of 1917, there remained some room for individual nationalities to express themselves, at least in the cultural sphere. Included in this provision was the possibility of nationality schools, with mother-tongue instruction, ethnic literary works, etc. With the rise of Stalinism, the republics and nationalities lost their sense of self-expression and self-determination. It is little wonder that with *perestroika* strong currents of nationality interests came to the fore as local groups protested against Russification and the so-called normative socialist ideals.

Significantly, the breakup of the Soviet Union has not solved the Russian Republic's ethnic problems. Even with independence, the issue of how to cope with approximately 130 ethnic groups within the Russian Republic borders remains unresolved. The educational solution being proposed by the Russian Republic Ministry of Education officials appears, on the surface, to solve the issue. This policy proposes to allow every nationality the right to self-expression and national development by defining itself and its schooling in terms of the nationalities group itself. On the face of things, this seems to be the only possible solution, but is it really a solution at all?

In its present formulation, the ethnic orientation of the Russian Republic may reinforce further fragmentation and isolation of groups. These fears may be misplaced, for it seems that ethnic tolerance in republics such as Ukraine is exemplary and progressive (Kupchan, 1994, p. M2). However, the Russian Republic ethnic policy is somewhat similar to that which existed in Yugoslavia for many years. Yugoslavia attempted to resolve its multiethnic condition by mandating a nationalities-oriented schooling programme, where preschools, primary schools, and secondary schools, if there were enough candidates, were to be provided with schooling in the native language. In 1977/78, for example, there was one secondary school in Bulgarian with 12 pupils, and three secondary schools in Ruthenian serving a total of 16 pupils (Holmes, 1983). And the country took on the obligation of preparing a full set of textbooks and materials in Ruthenian for those pupils, reflecting a full commitment to nationalities-oriented education. Recent events in Yugoslavia attest to the fact that such an educational orientation has not led to peace among the national groups. In fact, power blocks in some areas of Yugoslavia have so overwhelmed claims of harmony between groups that the order of the day has become to impose ethnic homogeneity forcefully in large areas of the country (Hyseni, 1993). In spite of this, some scholars still find, in the midst of military conflicts, certain local attempts to perpetuate the policy of equal treatment of minority groups (Domini, 1993).

In North America, a growing political movement is attempting to arrest the flow of ethnic and national minorities into the country. It is likely that Americans will experience a continuous series of ethnic, religious and national tensions. These tensions are related to enormous migrations of individuals and minority groups, that already represent one of the biggest movements of people in the history of Europe and North America.

Ethnic tensions are now replacing those of the East–West conflict which has existed in Europe since World War II and has created an inter-European identity crisis that in many ways is spreading hate toward foreigners in Central Europe. Large European cities are already multi-cultural and multi-religious. German professionals believe that in the next decade over 20 million people from Eastern Europe alone will come to Germany. This may fuel the feelings of dislike on the part of the Germans toward foreigners, even towards those who call themselves Germans. The migrations are posing such a threat that the Western European countries may establish a new wall to keep the Eastern Europeans in their place.

No single country is immune from such migrations. Even countries on the periphery of Europe, such as Norway, are being forced to liberalize their political views regarding migration politics. These countries are not yet prepared to deal with such large numbers of individuals and groups with cultural norms that deviate from their own. This is happening at a time when the internal population growth is beginning to decline. It has been estimated that the internal population in Western Europe will be reduced by about thirty million people in the next century (Jouvenel, 1988). This internal population decline will result in a reduction in the number of qualified professionals, and the necessity to rely heavily on foreign workers. There is already a great deal of tension in Europe that goes along with *Fortress Europe*, which is an attempt to create a Europe that maintains a free inner market but establishes protections against nations outside Europe. Some observers are already wondering if Europe will be able to maintain openness to the world while creating a protective climate intending to facilitate its own inner development.

All of this is occurring as the large transnational powers are disappearing. In earlier eras some cohesion was maintained, at least in Europe, by the Roman Catholic Church, royal alliances, and economic alliances, e.g. The Hansa Federation. In more recent years, the last empire to exist was the Soviet Union, and it has already disappeared. There is no new development that reflects the suppression of national and ethnic interests in favour of transnational powers. The danger today is that conflicts over resources, population, desire for land, and fundamental traditions are leading to sharp opposition without the balance of a superior political ideology.

Minority rights have a big appeal, particularly to smaller countries like Norway or the Czech Republic. The problems that confront the world today, from an uncontrollable international economy, to continuous unemployment, over-population, the environmental crisis and unchecked technological development, could more easily be solved by working together internationally. It is easy to state that co-operation is necessary, but it will not be possible without giving up a certain degree of sovereignty, both ethnic and national. Therefore, internationalism must be engaged in, while ensuring ethnic and religious minorities that their culture, language, and religious independence will be tolerated within the context of a binding international and regional frame.

Every European nation makes seemingly valid claims for its sovereignty: Norwegians wish to preserve their fragile fishing claims; the French wish to preserve their agricultural traditions; the Germans want their German Mark to remain strong. The way forward toward a unified European vision is still difficult and will take many more years to realize, but it is likely that a politically and economically united Europe will emerge.

The consequences are that Europeans will be forced to accept the challenge to live and work together with people from other cultures. Because the economy will be integrated to such a large degree, some foreign languages will be spoken throughout the region, even in smaller countries such as Denmark. Knowledge about other cultures and languages will be even more important than before. Above all, the tempo of change will be greater, the readjustments quicker, and the demands for the simple ability to think more openly will increase.

THE SOCIAL RELATIONSHIPS REVOLUTION

Today, there are an increasing number of different kinds of physical and psychological living arrangements. Definitions of family and home are expanding. The role of youth, especially with regard to its relationship to the adult generation, is changing; the role of the elderly in society is changing, as well. In the past two decades, fundamental questions about human relationships have been asked that were rarely questioned in the past.

Attitudes about social relationships are in large degree influenced by basic values and established wants. With the continuing influence of the internationalizing

movement, the media industry and the dawning of the multi-cultural society, fundamental questions are being raised concerning the types of social relationships that
should prevail in Western societies. It is far from certain that appropriate changes
will occur. Certain societies may become entrenched and reactionary in terms of
social relationships. What is certain is that cultures and social relationships are
everywhere being challenged.

Gender Issues

Few institutions in a society change as slowly as social relationships. Long-estab-
lished norms and feelings often create barriers against change. Nevertheless, few
relationships are undergoing more fundamental revision than that between men and
women, and in this section we shall concentrate on gender issues. The definition of
what is socially acceptable for a woman has often shifted for simple pragmatic reasons, because of the need to tap into reserve women resources in building up an
economy. The women's movement has now reached a turning point. After decades
of slow and frustrating progress, the movement has reached a critical mass, redefin-
ing relationships between men and women.

There is movement from a male-dominated society toward a society where
women's roles and new relationships between the sexes are now acceptable.
Women have finally become an accepted part of the political process. In 1991, Edith
Cresson became the first woman prime minister of France. Gro Harlem Brundtland
has been the prime minister of Norway for three terms and eight of her 18 cabinet
members are women. In 1991, 40 per cent of the seats in the Finnish parliament and
38 per cent of the seats in the Swedish parliament were held by women (Aburdene
and Naisbitt, 1992). In 1994, the two senators of the largest state in the US,
California, were women, and Kathleen Brown was the Democratic Party candidate
for governor. Of course, there are earlier examples as well, like Margaret Thatcher,
Golda Meir and Indira Ghandi. Even though the top echelon of major industrial firms
in America remains in the hands of men, half of the second-tier managerial group are
now women. By the end of this century, many of these women will begin to move
into the top echelon. Regina Herzlinger, of Harvard Business School, predicts that
by 2010 a large number of the CEOs of the Fortune 500 in America will be women.
Already more than 6.5 million women are at the top of small- to medium-sized businesses, many of which will become top companies in the near future. In 1992, the
number of people employed by women-owned businesses surpassed the number of
people employed by the Fortune 500.

Even such traditional bastions of male domination as religious organizations
have been challenged, including what many feel is a male interpretation of the
Bible. Since 1992, the Church of England has ordained women to its priesthood.
Women now serve as rabbis and cantors of Jewish synagogues and, according to
Rabbi Ellen Dreyfus, the 'ritual, theology, language and imagery' of Judaism is
undergoing transformation to reflect women's perspectives (quoted in Aburdene
and Naisbitt, 1992, p. 120).

Growing numbers of women are raising serious questions about the 'origins,
problematics, social meanings, agendas and theories of scientific knowledge-seek-
ing' (Harding, 1991, p. vii). Women are increasingly invading what was once
considered a bastion of masculinity: the sports world, not only as athletes but as

41

coaches, managers, recruiters and owners of professional sports teams.

The emancipation of women is occurring on a broken front. It is perhaps most evident in regions such as Scandinavia, and the schools should be given great credit in making possible the growing sense of equity between males and females. The situation has come to the point in the developed world that more girls than boys now complete compulsory schooling and upper secondary education. In the four years from 1936 to 1940, in Norway, 924 female secondary school certificates were awarded, compared with 1812 male certificates. This amounted to approximately 5 per cent (female) and 10 per cent (male) of an age cohort (SSB 1978). The educational growth in Norway since World War II has been enormous. In 1992, essentially all of the 200,000 students took some type of secondary school leaving examination, including 92,000 female students. Of the 24,000 secondary students taking the examination in the general track, which has traditionally led to university study, 13,000 were female (54 per cent). This is but one example of a quick change in society, which was never fully planned. It is an instance where a natural change has taken on significance greater than any planned and designed change. New knowledge and new lifestyles break the frame for what is socially acceptable. Over the last 10–15 years relationships and lifestyles have come to constitute one of the most important stimuli to further development of society.

THE ECONOMIC REVOLUTION

Two aspects of the economy will be discussed in this section. First, the base of the economy has shifted, from agriculture, to industry, to service; and second, from national to global.

Table 3.1. The Labour Force in OECD countries in the year 1900, 1940, 1990 (for Norway) and 2010

	1900 (OECD)	1940 (OECD)	1990 (Norway)	2010
Land Use	70%	30%	5%	4%
Manufacturing	20%	50%	25%	5%
Service	10%	20%	70%	

Sources: OECD (1989); Drucker (1993), p. 132

A Service-Based Economy

Table 3.1 shows the workforce profiles of the OECD countries in the years 1900, 1940 and 1990 (total for Norway). The shocking aspect of the economy is the rapid decline of the labour force in agriculture, followed by a decline just as sharply in the labour force of manufacturing. According to Peter Drucker (1993, p. 132), there is no parallel in history to the abrupt decline of the blue-collar worker in the past two decades, when the labour force in that sector has been cut in half. In fact, by 2010 the labour force in manufacturing will be no larger that the current labour force in agriculture. This has enormous implications for the work world. Technology has helped us reach a point in which agriculture and manufacturing will not require more than 10 per cent of the labour force. The one sector that has grown dramatically has been the service sector.

Whereas technology and innovation have reduced the need for farmers and industrial workers, even while farming and industrial productivity have increased, that has not been the case with regard to knowledge and service workers. In fact, the service sector has experienced dramatic increases in workplaces, especially in areas like education, research, media, healthcare and the hotel industry. What is interesting, is that innovations and new technology have so far not reduced the number of people required by the service sector (Drucker, 1993).

Even as the service sector has become more proficient, it appears to require more and more workers to maintain productivity. For example, as today's hospitals have invested growing sums of money in new, more efficient facilities and equipment, these investments have brought with them the need for expensive knowledge workers and growing numbers of service workers to administer and care for the facilities. And, while it was assumed that the computer and other office technology would have a dramatic negative effect on the number of clerical workers, even as dataprocessing machinery has become a common part of any office, the number of knowledge and service workers in those offices has increased dramatically. As Drucker points out, we have discovered that 'capital cannot be substituted for labour (i.e. for people) in knowledge and service work' (1993, pp. 95–6).

Additional aspects of the service sector will undoubtedly grow. The *human service sector*, which focuses on compassionate work, is a case in point. In the US, the human service sector provides part-time and full-time employment for many people, but public agencies are increasingly no longer able to give the kind of service that is wanted. Public institutions are often unable to issue pay-cheques on the date due, city governments are unable to sweep the streets, and law enforcement agencies are unable to ensure safety for citizens. An extensive need for many public servants is recognized. Up till now, the public service sector has often been a point of entry to the work world for many unemployed (not to mention the youth). Some of these public servants are paid by the public, often through unemployment contracts, but other public servants are paid by the industrial sector or by beneficiaries of the services.

In spite of the unique role the service sector is coming to play in the work world, it cannot absorb all of those wishing to engage in conventional work. Certain other means must be found to deal with unemployment. One solution would be to continue reducing the workweek, a process that has been ongoing since the 1920s. In the USA, in 1920, the workweek was 51.7 hours for the age group 20–24. It fell to 39.5 hours by 1977 (Owen, 1986). Many large businesses are now evaluating a four-day workweek, which is already a reality for Volkswagon employees.

Another way to find additional work places would be to create new spheres of work. One growing occupation is that of artists who provide a personal touch to manufactured products. Information technology is used in production and it can tailor products to the customer's needs. And, even though a automobile factory can produce 25 million different versions of a car, the consumer wants personal attention and is not satisfied with mechanical, technological solutions to these personal needs.

Unemployment among the Educated

Never have the OECD countries had so many students, and never have their future possibilities been more uncertain. In Germany, 1,800,000 students fill auditoriums which have a capacity of 900,000! An uncertain future awaits these students. For the many thousands of German students that are now beginning long years of university study, often on large student loans, the situation will become desperate. Typically, students in Germany apply for 200 to 800 jobs before they are offered an interview. In the year 2000, there probably will be between 600,000 and 800,000 more students flooding into German institutions of higher learning than are available workplaces. The disparity will continue to grow, into the next century.

In recent years, large companies have almost stopped recruiting new university graduates in favour of those with technical skills, or they have dramatically decreased recruiting; so, even though unemployment among the educated is lower than for other groups, the situation is beginning to reach the critical stage. In 1994, Daimler-Benz reduced its workforce by 44,000 jobs. Siemens normally recruited 8500 engineers and scientists, per year. In 1994, the number was 1500. In the chemical industry, many thousands of well-educated chemists are looking for a job.

This situation has serious implications for the rest of Europe, because Germany is the locomotive in the European market. The downturn comes at the time the two Germanys are being united, a process that has sharply increased the number of unemployed, including the highly educated, such as doctors, scientists, biologists, mechanical engineers, electrical engineers and teachers. It is projected that over half of today's medical students, will not be able to find work as a doctor in Germany, because positions will not be available. In Germany, as in other industrialized countries, a downturn in production shows up in tax revenues, leading to dramatic cuts in the funding of public administration. There is serious discussion about reducing the academic school track leading to a secondary school leaving-certificate, from 13 to 12 years. This would put 15,000 teachers on the streets and bring a reduction of 8–12 per cent in public expenses.

Germans are experiencing a dramatic mismatch between supply and demand for an educated workforce. One possibility is that universities and high schools have been in a world of their own producing students for which the market has no need. Those in German industry have long complained about the one-sided, theoretical education the young receive. One study showed that 84 per cent of those who hire academics complain that students lack practical experience and are too theoretical in orientation. People in the work world argue that the students are too often out after their own career and think little about the firm where they will work and even less about working together with others. Apparently, the higher educational system educates people with attitudes and qualifications that the work world neither wants nor needs. According to a well-known scientific theoretician, Professor Jürgen Mittelstraß: 'The university's courses, to a large degree, are created in the professor's minds without necessary contact with the world outside the universities' (*Der Spiegel*, 1993). Another explanation is that the job market is changing so rapidly, and the future market is so uncertain, that inevitably there will be a mismatch between the education process and production demands.

Ecologist Ernst Ulrich Von Weizsacher, at the Wuppertal Institute for Climate Research, a well-known activist working for an alternative work market, says that the end of industrial society is approaching faster than anyone could have predicted. Germany is forced to change its production system for two reasons:

1 The earth can no longer sustain continuing industrial growth. The inhabitants of the industrialized world must reduce consumption, because billions of people are demanding the same rights to the good life that Germans enjoy.

2 Highly qualified people in Eastern Europe and developing countries are quickly replacing expensive manpower in Germany.

Von Weizsacher's formula is to shift the taxation scheme from a tax on work to a tax on energy, which will make work cheaper and slow down the speed of de-industrialization. At the same time higher taxes on energy will stimulate the development of new technology. He foresees a strong tendency toward highly qualified persons not finding permanent employment, but establishing themselves as self-employed, and moving from salaried work, to their own work, to volunteer work in industry and in the larger society.

Uncertainty in the future work market has often led to the following counsel: 'Stay in the educational track as long as possible. Then your job opportunities will be greatest'. But, that counsel is not always sound. Germany has a big shortage of manual workers, and this need will climb in the next fifteen years. So, those in academics would do better in the crafts and technical fields. However, in all fields, a certain type of education remains highly valued. Those who are motivated, show initiative, co-operate and have practical experience have a decided edge in the competition for work places.

The Global Economy

Most people notice internationalization in their everyday lives simply by the goods and services they consume. In the past twenty years, businesses have been changing; restaurants have become more varied and shopping is more international. Tacos are no longer found only in Mexico, sushi is not only in Japan, Canadian crab is found everywhere and Norwegian raw salmon is eaten in some delis in Japan. More than 10,500 McDonald's fast-food restaurants are found in fifty countries. Ford Escort is sold in fifteen countries. Over 40 per cent of Japan's tape-recording industry was distributed to newly industrializing countries of Southeast Asia in a two-year period (1985–87). The brand names of Coca Cola, Sony, IBM, Volkswagen, Volvo and Nestlè are known by almost all consumers, in every country where the inhabitants have purchasing power.

The economy has become globalized. International interdependence already exists and it will become even more intertwined in the near future. Only ten years ago, most business people came in contact with what might be described as national businesses, but since then large numbers of businesses have become, at least in part, international. During the entire modern, industrial age, economic structures were centred around nation-states that behaved as if they were autonomous, self-sufficient entities. In recent years, that has all changed. Through the development of multinational companies, the free flow of information and the breakdown of trade barriers, the world is rapidly moving toward an interdependent, free trade system.

The economy of the world is now driven by some six hundred mega-firms which account for more than 20 per cent of the world's agricultural and industrial production. This development is so significant that Toffler suggests the term 'multinational' may be outdated, because these firms are more nearly non-national or transnational. Even Japanese firms are not immune to these developments: Ford owns 25 per cent of Mazda; Honda cars are increasingly built in the US and shipped to Japan; General Motors is the largest stockholder of Isuzu (Toffler, 1990, pp. 460–1).

The largest multinational companies have contributed to economic growth over the entire world. And they have also contributed to a process of considerable technological and expertise transfer throughout the world.

Parallel with the development of big multinational industries is the development of an enormous, international electronic finance market that operates 24 hours a day and that exchanges over one trillion dollars a day. This amount is much more than is necessary for daily import/export exchange. Some observers feel that 90 per cent of this business does not have any direct relationship with international trade, but is pure speculation in currency and paper money (Bergsten, 1988). In other words, a world economy exists that, in large degree, is driven by private economic interests. Above all, the large multinational companies have resources to utilize the most modern technology when it is appropriate, and they participate actively with smaller, nationally run companies. In fact, commercial and industrial structures will probably become so globally integrated that larger national firms will soon be consumed by international enterprises.

It is important to stress that international companies will impose their values on local environments. An executive of Coca Cola said: 'We don't sell a drink, we sell a way of life.' However, these firms increasingly maintain small, local subsidiaries, that have close contact with the customers, are attuned to the local culture and have a closer eye on the competition. This advantage gives them considerable leverage with head offices. A large multinational company is dependent on the fact that all the different national companies pull together. It becomes increasingly more difficult to dictate to the smaller, local firms.

The world is quickly becoming an open market. Of course, there are regional and national alliances, but these appear to be but transitional arrangements on a course toward a world dedicated to interdependence and free trade. The establishment of the European Community and the Single European Act symbolizes activities taking place everywhere. The Single European Act deals with four basic provisions:

1 free movement of capital,
2 service commodity exchange,
3 the freedom for people to live where they wish, and
4 the freedom to work where they desire.

In Europe, there is active discussion concerning the quality and competence level of workers in different parts the region, the need for a more uniform recognition of worker qualifications, the necessity of establishing a basic set of educational standards, especially for those moving from one country to another. Curricular, textbook and instructional modifications are being made. There is even a growing awareness of some greater integrative forces in the notion of a 'United States of Europe', which implies some level of commitment to a united sense of purpose, a certain patriotic feeling, an emotional and mental identification with being European (Budd and Jones, 1990).

Similar developments are taking place elsewhere. Trade agreements between Australia and New Zealand, in 1988, and between Brazil and Argentina are indicative of this movement. One of the major issues in the Pacific Rim region has to do with free trade, and there is, at present, a lively discussion focusing on the so-called North American Free Trade Agreement (NAFTA), which gained approval of the US House of Representatives in 1993 and involves Canada, the US, and Mexico. Discussions continue with regard to trade agreements with countries in the entire Pacific region (Brown *et al.*, 1992).

This process is the culmination of a dramatic growth in the economy and standard of living. Following World War II, the stability and certain economic growth was so self-evident, that few questioned if there would again be hindrances to economic development. The world's economy grew more after World War II than through the entire history of the world up until that time. From 1950 to 1980, the world's GNP quadrupled, from two to nine trillion dollars!

The global economic growth has contributed to economic turbulence rarely experienced before by certain national economies. The first oil crisis in 1973, when the price of oil quadrupled in only a few days, brought to consciousness a new phenomenon. Some highly developed countries, such as Norway, were thrown into a period of turbulent reassessment of their ability to dictate their own situation. They were forced to institute so-called car-free days where the streets were empty for one day a week. The Norwegians, and the entire developed world, entered into a new, turbulent period of time. Oil and gas nations experienced an enormous surge in development but, at the same time, their good fortune contributed to a stagnating economy in many developed countries.

The oil crisis has not been the only factor to contribute to turbulence. In September 1992, the Finnish Mark collapsed, mainly because approximately 20 per cent of Finnish exports had gone to the Soviet Union. When the Soviet Union collapsed, the economy of Finland also experienced near collapse and the Finnish Mark was immediately devalued by 13 per cent. The Swedish Crown faded away in the same period, and it required foreign capital intervention to help it survive. Interest on loans increased from 16 per cent to 24 per cent. During this period, the Norwegian currency remained relatively stable, because of the surplus in its balance of trade (mainly because of its oil and gas reserves), but even in Norway the value of the Crown declined, in large part because the European markets are so dependent on each other, that shifts in one country affect the markets of other economies (Udgaard, 1992).

In that period, the interest rate of the German Bundesbank was at a record high of 9.75 per cent, mostly to offset an inflation rate of 4 per cent. The Germans blamed this inflation on the unification of the two Germanys.

The power international speculators have on the world's economy is real and will characterize conditions into the postmodern era. Some specialists predict that the business world will gradually stop talking about national trade deficits and surpluses. Those are concepts for a period when economies were national in character. Naisbitt and Aburdene (1990, p. 4) point out that no one knows what the imbalance of trade is between Frankfurt and Düsseldorf, or between Denver and Dallas. In time, experts will stop asking what the imbalance is between the US and Japan. The question will be almost irrelevant in a global economy characterized by mega-corporations and free trade. Rather, the more important questions will relate to the ability of cultures to respond to accelerating economic requirements and demands.

Toffler (1990) suggests the emerging economic order is obliterating modernist categories of rich and poor, North and South, and has thrust the world into a division of what Toffler calls the fast and the slow, where advanced technology, particularly electronics, speeds production and distribution time, to the point that speed has become the most important element of our postmodern condition. In contrast, those societies which remain in the heavy production and traditional phase of development move at a glacial pace. This already manifests itself in the uneven sharing of the wealth of the world. The richest countries have GNPs that now provide each person with between $30,000 and $40,000 a year, while those in the poor countries of Africa earn about $200 a year and those in India about $350 a year (Kennedy, 1993).

While the developed countries stand before an economic restructuring process of gigantic dimensions, they must face the fact that they are a part of a world-wide community. Today, OECD countries have 17 per cent of the world's population and 70 per cent of its industrial production. It is projected that, in the year 2030, Asia will have 50 per cent of the global production. Asia is becoming, to a growing degree, the world's economic centre of gravity. This situation will require major readjustments on the part of Europe and North America. There are already a number of attempts to deregulate trade, lower pay standards, create more flexibility and a smaller public sector, and reduce social benefits. The challenge from both Asia and Eastern Europe requires quick and determined leaders. Thorbjørn Berntsen points out the following:

> In 1960 the richest 20 per cent of the world's population received 70 per cent of the global income. By 1989, the richest share had climbed to 83 per cent. The poorest 20 per cent of the population had, in the same period, experienced a decline in their share of income from barely 2.3 per cent to an unbelievable 1.4 per cent. The relationship between the richest and poorest fifth of the population had shifted from 30:1 in 1960 to 59:1 in 1989.
>
> (Berntsen, 1994)

The Organization of Work

The workplace of the future will most likely be organized in ways quite different than workplaces of the past. Work areas will be tailored to individual tastes and needs. Networks of flexible, simple organizations will dominate. Work will be closer to the worker's living quarters and to the customers. The authority structure may be radically different. Routine jobs will increasingly be taken over by automatic processes, and the competitive edge may be: understanding and helpfulness, relations, mankind development, and other so-called added-value services (Drucker, 1989).

Many industries are already engaged in dramatic readjustments, including the steel and automobile industries. The newer jobs promise to demand more education. More than half the jobs in the US already require a high-school or university education (Johnston and Packard, 1987, p. 98).

Much is happening with regard to job security. Since the 1970s, more independent, industry-driven, and self-regulated positions have been created, where people choose their own working time and working rhythm (Christensen, 1989;

Perelman, 1990). The well-educated parts of the population are more and more engaged in this sort of process, because of the electronic workplace, often in the home, while an underclass of uneducated workers is being forced to take any kind of job to be found.

The differences in work advantages are being accentuated. This is most evident today, in the difference in living standards between North and South, and East and West. Some of the basic reasons for this are the Western advantages in new technology and the integrated Western global economy. However, even within highly developed countries there are great differences. Norway provides a good case in point.

Norway must compete with cheaper manpower from the former Soviet Union and East Europe. Because of this growing threat, many Norwegians argue for protectionism. It may be possible for Norwegians to buy a little time because the economy is now supported so heavily by oil and gas but, eventually, the country will have to go through a structural transformation that will reorganize the entire economy. Norway currently has an exceptional position in the Western world because of its gas and oil reserves. In 1992, the export of oil provided Norway with 102 billion Crowns, which amounts to over 30 per cent of that country's total exports. The oil industry in Norway is nearing its maximum potential and it is estimated that this maximum production will continue for another decade before it begins to decline. Gas will soon overtake oil as the primary resource. It is anticipated that gas production will last for approximately eighty years, but it is unlikely that gas production can compensate for the decline in oil production. Norway will, because of its oil and gas reserves, be able to maintain a healthy standard of living for many years. At present, it has one of the highest standards of living in the world. That condition ought to continue for the next two decades. When the oil boom concludes in about 2020, Norwegians must ask themselves if they have taken advantage of this temporary abundance. Have they engaged in a process of economic development that will allow them to retain their station in the world? They must think more seriously of themselves as 'Norway without oil', so that they can use current resources to build a foundation for quite a different economy.

This is the case with many countries of the world. Of course, oil and gas will continue to be a considerable power factor far into the next century. With new technology, it may be possible that engineers will find additional oil and gas reserves. The reserves of Azerbaijan will finally begin to be fully exploited, and other reserves will likely be found elsewhere, as well. The use and the price of oil and gas increasingly depend on ecological factors and what happens with the growth and consumption in the newly industrialized countries in Asia. The further economic development of China, with its population of 1.2 billion people, will play an increasingly important role in the world.

THE TECHNOLOGICAL REVOLUTION

This century has witnessed many technological breakthroughs, the most recent of which are in biotechnology and telecommunications. These developments will continue at an increasing rate. But, technology has so often been regarded as the answer to current and future problems, that the real question has been forgotten. We shall look at some aspects of technology development that, in years to come, will likely be significant.

Economic development is closely tied to technological developments, which are related to an explosion in knowledge. There is no easy way from education to experimentation, or from experimentation to technology, or from technology to economic development. Many have the opinion that these relationships are unique and linear, but this is probably not the case. There are many examples of countries that have exploited other countries' investigations to their own advantage and in the process they have considerably increased their standard of living (SCANS, 1992; NCEE, 1990). There are other examples of countries, such as the former Soviet Union, with an enormous knowledge industry, which was neither able nor willing to market to the rest of the world.

Technology and the Environment

The history of technology can be an exciting vocation in creativity, embracing all people and activities, and with great meaning in different eras in the history of mankind. Technology has also increased the scope of war and destruction to a much larger degree than would have been possible without breakthroughs in technology. And economic and technological development have begun to threaten the capacity of the world to renew itself. On a typical day, humans destroy 115 square miles of tropical rain forest, create 72 square miles of desert, eliminate up to 100 species, erode 71 million tons of topsoil, and increase the population by 263,000 (Orr, 1992, p. 3). McCune et al., at the Midcontinent Regional Educational Laboratory in Colorado (1988, p. 8), claim the 'deforestation of our planet, the greenhouse effect, the loss of world topsoil essential for farming, air pollution and other environmental concerns raised by human activities have begun to threaten the basic habitability of the earth itself'. They argue that it must become a priority of all nations to educate policy makers and the general public to understand the environmental changes taking place.

In 1990, the California Superintendent of Public Instruction became so alarmed at the deteriorating environment that he sent a letter to every school and school district in the state appealing to them to dedicate themselves to the development of continuing and comprehensive programmes of environmental education (copy of letter in Clendon, 1993). The Vice-President of the US, Al Gore, claims the world ecosystem has reached such a state of crisis that human civilization must begin a global Marshall Plan. The strategic goals of the plan are (Gore, 1993, pp. 305–60):

1. the stabilization of the world population;

2. the rapid creation and development of environmentally appropriate technologies;

3. a change of the economic rules of the game by which we measure the impact of our decisions on the environment;

4. the negotiation and approval of a new generation of international agreements that would ensure global participation and adherence to positive action regarding the environment; and

5. the establishment of a co-operative plan for educating the world's citizens about our global environment.

The most critical of these goals for educators would be his plea that the world establish a plan for educating the world's citizens about the environment. Such a plan, of course, would only be possible and useful if the other four steps were at least partially adopted.

Land Use and Biotechnology

The growth of biotechnology will be used to illustrate what modern technology can contribute to economic, political and social activities and to the workplace, both in the northern and southern hemispheres. Between 1950 and 1984 the world's food production grew by a factor of 2.6, faster than the need for food. A close association between nations and international business centres, land-use opportunities, agricultural researchers and farmers led to what is known as the 'green revolution'. Annual rice production shot from 257 million tons to 468 million tons in twenty years, and is probably the single most important preventive of famine in many countries. Because of the green revolution, many developing countries are now less dependent on the rich countries and have been able to develop greater political stability (Johnstone, 1988).

The green revolution may have reached its limits. In the last decade population growth and its attendant demands for food have begun to exceed the ability of agricultural producers (World Resources, 1990–91). The growing population requires about 28 million more tons of wheat each year, while growth capacity of agriculture is only about 15 million tons. One of the major complications is the serious loss of cultivated soil. According to FAO, in the past twenty years, an area equivalent to three times the size of France has lost its worth as farmland. In the past hundred years, an area as large as all of Europe lost most of its productivity by depletion and over-pasturing. Further, an area as large as Australia has decayed. Only approximately 11 per cent of the earth's surface can be cultivated. Erosion eats yearly at this area – urban sprawl destroys farm lands, and ground water is being diverted to other uses – all of which has accelerated the loss of cultivated land by a factor of more than two. The reserves of rice in the world today are extremely depleted, reserves that would be used up in less than two months if they were not replenished.

There is still some possibility for growth, creating new farm land in areas such as Latin America, and by improving the productivity of farm land. An African farm produces only 600 kilograms of corn in a year, while an American farm produces 80 tons, i.e. 130 times more! In addition, further biotechnological breakthroughs may occur. Through manipulating DNA molecules, researchers may determine which parts of a plant or an animal are most useful to civilization, and these parts can be enhanced in the reproductive processes. Of course, there are both ethical and ecological consequences that must be confronted (Wald, 1992).

It is very tempting to turn always to the potential of biotechnology as a solution to the growth in the world's population. The economic promises and infrastructure of multinational companies make this alternative very tempting. The possible negative consequences must, however, be recognized, in terms of health and the environment. Even more difficult to solve is the large imbalance between production and distribution. The European Community is out of balance in terms of over-production of food, which contributes to the waste that plagues Western countries. One of the anomalies of this situation is the policy on the part of almost all OECD countries to subsidize farmers with $250 billion a year. Without these payments the number of farmers would continue to fall, and they already constitute a small part of the workforce in most countries. Only 3 per cent of American workers and 9.1 per cent of Italian workers are farmers. It is difficult to discuss the issue of food shortages throughout the world, when it is known that a large food surplus exists in the rich part of the world while a major shortage is found in many underdeveloped nations.

One consequence of biotechnology is that the borders between the farmers, researchers, fertilizer producers, the food industry and the organizational market become less evident. So-called 'vertical integration' continues steadily and pushes biotechnology production further and further. In the next century, this relationship will probably have even greater consequences. It will open new producers, new workplaces, give new form to organizations and probably substantially reduce the cost of food. It will have even more dramatic effects for those people who play the more traditional farmer roles. Biotechnology will clearly introduce a whole new type of economic development (Kennedy, 1993).

Land, natural resources and qualified manpower have, through the millennia, constituted the most important factors in economic development. These factors will be less and less important as automatic factories, laboratories and service industries come to dominate the economy, even though the farming lobby groups will do everything possible to stop or change this development.

Technological developments, coupled with the multinational companies, have their own dynamics. Young researchers will be attracted to new possibilities in research that these large companies can offer. Companies will likely migrate to countries that have the most liberal laws, creating new and different kinds of imbalance, including still another type of dependence on the developed world. Today, it is possible, for example, to produce synthetic rubber much more cheaply than real rubber. This has important consequences for the 16 million Malaysians and Indonesians, whose way of life is based on rubber production. Such developments raise serious questions about the role of biotechnology in the next century (Kennedy, 1993).

International Consequences of Technology

Countries with technological advantage and new organizational knowledge, are able to increase their advantage over other countries, accelerating the distance between the 'have's and the 'have not's. Many international organizations (e.g. the World Bank), and many large companies, such as International Partnership Initiative, are looking to develop new strategies that can close the gap between South and North, and between East and West.

The emerging job market is highly dynamic. There is no zero-sum gain in the situation, so that one person's job costs another person a job. As other parts of the world, such as Asia and Eastern Europe, begin producing, their markets also open new doors.

Care must be taken to reduce the imbalance in the world economy. The one hundred largest companies in the world produced in 1985 more than the combined output of the 50 poorest countries, where more then 67 per cent of the worlds population live (Goeudevert, 1992). These companies are located in the highly industrialized countries and are leading the way in the development of future technology.

The problems in relation to underdeveloped countries are many and complex. There is a big danger that these countries will obtain outdated technology that, often, is neither energy efficient nor safe for the environment. The poorest countries have, sadly, a considerable economic handicap in terms of their starting point, and the gap between them and the developed countries is increasing. In the decade of 1981–1991, the gap between these two groups increased from 751 billion dollars to 1.351 billion dollars (an 80 per cent increase). Even though new technology would be desirable, it is inconceivable for many countries.

Technology and Values

Technology is not value neutral. It changes our culture. Postman (1987), in writing about America, makes the following claim:

> We have turned our culture over to our engineers, who have convinced us that technology innovation is the same as human progress. Or perhaps we have convinced our engineers that this is so. In any case, in America we love our technology more than we respect our history or our traditions or our children or our political system. And, as you know, when someone is in love he sees no faults in his beloved, . . . as a result he usually knows very little about her . . . .

New technology is being introduced into our own countries so quickly that there is almost no time to ask calmly what the consequences may be. A culture always pays a price for new technology.

The five revolutions discussed thus far (the knowledge and information revolution, the population explosion, the globalizing and localizing revolution, the social revolution and the economic revolution) work together. They not only increase differences between individuals, groups, countries and continents but create growing dissatisfaction on the part of those who are not on the cutting edge of technological advances. Believing the good life must be just around the corner, they are continually disappointed. Technology creates a climate for social rebellion, emigration and social dislocation.

THE ECOLOGICAL REVOLUTION

A discussion of the ecological revolution must take as its starting point the simple fact that the world's population will increase to over three billion in this century, industrial production is more than four times what it was in 1950 and the Western lifestyle has spread itself as an ideal to increasingly more countries. While industrialism and the Western life-style are highly valued aspects of modern life, their consequences, when magnified to the world's surface and population, are as negative as they are positive. Negative consequences can be observed in nearly all countries.

While the so-called green revolution contributed to a temporary alleviation of food shortages, food production can no longer keep up with the world's population growth. In addition, pollution, erosion, destruction of ground water, destruction of wildlife, change of climate, reduction of the ozone layer and depletion of the land are taking their toll on the ability of the world to produce enough food. People are destroying their own basic requirements for life on earth. Reduction of the animal habitat is happening at an increasing pace. More than one hundred animal species are eliminated every day! The agricultural industry has concentrated its efforts on a small selection of plant species to satisfy approximately 90 per cent of the food supply, including wheat, rice, corn and soybeans, which serve as food staples. Most agriculture is now concentrated on only twenty plant species, even though there are more than 80,000 eatable species on earth. This exaggerated specialization itself has become a threat to the richness of the world's food plate (Mathismoen, 1993).

Civilization has so disturbed the ecological balance, that our descendants may suffer untold ills. The so-called greenhouse effect is one of the many serious threats to the environment. It results from increasing concentrations of carbon dioxide in the atmosphere and will probably result in the temperature increasing by 1.5–4.5°C. That could result in the melting of the ice cap, increasing the ocean's water mass by up to 2–3 metres, changing possibilities for food production because of the changing climate, and the character of life for large parts of the world's population. Of course, while most researchers agree with this analysis, there remain some sceptics, also among highly qualified researchers, who are of the opinion that much of the variation is due to nature itself and has little to do with human activities.

There is not room here for a full description and analysis of the many ecological problems that confront humankind today. The Norwegian Brundtland Report (Berntsen, 1994) and Vice-President Al Gore's study (1992) provides adequate documentation of the situation. We maintain that the world's environment must become a major factor in development activities in the coming years. The world cannot continue to engage in a development process in the same way that the US and Western Europe have done. Because nature sets boundaries and because civilization may not survive enormous economic and social differences, a new course must be found where all countries take part. The world stands at the beginning of an ecologically sensitive new world order.

The ecological debate has up until now been caught up in a description and analysis of the earth's situation, which has become increasingly bleak. There is general agreement that the developed world is acting rather selfishly and that there are no easy alternatives. The German ecologist, Ernst Ulrich von Weizsacher, argues that the industrialized countries must take the first steps (Weizsacker, 1992). He claims that the demands for industrial development in the world will continue, with such a great energy use, that by the year 2030 the production of carbon dioxide will more than double. This will result in an ecological disaster. He also shows that work productivity in OECD countries has doubled twenty times in the last 150 years. The technological productivity development has been equally great. However, we have not been paying real costs for resources like energy, water, minerals, etc. Weizsacker shows that the countries which, to the largest degree, have subsidized energy and water, mainly the socialist countries, are those where the economy and ecological balance have eventually collapsed.

Weizsacker shows that those countries that are the most realistic in pricing of natural resources in relation to the costs, are the countries that have the strongest economies. He has shown that environmentally sensitive structural and economic reforms contribute to a sound economy, at the same time, they contribute to ecological balance.

The problem today is to establish rules on which all countries can agree. This is difficult, because it is not easy to predict the course of nature. And, also, some countries have barely used their resources and they have a hard time understanding that they have to restrict themselves while the rich world continues to live in abundance.

There are really only two scenarios for the future: either humankind decides to change its course and live within the boundaries that nature sets for human activities or it does not. If we decide to change, it is possible to catch a glimpse of a world with people in harmony with nature and themselves. If we do not change direction, we will send an unmanageable bill down to our children and grandchildren.

There can be no doubt that the school must support the alternative of a world in balance.

THE AESTHETICS REVOLUTION

In some respects, the twentieth century might be characterized as the dark ages of art, while technology, totalitarianism and war have dominated lives, but that appears to be changing. Already the world is witnessing a renaissance in the visual arts, poetry, dance, theatre, and music throughout the developed world. Part of this may be because of the growing leisure time people enjoy, but that is only part of the story. Given a choice, it is significant what people choose to do with their time. In the past, sports has received the largest piece of the economic pie in America, but the arts are catching up. In the US, corporate donations for the arts exceeded one billion dollars in 1988. Since 1965, museum attendance has increased from 200 million to 500 million annually. The Alabama Shakespeare Festival has grown from 3000 in 1972 to 300,000 in 1989 and since 1970, attendance at operas has tripled. Whereas, there were only a handful of opera companies in the 1970s, there are now over 654 companies across the land. Chamber music groups have grown from 393 in 1985 to 578 in 1989. More than 25 million people attend the top 280 symphony orchestras, annually. There are 700 per cent more professional dancers today than in 1972. This growth in the arts is not restricted to the US. In the last ten years, Germany has built 300 new museums. In Great Britain, a new museum opens every 18 days.

An aesthetic revolution is taking place that represents a reaction against the standardized, mass-industrialized consumer society. Such a trend is championed by people like Charles Jencks, who claims the world is moving:

> . . . from mass-production to many fragmented taste cultures; from centralized control in government and business to peripheral decision-making; from repetitive manufacture of identical objects to the fast-changing manufacture of varying objects; from few styles to many genres; from national to global consciousness and, at the same time, local identification.
>
> (Jencks, 1987, p. 43)

Frederic Jameson sees certain negative implications of the new age, claiming that as aesthetic production has become integrated into commodity production generally and has participated in the multinational economic domination throughout the world, there comes to reign:

> a whole 'degraded' landscape of schlock and kitsch, of TV series and Readers' Digest culture, of advertising and motels, of the late show and the grade-B Hollywood film, of so-called paraliterature with its airport paperback categories of the gothic and the romance, the popular biography, the murder mystery and science fiction or fantasy novel.
>
> (Jameson, 1984, p. 55)

In contrast to anti-modern expositors, others have a more balanced perspective. While agreeing that the cultural and the social have fused, these interpreters claim that anti-modernism has shifted and is now able to proclaim its own positive identity (Huyssen, 1986, p. 219). Its genius appears to be its ability to transcend time and space, history and geography. It is characterized by the synthesis of various traditions, by simultaneity, incorporating the past into the present, and the distant into the local. Architecture is an important case in point. It has broken from the strait-jacket of modernism and has flourished in an eclecticism of various styles and tastes. Stylistic shifts appear to be kaleidoscopic and simultaneous. Huyssen recognizes a breaking away from safe categories and established institutions which harboured art, including the academy, the museum, the art gallery, the concert hall to allow 'a new freedom, a cultural liberation' (Huyssen, 1986, p. 219).

What North America and Europe are now experiencing is a turning back to the arts in all its forms. Art in the US received more than one billion dollars from private donors in 1988 and public budgets show evidence that people are on the way to a society where aesthetic values are taken seriously. There is strong evidence that an aesthetic revolution is beginning and that it will make a contribution to an increased understanding in the heterogeneous future society. Aesthetic forms of expression have their own communication channels and can build bridges between people and nations. A consumer orientation can gradually give way to artistic sensibilities and forms of expression, that have both ecological and economic effects and can provide a richer life for all people.

THE POLITICAL REVOLUTION

The modern age has been characterized by the emergence of the nation state, which successfully rationalized and centralized all political authority within its geographical boundaries. Modern democracies have a singular characteristic in that they have regularly become mass movements. In the political sphere, we also witnessed the development of something Alvin Toffler (1990) calls 'mass democracy'.

In recent years, mass society has begun to de-massify. In the economic sphere, there has been a dispersal rather than the concentration of production, and in the political sphere, at least in Europe and North America, a whole string of liberation and self-determination movements, involving ethnic groups, minority groups, neighbourhoods, alternative lifestyle groups, as well as single-issue groups, representing gay and lesbian rights, feminists, a non-nuclear world, 'Right to Life' legislation and religious revival, have asserted themselves with a force that at times has resulted in physical violence (Owens, 1983; Moi, 1988; Nicholson, 1989). Education is not exempt from this list. Parent associations and students' rights groups demand participation in school management policy and other decisions, challenging the established system.

Of course, social movements are not new. Throughout the modern age, Europe and America have experienced movements similar to those of today. Klaus Eder divides these into so-called romantic and populist movements (Eder, 1982). Romantic movements represent a continuing backlash against the age of reason and the attempt to rationalize social life, advocating a more natural life and a society based on co-operation and sharing.

Populist movements have challenged the corporate structure of our economy and the stifling bureaucracies of the state apparatus. They demand participation in decision making in all forms of social and political life, including the school, the workplace and the local government. What is at stake with these movements is the demand that minority voices count and that political systems must be restructured in such a way that minority interests can be taken into account. The most obvious political symbol of the new age is the obsolescence of the notion of majority rule, which blunts variety, openness and diversity. Without a concerted commitment to minority rights, majority rule relies on the tyranny of mass-society, including so-called representative government which, from the perspective of minorities, has rarely been representative.

Conventional authority, which is typically state authority, is failing. Superpower authority is becoming a thing of the past. Increasingly, the world order is shifting from what was once a bipolar to a multipolar power configuration, and power within this framework is so broadly distributed, that even the great powers are no longer able to enforce their will on others (*LA Times*, 1990, p. H2).

This presents the world with a terrible, double-edged sword. On the one hand, there is a developing possibility, that solidarity between groups can come through the participation of fringe groups in all forms of social life. There is a growing possibility for the emergence of a type of direct democracy, a sense of connectedness with life's events and decisions. There is a possibility of a global context, with the breakdown of national boundaries, the creation of global markets, the emergence of world concern through local involvement. On the other hand, there is a possibility of the demise of any attempt at rational policy-making, this having been replaced by relativized preference dictated by peculiarity of taste, and decision making based on specific group identity rather than from any globalized, general concern or perspective.

THE VALUES REVOLUTION

Plurality and even social fragmentation, above all, have characterized the end of this century. Earlier societies were influenced to a considerable degree by pervasive values and standards, often based on religious tradition. Western society was influenced by Judeo-Christian and humanistic values which included a distinct Puritan ethic.

With the knowledge revolution and the continuing international trade and dialogue, alternative ideologies, values and standards, critical questions have been raised regarding established values, particularly expectations about conformity and deference to established authority. This questioning spirit has contributed to a breakdown of the conventional values and norms that have defined society. In the contemporary world, educators working with children and youth generally sense a pervasive confusion of values and standards both among the youth and among those responsible for working with the youth. Youth is left, to a large degree, to develop its own values and standards, and the experiences passed on by the adult generation are often vague and contradictory. This situation has reached a point of crisis, because values and norms are vital for social well-being and health.

Certain recent developments hint at the development of a more fundamental value orientation. Many young people develop a relationship with the religious sector, in different mystic and spiritual groups or in the extreme-left or radical-right political groups. This quest for a more certain grounding includes affiliation with non-Western religious traditions, including Islamic and Asian spiritual expressions.

Fundamentalism is another type of orientation with which many are coming to identify, as it promises priesthood power and social control. It also represents a powerful reaction against the Western consumer and technological society. Many react negatively, for example, to what they feel are the unrighteous or unjust distribution of the benefits of a highly technological society.

As societies move into the postmodern era, they will begin to define conditions out of which values and standards might emerge; however, the source of basic social values can no longer be left to religious traditions, because for those who do not identify with religious groups, this would represent externally imposed norms. Of course, value definition must include religious impulses but it must also be meaningful to those who have no religious identity. It will also be impossible for the state administrative mechanism to define and impose a set of values and standards. If a sense of legitimate authority is to be restored to the state, it cannot act capriciously or coercively over the citizenry. The state can only facilitate a collective debate and support the emergence of shared understandings, moral practices, and the common aspirations of its citizenry. If there is no such dialogue, social fragmentation will continue and become even more confrontational (Küng, 1990).

The coming era will likely never by guided by a state of value homogeneity. The norms and standards reflected in society will likely be the constant subject of dialogue and discussion.

Chapter 4

Visions for the Next Century

In earlier chapters, discussion has centred on forces contributing to the transformation of society. Predictions have been avoided. Some elements of the future are reasonably sure (e.g. population growth), but some elements can develop quite differently from what might be anticipated. The world stands before an unsure future, a future that holds a number of possibilities, but it would be foolish simply to let history take its course, without intervening where and when it is possible. But, if we are to help mould our future, we need a vision of what we wish to happen, and we must do what we can to make it happen. A vision is not just an idea or a product of fantasy. A vision is something that grips and drives people, that they can believe in and fight for. A vision is the answer to the question: 'What do we wish to create?'

A vision that is developed by one person – a leader, a politician, or a researcher – has little importance unless it becomes shared. But when people are bound together, working for a common goal and ambition, they can help turn a vision into a reality. A vision is of little value, if it does not create a community, binding people together in a common cause.

Critical mass is the phenomenon that occurs when forces pull in the same direction. When this happens, constructive development is more likely. The danger is, that the complex world we have outlined may not be capable of a unified movement toward a new future, resulting in catastrophe and chaos in different parts of the world. The world needs a more common vision and a set of ethical norms, otherwise it will be difficult to bring about fundamental changes. This will certainly require more insight than any one person or field of study possesses. Each of the various academic disciplines, for instance, appears to have a partial grasp of changing reality but is unable, of itself, to provide a suitable conception of things to come. Peter M. Senge suggests a fifth discipline must be adopted that moves individual disciplines toward a systematic interdependency and view of the whole (Senge, 1990). Of course, such a conception must allow individual groups to shape themselves and should encourage open-ended systems where change and purpose-seeking are the norm.

A common vision must transcend the tendency to deal only with immediate imperatives and to put off accountability for decisions. There is already an awareness that the world's financial debts are being pushed off on its children. And more subtle social and political debts are piling up and must also one day be paid. To change our course of development will not happen without conflict. The most serious enemy to be faced, is ourselves. Those in the developed world must accept responsibility for the fact that each person pours fifty times more pollutants into the air than those in the developing world. Each uses 1000 times as much energy and resources as a person in a typical developing country (Weizsacker, 1992). Somehow, those in the developed world must help those in the developing world to gain a better standard of living, while at the same time exhibiting self-discipline and not living with excess.

Those who live in large countries, such as the US, may tend to feel that they have all they can cope with in dealing with their own enormous problems. Those who live in countries with small populations may take quite a different point of view. Special attention has been given in this volume to Norway, which is a small country with a relatively stable homogenous population, with democratic traditions where individuals, groups, businesses, institutions and organizations take part in decisions. Norwegians have relatively small problems, and they are blessed with a beautiful country that is to their economic advantage. In Norway, it is possible to go in a direction that is counter to the more general one and takes Norway into its own alternative future. Those living in both large and small communities must recognize that everyone is in a global community and none can be divorced from that world community. All must participate in defining and building a valid world vision.

Part of that vision is the realization that personal values and internal wealth are no less important than material possessions. Even though powerful forces may be working against this insight, we must discover how exciting it can be simultaneously to experience direct profit and social justice, what social and cultural development of society can mean. The central pedagogical duty educators have, is to contribute to the creation of new and productive ideals which can help, anchor people's lives, that motivate them to work individually and with others toward a better future.

Is there a group or a country really prepared for the twenty-first century? Probably not. The dimensions and complications are overwhelming, and reactions are all too often 'business as usual'. Educators must play a decisive roll in the preparation for the next century. They work with the future. 'The future is in our hands,' said Erik Dammen, who began the 'alternative movement' in Norway in 1972. Educators must do what they can to give the next generation the tools that prepare them for a whole new life situation. Education is central to the realization of a viable vision. The school is the only institution that brings the whole population through a systematic learning process.

Both attitude and behaviour changes are required. The school is critical in bringing about these changes. Unfortunately, all too often, the school has relied on the one-sided use of words to affect new attitudes and behaviours. Words have powerful potential, but they have limitations in their capacity to change attitudes and behaviours. Researchers Conrad and Hedin (1981), of the University of Minnesota, mapped out how teenagers in the US change attitudes toward the sick and old. Similarly, traditional ethics instruction in the classroom has demonstrated practical work with elderly and the sick helped to develop positive attitudes. Attitude change did not come before action. Practice, supported by reflection and assessment, is a powerful way to develop appropriate attitudes.

A sound vision of the future ought to include a number of elements; ten of which will, be discussed now.

1 An ecological vision: life in harmony with nature

2 A vision of a fair, democratic society

3 From dominance to partnership in social relations

4 From a war to a peace economy

5 A worthwhile life for the world's poor

6 From monoculturalism to multiculturalism

7 The vision of work

8 Technology in the service of human growth

9 Life skills in the service of health

10 From standarization to creativity

AN ECOLOGICAL VISION: LIFE IN HARMONY WITH NATURE

One critical vision, is of a world society that lives in accordance with the possibilities and boundaries nature itself has set. Contemporary adults cannot shove ecological problems on to the next generation. They must find harmony between people and the rest of life; they must avoid assumptions that they can disregard, abuse and destroy nature.

An ecological vision must be rooted deeply within the lifestyles of people. It must have consequences for a daily way-of-life. It must help us understand what is valuable and how to regulate consumption of nature's goods.

The dilemma in this vision is that humankind must begin to change its lifestyles before it becomes fully apparent what humankind must do. Many will feel it is possible to live on the world's sunny side and disregard its shadowy side. Because those in Europe and the US stand presently in such a good position compared with the rest of the world, they may be tempted to assume they can retain that advantage. A long-range perspective demands that the advantaged behave ecologically, not only with regard to less advantaged people but also with regard to nature. They must begin to practise new behaviours that support harmony with nature. We cannot assume, that whatever is good for large corporations and industry is, automatically, good for society.

There are many groups and organizations that have been working, for several decades, to formulate a more ecological design for society. Greenpeace is the world's largest environmental group, numbering several million people. A dominant political group committed to an environmentally safe world is the so-called Green Party, found throughout Europe. In the US alone, there are almost two hundred organizations dedicated to environmental issues, such as Alliance to Save Energy, Institute for Earth Education, The Oceanic Society, Rainforest Action Network, Sierra Club, Treepeople, and Zero Population Growth (*Your Resource Guide*, 1991). There can be no doubt that the single citizen is more aware today of ecological questions than twenty years ago. The question is: What the consequences are for our lifestyle? At the present time, all is not positive. One of the most beautiful and environmentally conscious countries in the world, Norway, is also guilty of consuming more energy per capita than almost any other country. Its people have plenty of energy, so they use it as if it were an unlimited resource. Even the Norwegians must gain a new vision and begin putting it into practice.

The school must play an important educational role. It will not be enough for teachers to talk about the environment or to organize a new subject field, such as ecology. The task is to begin engaging the youth in environmentally sensitive activities.

A VISION OF A FAIR, DEMOCRATIC SOCIETY

A critical vision of future society includes the notion that political life is governed by fair, democratic processes. Democracy is never completely defined, but John Dewey's notions (1916, p. 101) are helpful. He claims democracy is "more than a form of government, it is a mode of associated living, a conjoint communicated experience.' A democratic society resists excessive hierarchy in favour of more horizontal forms of shared governance, where all citizens are able to join together in formulating and interpreting a common standard for society.

Some maintain that democracy is an aberration, that society is more likely to be guided by authoritarian, dictatorial rule. If this is the case, those living in democracies must work all the harder to ensure that the world of the future is governed according to the rule of democracy. One of the significant outcomes of the collapse of the Soviet Union has been the declaration on the part of every republic and state in Central and Eastern Europe, claiming that it is striving toward democratic rule. These new democracies are fragile and need support and resources for a long period if they are to move toward prosperity and stability.

Political democracy is not without its shadowy side. Some countries tend to stress individualism at the expense of communal values and social welfare. While individualism is critically important, the dangers of our increasingly pluralistic society is that there may be no common ground on which all can agree. A challenge of Western democracies, is that they need a new vision and new stimulation toward democratic participation. Something is wrong, when only 50 per cent of an adult population takes on the responsibility to vote in a general election. Something is wrong, when minority groups feel so disenfranchized that they do not engage in democratic political processes.

If future societies are to be characterized by democracy, some mechanism must be available to ensure that democratic attitudes and values are instilled in the younger members of society. Further, some mechanism must be available to help young people to practise behaviours that are widely perceived as consistent with democracy. Tradition dictates that many institutions that serve youth are not always democratic. Clearly, many families and religious institutions are characterized by hierarchy, authoritarianism and patriarchy that are usually antithetical to democratic expression (Levin, 1993, p. 2). Amy Gutmann (1987, pp. 282–3) also points out that many workplaces do not reflect the characteristics of democracy. Employers often expect workers to practise absolute obedience to arbitrary rules. Those at the higher levels of an authority pyramid in firms often expect workers to perform a limited number of operations, to be uninventive in their behaviour and to accept mandates without question.

Even though institutional patterns are changing, it is risky to rely on families, churches and the workplace to help youth learn democratic values and practise democratic behaviours. Unfortunately, a similar indictment could be made of the school. It has not always been a good institution for instilling democratic values in its youth. Most schools are organized in an authoritarian and hierarchical fashion. Important decisions are typically made at the upper levels of this hierarchy and passed down to lower levels of the structure, where teachers and students form the lowest tier. Even so, as humanity faces the future, its greatest hope for developing democracy among the youth ought to be the schools.

Those measures taken by parliamentary democracies to ensure that schools instil democratic values, attitudes and behaviours have, to this point, been disappointing (Jennings and Niemi, 1974). Typically, schools have adopted formal curriculum units to teach youth about the struggle for democracy, about the democratic processes in government, including laws and governance practices, and about the role of the general citizen in a democracy. It is not surprising that empirical evidence related to political and civic knowledge has not been positive. The Central and Eastern Europeans, who are attempting to democratize their societies through education, are acutely aware that preparation for democracy is more than teaching about democracy. Of course, it includes having knowledge about the rights and obligations of citizens, but it also includes competence about human relationships and standards of behaviour. Democratic education may best occur through democratic practice (Lóránd, 1993, p. 2).

Democratic education can best happen in a school that itself functions democratically, a school that takes both students and teachers seriously. Schools are capable of helping students to play an active role in developing the school and instruction. It is first and foremost through activities and personal experiences that attitudes form. Our vision is of an active democratic society, where the state has legitimacy. There the state steers, but all citizens, both from minorities and majorities, must participate in all facets of the political process and feel equally treated in an open and fair system.

FROM DOMINANCE TO PARTNERSHIP IN SOCIAL RELATIONS

Another vision of the future, is that reliance on male dominated societies will give way to societies where both men and women play an equal part in their personal lives and also in most facets of social life. Those in the developed world must eliminate the barriers that still exist in their own societies and work to provide those in the Third World with a sense of equal worth and equal opportunity.

Riane Eisler has, more than most, shown to what degree Western industrialized societies have been built on a dominance theory (Eisler, 1987; Schierbeck, 1994). She has determined that European society, during pre-Hellenistic times (about 7000 to 3500 BC), was characterized by a partnership model in terms of social interaction. Authority relationships were based on an equal position between the genders and were neither focused on violence nor war. Eisler claims archeologists have found almost no weapons from this period, which was characterized by an advanced farming culture.

Eisler demonstrates that European culture gradually moved toward a dominance-oriented culture, characterized by a domineering male, who used violence and war as a means of conflict resolution. Above all, Eisler demonstrates the possibilities of a partnership model in regards to the fundamental problems the world as it faces the beginning of the twenty-first century.

It is a travesty, when half the population either does not have a say or is strongly under-represented in the groups that engage in the fundamental questions of society. The world needs to take advantage of the energies and resourcefulness of all its people.

Some of the main problems the world can best be solved in fellowship, where all parts of society are included in arriving at solutions to these problems. No one

63

can sit on the sidelines. Women and men must contribute in an equal way with their resources and perspectives to solve the enormous problems that confront us.

Aburdene and Naisbitt (1992) maintain a broader collaborative social process must begin with collaboration between couples bonded in marriage. Even though there has been great debate about the role Hillary Clinton plays in the American White House, the Clintons reflect the wave of the future, when couples work together rather than in their separate spheres of life. They typify an increasing number of couples, who are sharing larger and larger aspects of their lives with one another, rather than compartmentalizing their lives, as was so often the case in the industrial age. Aburdene and Naisbitt suggest a number of reasons for this shift, including the roles of the computer and telecommunications, which increase the potential of small groups to effect change; new attitudes, that allow women to work as equals with men in the home as well as the workplace, and which allow people to communicate immediately with one another wherever they wish and whenever they wish.

The school has an important part in moving society toward a partnership ideal. Unfortunately, there is sufficient documentation at hand of different and discriminatory treatment of girls and boys. Classrooms must be so organized that no young person feels the heavy hand of discrimination and exclusion, simply because of gender or ethnic background.

FROM A WAR TO A PEACE ECONOMY

Another vision is of a world economy oriented toward peace. Humankind must find a way that leads toward peace, takes the world away from violence, and builds a solid fellowship. The cold war created a whole new economic assumption about solutions to the world's fundamental problems. In fact, a significant source of strength in cold-war economy was its dependence on military preparedness. This is most evident in the former Soviet Union, where tens of millions of people worked in an economy devoted to war. About 80 per cent of the economy was committed to industrial production and about half of that was devoted to war production. For those in California, where a disproportionate amount of military production has been located, the movement toward a peace economy in the 1990s has been both difficult and painful, leading to temporary and permanent unemployment.

In the past, a large part of research and development resources was directed toward defence jobs. Space travel has also largely been committed to military purposes. As the peace economy takes over, commitment to these endeavours suddenly disappears, along with the technological innovations and the potential jobs the peace economy might enjoy.

War is not a productive way to solve conflicts. Those committed to peace must take control of the power structure and reduce the resources committed to war. They must work to build a political process that works for peace and a peaceful economy that supports it, to create the same commitments around peace that nations have had towards war. The alternative to building towards peace is to restore a commitment to war. The school must play a basic role in peace education. Attitudes, including aggressive attitudes, are formed early in life. The violence surrounding children and youth represents a serious problem in many large communities. Schools must engage in intensive efforts to channel aggression in useful ways, and to develop strategies to solve conflicts.

A WORTHWHILE LIFE FOR THE WORLD'S POOR

The prognosis is, that the number of hungry people may increase by a factor of three or four in the next thirty years if the present course is maintained. The poor will likely be poorer and the rich, wealthier. The poor may be even more exploited than they now are.

Practical solutions do exist. For example, the production of sufficient food is not as serious a problem as distribution of food, which must be resolved if the world is to avoid an ecological catastrophe. If leaders are to take a positive view of the future, they must find ways to reduce the number of the world's poor. Aid and development efforts have, so far, been a miserable failure. The poorest countries have gone so deeply into debt that the interest on their investments and loans soon eat up all the development resources. The world's trade remains characterized by tariff barriers that dictate disadvantage to the poorest countries. If the need for a new world order is not resolved by today's leaders, the problems will be deferred to the children, who will be left to solve a crisis that will have grown even greater.

One breakthrough for improving the economies of underdeveloped countries may be the so-called, 'Uruguay Round', of the General Agreement on Tariffs and Trade (GATT). There remains uncertainty about the consequences of these talks for different economies, but the intentions are in the right direction.

The world must dramatically reduce the differences between the powerful and the powerless, the powers and structures that bring poverty must be studied and understood, and mechanisms to counteract them must be found. In democracies, freedom is taken for granted, but certain freedoms are exercised at a cost to others. Today, the most important agenda is to express solidarity with the poor people of the earth, and laws, rules and ordinances, that hinder this commitment, should be revised.

The school has a unique, important duty to play, namely to show the practice of solidarity. In some countries, individual teachers and students already express such solidarity. Some schools in the developed world adopt schools in developing countries and attempt to work co-operatively with them. Those in the developed world must do what we can to share study places with those from poor countries. Those from poor countries must be able to take advantage of these places, without paying the kinds of fees only the wealthy can pay.

FROM MONOCULTURALISM TO MULTICULTURALISM

In the future, children must learn to live in the context of plural cultures. They must learn to associate with, and work together with, people with other skin colours, from other cultures and with other customs, perceptions and values. In the next decades, migrations of people will increase. It would be absurd to try to build psychological and physical walls to keep those on the periphery away. It is not a question of whether societies will be more pluralistic. This issue has already been resolved. The question, now, is how people of differing cultures will live together. Hans Küng states:

> There must be a reconciliation of a great many cultures. We must get away from the dividing line characterized by resistance, ethnic and cultural discrimination, away from marginal changes of two thirds of the world's population, away from anti-Semitism and racism.
>
> (Küng, 1990)

The vision of uniting those of different cultures is not unique. Some cultures have exercised their power to create an equable and fair society. They have created conditions where everyone makes the same claim to legal rights, culture, language, religion, economy and politics. Even so, this vision has never been instituted on a global scale.

If multicultural societies are to function successfully, they must learn to live in a world that tolerates groups with different values and aims in life. This can only be accomplished if all groups accept some basic common ground on which relationships are built. It will be difficult. It may be, for example, that some groups will work in opposition to cultures where women are not seen as equal to men. Will behaviours be accepted that are in violation of individual national laws? Shall the largest culture, whichever that is, exercise the right to establish standards for immigrants and others? It is difficult to find good models for multicultural societies. Though plurality would be the norm, it is not easy to combine plurality with common values and norms.

The assignment is, to learn to live together; this will be a central duty of the future schools. Again, new practices in the school will be necessary. Multicultural schools will be a distinct resource in the future because they represent microcosms of tomorrow's society.

THE VISION OF WORK

In the future, the economy will not require the commitments to conventional work and labour that were required in the industrial age. During the industrial age, conventional work was seen as a valuable and important aspect of social and economic life. It provided wealth, personal and social resources, a sense of personal identity, and a reason to live and be productive. In the new vision of the future, work will take quite a different place in society than it has done during the industrial age. Technological and scientific rationality have created conditions such that the material wants of humankind can be satisfied without requiring such extensive devotion to conventional labour.

In the next century, most people will engage in three types of work:

1 They will engage in conventional labour that is somewhat similar to current definitions of work.

2 They will engage in what might be designated as self-employment or work to enhance conditions for themselves and their families.

3 They will engage in what has been known during the industrial age as volunteer work, which is work and activities in the service of the community and society.

We anticipate that, in the coming era, all three forms of work will be valued. They will give rich opportunities to learn and for personal and social contributions and development. These types of activities are certainly not new. In fact, they typify the lifestyle of large numbers of women, who now find it necessary to engage in conventional work, to engage in personal development and compassionate activities in the home, and act as volunteers in the broader social context. However, two things are likely to change in the coming era. All three types of activity shall be defined as legitimate work and be part of economic investment and productivity. And, both men and women will participate actively in all three types of work.

Until recently, work has been juxtaposed with free time, and free time has been defined in the context of that relationship. Free time has been considered a time to rejuvenate or to rest and recover from the stresses and physical fatigue that work has brought. Free time has been defined as 'not work'. But, the relationship between work and free time will begin to blend and even disappear. People will engage continuously both in activities that have a paycheque connected with them and in those which are not paid. This will include short- and long-term activities. On the one hand, some may devote years to self and family, years to service, and years to conventional work. Some people may be engaged quite differently during different phases of life, some may be involved in different realms simultaneously, and there will be those who devote themselves exclusively to one or another kind of activity.

The notion of economic investment and productivity must be expanded and would include highly personal contributions to self and society. A haircut at home is as much a contribution to the economy as a haircut in the barber shop. Humankind must also work more diligently to define quality as a part of economic productivity. Is it realistic, for example, to include destructive activity as economic productivity? Do we enhance society by producing an atomic bomb or a machine gun? Of course, there are differences of opinion about what is destructive and what is socially enhancing, but the discussion must be initiated. Ecologists may focus too exclusively on the environment, while medical people may focus on physical and mental health. It is difficult to understand what is meant by economic development, but one vision is to develop a common understanding for the direction of economic development. The starting point must be central values that can steer notions of what development is.

As with other visions, the challenge to schooling is that it must take responsibility to prepare youth for professional careers, provide a solid foundation of knowledge and general proficiency, and prepare students to master changes in work and life. This can be accomplished, in part, by organizing broad learning rather than narrow and specialized learning. New and unusual combinations of education will give possibilities to different arenas, for the paid work market, the volunteer work market, and self-employment. Equally important is, perhaps, mental preparation for work life. The ability to master new changes is not dependent just on good professional assumptions. It also depends on self-confidence and flexibility. Here, the school can do something, but its viability depends on co-operation with home and the industrial environment.

TECHNOLOGY IN THE SERVICE OF HUMAN GROWTH

Technology should serve human growth. The modern age has been characterized by the use of technology in ways that have, at times, been destructive. Throughout most of history, technology has been seen as a tool that could be used as a labour-saving device to supply people with an increasing number of material goods. For most of the modern age, technological mechanisms were so successful that they came to symbolize a model of economic organization and efficiency. In fact, technology came to symbolize social, as well as mechanical, organization. While technology was once viewed only as a tool to be used by intelligent and sound leaders, it has recently come to be seen as much more insidious, in that technological society appears to have emancipated itself from human control and set in motion its own imperatives.

This orientation toward technique ought to shift in the coming era, so that technology will be focused on helping people to engage in more meaningful and fulfilling work. In many jobs, especially in the service industry, the primary quality factor ought to be the quality of people's work, and not just the effectiveness of material production. The human factor must become increasingly critical as a criterion of effectiveness and productivity. Technology must operate in the service of human beings. To an increasing degree, the development of creativity and the ability to innovate become the criteria for competence.

The challenge to the school, and especially to the trade school sector, will be even greater than it is today. The task of the school will not just be to master new technology, but to create possibilities that enhance the value and recognition of creativity and innovation.

LIFE SKILLS IN THE SERVICE OF HEALTH

Human beings should be in a position to make life choices that will help to maintain the kind of physical and emotional health necessary to play constructive, productive and satisfying roles in postmodern society. Maturely modern nations have lived a two-edged form of life. While their material wants and creature comforts have been increasingly satisfied, they have also increasingly engaged in behaviours that posed a serious threat to their health and well-being. People's health standard has been placed in jeopardy through health-damaging activities. Beatrix A. Hamburg (1994) outlines some of the most serious health problems of our time:

- the use of tobacco increases the risk of cancer, lung disease, cardiac and vascular disorders;
- the use of alcohol and certain other drugs increases risk of injury due to automobile and other accidents, as well as intentional injury such as assault, homicide or suicide;
- the use of alcohol and other drugs increases the likelihood of impulsive or inappropriate sexual behaviours with possible outcomes of unplanned pregnancy, sexually transmitted diseases, or HIV infection;
- dietary habits of over-eating rich foods predispose to diabetes and a range of cardiovascular conditions;
- the fad diets, bulimic behaviour or excessive dieting leads to significant nutritional deficiencies; any of these can also be linked to behaviour disorder; and
- alcoholism causes liver disease and/or neurological disorders.

The requirements of the future must include provision for responsible care of the human body. Physical and emotional health will become a high priority in the value structure of society. This requires a broad fund of knowledge of human biology and social competencies, including problem-solving abilities, conflict resolution skills, decision-making capacities, and the skill to evaluate messages coming from the media and other sources.

Health education presents some challenge to schools, which have historically neglected health sciences within their general education programmes. Programmes must be initiated related to human biology and its relationship to health, the environment and society in general, specifically targeting the effects of drug abuse, problems and possibilities related to human sexuality, disease, and healthy behaviour.

FROM STANDARDIZATION TO CREATIVITY

Aesthetic expression should occupy an increasing role in life. Industrialization brought with it standardized mass production. People's creativity has all too often been restricted to free time, to special and unrestrictive activities, such as art, that were largely reserved for the few and had little to do with the conventional economy. In cultures not yet industrialized, creative forms of expression often play a considerable role in society. Even in earlier forms of maturely modern societies, the crafts occupations were characterized by complex and individual expression.

Today, mass production has led to computer technology that is able to tailor production more to the customer's desire, than to standardized forms of mass production. But, the need to find expression of the aesthetic in everyday life, in the production process, in free time, and in the personal sphere, is becoming stronger. Society is, to an increasingly greater degree, characterized by aesthetics. Artistic displays, museums, music festivals local theatres, and song groups are thriving.

In this vision of the future, aesthetic needs will be encouraged to a much greater degree in all facets of life. Creativity will be encouraged and personal aesthetic expression will be highly valued in the school as in society. This will open possibilities for everyone and will change the picture of winners and losers. To make room for creativity, therefore, also means to make room for more of the humane.

SUMMARY: TOWARD A NEW ETHIC

The ten visions outlined require a new ethics to govern societies and the world (Küng, 1990). Ethics, here, is conceptualized as a means of establishing and defining standards and regular rules for welfare. Cultures can live together only if there is some consensus about guiding norms. Without a common ground, no democracy is able to function. A minimum of common values, standards and attitudes is necessary in every democracy.

All these visions raise the fundamental question of values. In any paradigm shift there will be considerable debate about rights and boundaries. Are we today, as members of nations, equipped to understand and debate the fundamental questions that must be answered in order to have an active relationship to the future?

The need for an ethical foundation with implications for everyday life can best be illustrated by the work of the medical doctor and the modern researcher. Research and technology open a whole new perspective for society's development, gene technology and biotechnology. Researching and practising doctors must often take a position, set boundaries and redefine what is right and what is wrong, what is moral and immoral.

In the future society, research and practice should not develop their own dynamic but all, in an open dialogue, should work toward agreement of where the boundaries are and which choices we are free to make. The alternative is to allow the future to evolve without direction, or to turn the conclusions over to power elites or to the experts. Elites must, without a doubt, play a major part, but each one of us must be responsible for helping to define the choices being made.

We must develop non-negotiable standards, some basic, common standards, perhaps as defined by documents such as the Universal Declaration of Human Rights, adopted by the United Nations in 1948, and the Covenant on Civil and Political Rights, agreed on by the United Nations in 1966. These basic standards that should not undermine the inalienable rights and worth of human beings. Each democracy depends on a clear framework and rules; societies and the world must begin to develop such a common, binding ethic. Hans Küng (1990, p. 89) writes of the essence of ethics:

> Man must never forget: ethics are neither technique (the learning of hypotheses and dogma) nor tactics, neither legal ethics nor situational ethics. For standards without context are difficult, but context without standards is blind. The norms should, therefore, enlighten the context, and the context define norms.

The school of the future must take on an even greater degree of responsibility than it does today, working with the question of values and integrating values into every part of its programme. This responsibility does not rest with the school alone to solve. It requires the mobilization of students, parents, social organizations and the political apparatus.

Chapter 5

Educational Needs of Children and Youth

The home and neighbourhood, church, media and workplace are the institutions that exercise the most influence on the young. Although the so-called ten revolutions (see Chapter 2) will have dramatic effects on these institutions as well as on the educational needs of children and youth, it is impossible to define exactly what those effects will be. Further, appropriate behaviours vary from one local environment to another; it is not inconsequential, for example, if a person lives in a little mountain community in Italy or in a major German city. But, there are some general conclusions to be drawn about the direction of the changes which are to come and what the consequences will be in terms of educational needs.

In the future, the primary institutions now serving the young promise to continue to play important roles, but there will be a general reconfiguration of these roles and the influence they exert. For example, the nuclear family will likely continue to decline in importance, but a variety of other family configurations will emerge. Families will be characterized by choice and variety. At the same time, the Western world will likely witness the further decline of mainstream religions, while fundamentalist and storefront institutions, as well as a spiritual awakening outside organized religious institutions, will likely increase. A further intermixing of cultures, races, and ethnic groups will likely continue, so that it will be impossible to expect a common national value system to be transmitted through homogeneous neighbourhoods and communities. The media will probably also lose its ability to communicate a single, pervasive value message. The media will fragment even further than it now has, so that most people will interact with a small, selfdetermined source of messages. At the same time, workplaces will become more and more localized. The wave of the economic future is small, self-styled firms and industries, each with a distinctive value orientation.

The family, church, local culture, media or workplace cannot be counted on to instil a uniform, general value orientation. None of these institutions will likely be able to define the attitudes of the broad spectrum of the people. Even though a general state of instability now characterizes Western society, by 2020 we expect the transition period to have stabilized so that more consistent value orientations will be found. While strong value orientations will once again begin to characterize institutions, these may be so localized and individualized that no single or general value orientation will dominate.

How will nations and regions be held together? If all the traditional institutions that affect the youth impart only special and specific values, what will be the source of glue that holds people together in a common sense of community? Where does this leave the role of the school? Should it take on this special role? Schools reflect the social environments in which they are located. They cannot deviate markedly from the emerging pluralistic value orientation and expect to survive. Consequently, schools will, also, tend to fragment, break up and serve small pockets of individuals who share similar value orientations. However, schools can and should be in the service of a vast variety of educational imperatives.

THE HOME AND NEIGHBOURHOOD

Recent developments have contributed to a deterioration of social capital available to youth, especially in large communities. The home has lost influence in relation to the power the electronic media and other institutions exercise over youth, and the community's increasing tendency toward specialization and fragmentation. Will this negative development continue? There are some signs that this trend may begin to reverse. New types of family constellations demonstrate they can, indeed, be productive and fulfilling. There is increased activism in local environments, in volunteer organizations, and a willingness on the part of people to devote considerable time to local educational institutions. For example, as part of a renewal programme of one school in a very poor area of Los Angeles, each parent has been obliged to sign a contract with the school to be involved and to contribute thirty hours of volunteer work. The approach has done wonders for the school (Wallis, 1994, p. 55). The future may be characterized by secure home environments and supportive neighbourhoods, even though these may have a multitude of forms. Families may be actively engaged in all of the institutions affecting the youth, participating with them wherever possible, to ensure that the growth and development of the child is as productive as it can be. The day when specialized institutions take over entire spheres of activity of children and youth is coming to a close. A close working relationship between institutions is important for two reasons. First, it provides a possibility for parents actively to support and participate in aspects of their child's education and development. Second, co-operation between institutions such as the home and school is necessary, because the future depends the development of a new story line, the development of a new myth that defines the world and changing values in order to provide the fullest measure of welfare for children and youth. The school needs to form alliances between itself and the family, to help to direct the input to the children of the media, and to give value content to the one-sided technological solutions that so often impress themselves on the education enterprise. In all of this, parents are the school's most important partner.

Families remain the surest possible force to counteract external challenges that strain to exercise negative influences on the lives of the young. The development of the young requires the fullest possible contribution of social capital, including time and finances. The family and home promise to remain the main institutional resource that funnels social capital into the lives of children and youth. In postmodernity, because the notion that productive work will include personally productive time, the norm will be that families spend considerable time engaged in learning experiences with their sons and daughters.

It has been projected that in tomorrow's society, the concept of work will expand to include not only conventional, paid work, but self-employment and self-development, volunteer work in the local environment and in wider society. This broadened definition of legitimate work promises new possibilities for more flexible roles and for the valuing of activities in the home and neighbourhood involving children and the youth.

Even with all the changes that have taken place in society, the home has continued to be the main institution for instilling a sense of responsibility, values and norms in the children. Historically, it has been the mother who has carried the main burden for this task. According to Bellah (1985, p. 88): 'While men's work was turning into a career or a job, women's work had the old meaning of a calling, an occupation defined essentially in terms of its contribution to the common good.' The definition of family has been changing, but the home remains, in many respects, the place where the most important models can be found for a productive and fulfilling life. A superior social and ecological vision is typically found in the home. The partnership between spousal partners ought to become the standard human relationship. The learning tasks that have traditionally been the responsibility of the family, such as reading in the home, travelling, and the learning of a second language, will continue to be important ways parents help children to develop. But, there will be large numbers of single-parent homes and many homes where children are forced to spend much of their time alone. Additional support for the family must be available. The home cannot be expected to be the only institution that provides acceptable models for life in the community and society.

The home also will take on an increased importance in terms of serving as a primary institution for translating and giving meaning to the knowledge revolution. What might now be considered to be more innovative aspects of interaction will be taken for granted. Electronic technology will play a much greater role than it does today. Through the use of home computers, for example, parents will have at their finger tips a full-range of programmes now falling under the label of *edutainment*. Technological information and new knowledge promise to provide opportunities for new types of learning that go far beyond that which typically is found in contemporary school. In fact, parents will be faced with the task of finding and channelling their children through a wide variety of alternative learning environments that will be available outside conventional schooling. The home will be able to use this future capacity for students with special learning needs and talents and to support the school's more conventional work.

The school will, in other words, be dependent on a close interaction with home and neighbourhood to develop social capital, in part, because fundamental attitudes, including broad visions for the future, develop in practice in the home and the neighbourhood.

Religious institutions

Religious institutions no longer function as the single most important organizations determining institutional norms and values. Even though religious institutions will continue to touch the spiritual in people – their longing after the eternal, their need for charity, their striving after the good, their search to set something in the centre of their lives – they will likely work in harmony with other institutions in accomplishing this task. Individual religious institutions will have many partners, and many of these will come from other cultures and religions. Religious institutions must lead a dialogue, not because the church has all the answers, but because they provide a forum of faith and strength to help to focus lives on important questions. Youth require role models, those who can help them in their search for answers to the central questions of life and help them to find new avenues to travel.

But, rather than working in a spirit of co-operation and harmony, some religious institution leaders have all too often been uncompromising and their actions have contributed to hostility and conflict. There is the possibility that hatred will continue to reign in tomorrow's world. It is difficult, for example, to see hope in today's ethnic and religious conflicts in Europe and Central Asia. In the next decade or two, there is the real possibility that many more religious conflicts will erupt. Those parts of Europe, which have relatively homogenous population groups, cannot live with the complacent thought that religious problems will only occur elsewhere. Religious institutions must become places where the young are taught to develop a sense of ethics and goodness even as they recognize that they live in an increasingly pluralistic society, a society in which others may have quite a different sense of the ethical and the good.

A number of recent works have stressed the growing need for some set of common values, especially in terms of a functioning democracy (Bellah *et al.*, 1985). These are necessary for solidarity with the world's poor, with the downtrodden and disadvantaged, with people of all races and cultures. If this is to happen, religious institutions must take a pro-active role and, in recent years, they have in many areas of the world.

Guidance from religious institutions must also continue with regard to new technological and educational boundaries, such as gene technology and medical technology. They must be productive partners in helping people to make sound judgments concerning information pressing through the media. They must give leadership in formulating sound and viable positions regarding economic growth, social development and ecological health.

The young cannot be expected to sit quietly but must become actively engaged in religious institution-led dialogue with those in other social institutions. One of these partners is certainly the school, for without a common ethic a school is dysfunctional. A school depends on partners that struggle with the ethical questions and give guidance with regard to value questions. Without a common value foundation and common vision, a school's work is impaired. In a multicultural society with many religious groups, this is the great challenge.

The Media

The TV media continues to be a growing influence in the contemporary world. The young are reaching out to TV and video. In the future, the media market will become even more influential than it is today, but we predict it will also be more differentiated than today. Advertisements will become more geared to specific user groups, with the net effect that the overall message will be increasingly jumbled. In addition, that aspect of the media market primarily dedicated to information and learning will become more competitive. A combination of communications and computer technology will increasingly be able to take advantage of the knowledge revolution in a more effective way than today. In the past, Europe has been sheltered from commercial inputs into media but there, too, advertisements will grow, becoming a part of everyday life.

Entertainment and the so-called home market will likely grow most rapidly. Through the help of the home computer and TV/video, local support groups will build and expand radically the number of so-called home schools and/or neighbourhood schools, and these schools might well rely on media outlets for their major global information inputs. Distance education will become big business, competing for the in-service and on-service markets.

The behaviour of children and youth will likely be increasingly coloured by what is served on TV and videos. So far, it has been almost impossible to agree on the boundaries of ethical standards for what is produced and disseminated. Even long-standing advocates of freedom of the press, individual freedom of choice and other central democracy values feel some guidelines are in order, at least for children and youth. The living room is no longer a private domain but a window on an electronic world-living room. The media will likely play a central role in the education society towards which humankind is moving, but there is a negative side of that influence, particularly the number of violent, immoral roles being projected. In response, institutions representing important norms and values probably will become increasingly involved in the production and projection of messages in the media.

The Workplace

The labour market of the future will likely become more flexible and whereas professional boundaries were once relatively strongly defined, the professional boundaries of the future will be less and less distinguishable. It will be more and more difficult to defend specific skills and competencies as something belonging to this or that profession. Competence will be more broadly defined and adhere to less local and more internationally developed standards.

Unemployment will probably not decline, at least in the next two decades. The reason for this, is that the economy is one of continual shifts and readjustments. Occupations will quickly disappear and be invented, which means that some part of the workforce will be in a transition state at all times. It may be inevitable that a standard at something near 5 per cent unemployment will always be the norm.

Work will also no longer be tied to large urban industrial centres. One important development is that small co-operatives have recently experienced a renaissance. With good communications and computer skills, local resource persons can create products and services in micro shops that are competitive on the world market. After World War II, new knowledge and technology was dedicated to processes that led to greater centralization and huge urban centres, but the more recent technology has transcended those imperatives and allows the world to be brought to sparsely populated areas.

As has been discussed, the whole concept of work will also undergo radical redefinition, and will eventually include so-called self-employment, volunteer work and more conventional work. A large part of the current informal sector will be redefined as work in the formal economic sector.

Another important development is that not just more expertise, but a deeper insight and increased understanding will be required in the workplace. Education, or expertise development for people in all age groups, performing different functions, will come to play a totally different role in the adjustment process. This raises the general question about how we will organize learning in companies, in organizations, and in the public sector. In the next century, what will be meant by a good school?

LEARNING NEEDS OF CHILDREN AND YOUTH

The starting point of any educational analysis must be the learning needs of children and youth, with the needs of both contemporary and future society being included. Of course, most teachers can find more than enough content and activities that are directly related to the needs of students today. And we agree that contemporary issues must be of great importance to the schools. School life is real life. It should give essential impulses to our life here and now. It should provide room for students with different talents, as well as emotional and intellectual inclinations. The school must direct its attention to today's needs, but it should also prepare for the future. Therefore, we must meet the challenge: to think through the implications of tomorrow's developments for today's school.

In addition to addressing the learning needs of children and youth in schools, a number of learning needs in everyday life must be addressed. Think about the fantastic task a baby has to master a language! It is probably one of the most complex tasks learned by a human. But, most children do it. All they require is a rich and stimulating environment. Each of us learns a great deal each day and most of this learning is tied directly to the tasks we are attempting to satisfy each day. These tasks may be tied to new technologies (e.g. advances in the telephone), new laws (e.g. new traffic laws), new processes, (e.g. new ways to pay bills), or new standards, (such as new social relationships). Everyday learning is also often tied to assignments that can best be solved together with others. Everyday learning happens by use of common sense, in co-operation with others and in assignments we have interests in solving. As a rule, many talents can be used. The duties often lead to co-operation and new thinking (Resnick, 1983).

In the future, children and youth will still work with everyday learning. One of the questions confronting educators is which learning needs of children and youth must be met by the school. Are there contemporary everyday needs that must be taken over by the school? John Dewey's conception of the new education at the turn of this past century was that an understanding of everyday life had never been a task of the school, but that society had grown to be too complex for young people to understand society without some systematic, formal introduction to that society (Dewey, 1899). He recommended quite a different school than had hitherto existed to satisfy this new need. Are the schools of today up the challenge of adjusting themselves to meet both the formal and everyday needs of children and youth? Humanity lives today on the borders of an important experiment. We are organizing a great educational experience in uncharted grounds. This will require sensitive reflection, co-operation, interdependence and a sense of adventure.

BASIC KNOWLEDGE AND SKILLS

The young need to learn basic knowledge and skills. The basic question is what that knowledge and those skills are. What will be basic for students living in tomorrow's society? It will, without a doubt, continue to be an ability to master their mother's language, both in spoken and written form. Research has demonstrated that good readers are necessary if the child is to do well in other academic areas (Brown,

1980). In addition, basic knowledge would also include basic numerical competence, the ability to understand the natural and social sciences, and the ability to deal with more than one language. But will there be more?

It is increasingly clear that encyclopedic knowledge, facts and simple data will be important but they certainly will not be sufficient. The so-called information society requires that we be able to digest huge amounts of information and make sense of it, that we can cope with the inputs of the media, which has enormous resources and will steadily increase its part in the schools. Facts and concepts are but a starting point and they must be a part of broad theoretical and conceptual frameworks that give meaning and understanding to facts and concepts.

One argument against factual knowledge is that our knowledge base is developing so quickly that educators are able to remain current only by accessing updated databases. This is a tempting argument but it is fundamentally wrong. Raw data from knowledge research is no more pure and clean than interpretations of that data. Facts are always collected in the context of specific scientific paradigms and frameworks. The fundamentals of science change, and in a generation's time they may appear to be quite stable, but they do change. What becomes essential, is for the students to understand the structure of scientific paradigms, with their attendant facts and concepts, and not be drawn into peripheral issues and changes that may be happening very fast. Students must have a wide and stable grasp of basic frameworks and the facts attendant to them (Anderson, 1981).

Information is like the food we eat. The process does not just involve swallowing the food. It must be digested. We need a digestive system that functions. The school is our digestive system. It is the school's responsibility critically to separate bits of information from each other, analyse them, then put them back together again, so as to create meaning and contribute to creating energy or motivation to continue growth and development.

Much of the information, that bombards us each day, is more distracting than it is guiding. Many children and youth have weak intellectual frames of reference. They lack clear cognitive structures. They need help to see the connections; they need help to analyse and synthesize. Such help assumes a wide vocabulary and working conceptions. The school must make sure all students have this. Many students come from homes where both reading and intellectual discussions are a standard, but many have a lot smaller vocabulary from the home. Therefore, it must be a priority assignment for the school.

It goes without saying that information is everywhere available. It is not the task of the school to deliver this information in digested form. The school must help the student to do that digesting and interpreting. The information found in newspaper clippings, books, media, or even a data bank is of little value in itself. School must act as a clearing house, an information processing and analysis institution, to help it to become useful for a community. Schools of the future have a special role to fulfil. Schools are institutions where individuals can totally concentrate on their own development. It will be an institution that gives each learner approximately 15,000 hours to engage in such development and the personnel and physical resources necessary to engage in that process. There will be no final definition of a school. First and foremost, the school of the future must allow learners the possibility to have a say in their own thinking life, to receive a variety of bits of information in connection with their interests, to assure learners that they can discover and use their talents. The school is the only place where people, with good conscience, can work for themselves. And it can happen in safety without people saying they are selfish and only looking out for themselves.

Gunilla Svingby (1993) distinguishes between surface learning and deep learning – the difference between the acquisition of superficial knowledge, or the products of knowledge, and learning related to deep knowledge, knowledge that is connected with an understanding of parts and the whole, with understanding both intellectual and emotional sides of processes, and the development of empathic understanding. Deep knowledge is the perspective on school learning that we feel will be critical in tomorrow's school. We now explore various aspects of this kind of learning.

Learning to Learn

The difference between good students and poor students is not necessarily a matter of intelligence. The difference can have a good deal to do with the student's background or the type of instruction taking place in the school. An essential aspect of learners that are successful is their ability to engage in a systematic introduction into a subject field.

The deciding factor between successful and unsuccessful students is their ability to connect new information with an existing understanding of the structure of a subject field. They have learned to figure out how things work or under what conditions they function (understanding procedures) and in what context those conditions exist to function successfully (context understanding). They have also learned for themselves, effective and different ways to reason. They know when to attend and when to screen information. They know how to set goals, develop positive relationships in learning and be self-critical (Dalin, 1991a).

Some students have a natural ability to engage in these activities and need little support to teach themselves to learn. However, most students need help. Some learn to incorporate work in systematic ways while engaged in studying a particular subject. Others do not know where to begin. Because all people must be able to deal with increasing amounts of information, all students must eventually receive extensive help in learning to learn. From the time they are in pre-school they must be continually engaged in learning how to learn. It will never be too early to start. A year-old baby may already have gained crucial skills in learning to learn. A student that has had problems through the years arranging information in a meaningful pattern, has already begun to experience discouragement and easily begins a bad cycle. Part of the difficulty is not just learning techniques, but to working through feelings of anxiety and lack of confidence.

Schooling must begin to model learning to learn. It must go beyond itself as a knowledge machine and begin to focus on understanding and problem solving. In the future society it will, to a larger degree, demand intimate understanding. We must have the ability to realize, use our intuition, understand our feelings, empathize with another's pain and to live with other cultures. Should the school continue to monopolize, to select the young in future trades (and we are strongly in doubt of the need), then we must inevitably help the learning culture in the school to change itself dramatically. We must begin to question other relationships than excelling in school.

Such a change is similar to the medical field. A medical doctor must have a great deal of knowledge and be continually engaged in updating that knowledge. But a good doctor is also a person the patient can talk with, one who has ability and insight, one who understands. The question is as follows: Is the best candidate for the medical profession a person with one-sided development in excelling in school?

Discipline in Distinct Subject Fields

The history of learning has always been imbedded in fields of knowledge. It will not be otherwise in the future. All learners must have some competence in the logic of basic fields of study, in the procedures which those in the field use, the models that are necessary to understand. Many students have great knowledge from a field of study, but they may have almost no understanding of the basic structure of the discipline. The task of the school is both to provide a overview of the world around us and the sequential and structural dimensions of various fields of study. It is not easy to learn the structure of a field of study. The learning of any field can be both boring or exciting. This does not diminish the importance of such learnings. One task of the school is to help the student to engage in such a process of learning.

Combined with the learning of learning, the learning of the structure of fields of study must constitute a central aspect of schooling, and it is becoming more and more important. Students are being fed so much information that they must have conceptual frameworks in which to place most of this information. If we are correct in our assessment that the social capital of most students is shrinking, then the school must take up that slack. If the student's potential is to be fulfilled, then the school must provide the framework for learning.

Problem Solving

The students in today's terribly complex society must solve problems and deal with difficulties that require a comprehensive understanding of the situation. Problems and challenges do not come with ready-made solutions and connections with fields of study. Students today confront problems for which specialists have only partial solutions or no solution at all. Often, their work is devoted, not to solutions, but to gaining a grasp of the problems themselves. However important an understanding of subject fields is, that is not sufficient in today's world, and it will certainly not be sufficient in tomorrow's world. Howard Gardner suggests that most adults do not use more knowledge than a five-year-old uses, when confronting problems that are interdisciplinary in nature (Gardner, 1993).

Answers to many problems are, according to certain scholars, more an authentic learning experience when the issues are complicated. This has begun to translate itself into school learning, where teachers are seeking to engage students in tasks that require an authentic learning experience, in that complex problems require creative problem-solving activities, relevant to the world today. Teachers must begin to help young people to learn how to solve problems. The vocational schools of many European countries have long taken advantage of the real world in exposing future craftspeople to the world of work. It may be that primary and general secondary schools could learn a great deal from vocational practices as they rethink school programmes of the future, and how to help engage young people in solving problems for which there are no pre-set answers.

Communication

It is likely that society will continue to develop horizontal structures that have no clear lines of authority structure. In a horizontal society, it becomes important to be able to communicate, to have the ability to tackle challenges between people, and to be able to understand and use information effectively. Proficiency in interpersonal communication becomes increasingly more important. Interaction between people requires the ability to work out practical solutions to work as a team in deciding how to proceed. A school that does not have programmes for systematic learning in this area, does not prepare students for future roles.

Interpersonal communication skills are often learned in daily life. It is appropriate that this be so and it is likely to continue to be so. But many students do not have the internal capacity to learn communication skills simply by living in today's world. They fail to meet the challenges of often tough peer pressure or of resolving conflicts with parents in the home. They require some guidance in learning how to increase their own insights. Therefore, good interpersonal proficiency is an ongoing experiment in how to learn together.

The more technical side of communication is also important. A solid understanding of a person's own language is a must. As we have said, unfortunately the standard in the teaching of the mother language is weak for a number of students. In the society we are moving toward, it becomes also important to master at least one, and ideally many, foreign languages. English is, of course, almost an imperative in the world today, but English speakers must also learn German, French or Spanish. Understanding of languages is tied together with understanding different cultures. Therefore, we see that understanding different cultures becomes an important basic course to learn. It is not possible to communicate effectively in another language without having a minimal understanding of the culture in question.

Communication does not depend only on language and cultural understanding. In tomorrow's society, it will become even more important than today to understand computer language and to be able to interpret and use pictures. It is probable that it will become easier to use computers, and that the relationship with the computer becomes a consumer task. It will be increasingly important for people to take advantage of the possibilities of computer technology. Here the schools have a responsibility, a duty that could be solved through close co-operation with others (Rolff, 1988).

Because of TV, the picture is a basic communication medium of the media, and because behind every picture is a purpose, a meaning often hidden from the viewer, it is important to master the analysis of what the picture media is trying to say. The danger that the picture is able to manipulate people is real. In view of the fact that so much time is taken up by TV and videos, and the trend scarcely appears to be diminishing, then to provide a knowledge of and proficiency in picture interpretation, must be a basic duty of the school.

In this interdependence, it is natural to assign a technological information role to the school. Certain countries, such as Norway, were very early in undertaking basic research with regard to technology in the school, and Norwegian schools have today one of the richest supplies of electronic equipment, software, etc. in the world. That has been a great aid in helping young people become computer literate. Technological information has become an integral part of the student's daily life, both at home as well as in school. It is particularly in relationship to the computer's enormous possibilities for accessing information and processing that information (e.g. CD-ROM's ability to store and share information) that has attracted schools.

Electronic technology has already demonstrated enormous capacity to simulate real, concrete work situations in the world of work, to allow individuals to discover paths that might be dead-ends and to play with ideas and possibilities that at one time required years of training and expertise.

The school will increasingly be in competition with the so-called home market where each home becomes a veritable electronics station, with modems, faxes, e-mail, etc. that make possible interaction with the world at large. The *edutainment* concept combines entertainment and learning in new and exciting ways. All the more reason, then, that the school provides the latest opportunities in learning and exploration.

KNOWLEDGE AND UNDERSTANDING

One can study love from every possible perspective, from a theological, an anthropological, a psychological and a biological perspective. It can happen that one could know everything there is to know about love but still not understand it. That requires direct experience with being in love.

School culture is built on the misconception that understanding is synonymous with knowing. In school, we learn to describe a phenomenon, and we learn to explain it. So far, schools have not done a very good job in helping young people, learn to understand. Understanding is something more than knowing. It has to do with putting knowledge into practice. We understand something first when it has meaning, when it leads to practical use, when it leads to insight. This does not mean that knowledge is not important. Rather, it is tied together to the intimate understanding (Max-Neef, 1992).

An increase in theoretical knowledge can easily lead away from the central idea of understanding. It may be that the current generation knows more than other generations, but it is not certain if the current generation has more understanding. Knowing something about poverty does not mean we understand what it means to be poor or are able to empathize with others' pain. We may know much about the world that surrounds us, but have very little understanding of it. The picture of the wide world swings before us on TV every night. The school has the great task of contributing to putting the puzzle of the world together, of describing it, explaining it and helping learners to learn how to make sense of it.

If learners are to become more understanding, they must internalize the knowledge, the explanations and the insights from formal learning. For example, it is not enough simply to learn how ecological factors work with each other, but one must learn how critical ecological understanding is. The young, as well as adults, must become directly involved in ecological preservation by working with conservation organizations.

To learn requires both knowing, explaining, insight and the relating of important matters to oneself. The problem with school learning is that the meaning is difficult to relate to, because students do not leave the schoolroom and engage the phenomena directly. A consequence is superficial learning, lack of motivation and failure to engage an issue. Curiously, everyone knows that everyday learning occurs quite differently from school learning. That learning takes place in a natural context.

81

The school lacks connectedness with the rest of the world. It focuses on duties and behaviours rather than genuine problems the world confronts.

How often one hears in the school: 'You will use this later in your life.' That ought to be somewhat unsettling. Schooling must be self-engaging. Learners must be engaged in real issues today. Will students really 'have use for it later in life'? Must the school have such a one-sided approach?

The school also has another problem: even while the world invades and engages the life of youth, the school all too often is isolated. While we talk of conservation and lay out theoretical frameworks, the reality of life and the importance of ecology is self-evident. The young people's energies are often consumed by the very things the school tries, unsuccessfully, to focus on. That is perhaps one of the most important reasons that youth's energy in large degree goes to things other than school learning. The distance becomes too great between theory and reality. Some students are engaged in exciting international popular youth environments, some engage themselves in conservation work, others in religious organizations and others in sports. And all the time, schools remain as they were before, just a modest part of the youth's motivation and energy. Young people, even when they are committed to schooling, usually fulfil a minimum contract with the school. This is a serious loss of resources.

We luckily find many good examples of schools engaged in their local environment in that they are involved in practical projects in which students can become deeply engaged. Some countries are exemplary. Norwegian schools are, for example, forerunners in the way schools can touch the world around the school. They are putting the young people outside the classroom into the local environments, insisting that they be personally engaged with local undertakings in history, local preservation, action groups, etc. They are moving in the direction of learning by participation (Dalin and Skrindo, 1981).

If schools are successful in breaking down their isolation, they must form alliances with the volunteer organizations, with the music field, with conservation groups, with immigrant organizations and with the political organizations. To master the enormous challenges the next generation faces, youth needs, first and foremost, more understanding. The young need to use their whole selves, they need to understand before they act. If we were able to create a safe world with less suffering and more justice in the next century, we need more knowledge, but, first and foremost, more understanding.

If the school is to become more than an institution devoted to books, it must take this challenge seriously. Especially important is that this includes a new view of the role of the school.

Independence and Responsibility

Children and youth are maturing physically at an earlier age, and they often have responsibility early for their own life away from school. At the same time, they remain economically dependent on their parents for longer periods of time, because they are expected to remain in school and experience difficulty finding work.

If the school is to be successful in combining knowledge with understanding, it must help students to become more responsible for their own and other's learning. This is the major concern of studies which advocate learning by participation (Dalin and Skrindo, 1981). Closely related to this, is a movement for co-operative learning, which is a systematic way to encourage learning in groups (Johnson, Johnson and Holübec, 1991). Learning by participation and co-operative learning are examples of a form of instructing that creates possibilities for increasing understanding.

Closeness and Belonging

Many students develop low self-esteem and self-confidence because they are not as close to their parents and other adults as they need to be. The experience of being alone, of being deserted in a foreign world, contributes to the breakdown of learning on the part of children and youth.

If the young are to grow and develop understanding, they must experience closeness and belonging. In the past, it was assumed that these experiences would be found in the home and neighbourhood, but the decline in social capital no longer allows us to make such an assumption. The school must assume responsibility for some of those necessary experiences. This may sound like a strange task for the school, but that only points out the fact that we have scarcely begun to think how the school can contribute to the issue of closeness and support in the lives of children and youth.

Role Models

Children and youth have the need for role models. In contemporary society, children and youth are all too often not able to live and associate with people who can serve as role models. Many fathers spend almost all of their time away from the family. Mothers may work or be so involved in other affairs that their children are left to their own devices. Fortunately, day-care centres or even nannies may provide appropriate role models, but some young people only have other peers with whom to associate. The young themselves function as role models, and these role models are reinforced by the entertainment and youth industries to which the particular youth group is attracted. These alliances can be powerful.

The problem is that the youth need to develop understanding, so they demand the insight and intimate understanding and education that older people may have. But, because the adults with whom the youth come in contact with are uncertain and perhaps have not had experience in things the youth find necessary, the young often stand without a clear and positive adult role model.

The teacher, therefore, has a big challenge, through their practice and daily work, to be a role model for their students. Students need to meet different kinds of people so that they have a choice between different values and models.

THE CONSUMER AND THE PRODUCER

An important distinction in the future society will be between the group that might be designated as the consumer group and, on the other hand, the group that might be designated as the producer group. The producer group consists not just of those who produce goods and services but those who are engaged in the production of ideas, new insights, art, politics, research, free-time outlets, etc. There is a growing difference in those who are generating what the society is and what it provides and those who are recipients of the producers. Many people are little more than consumers. Their roles are to buy and use the materials that producers, in their wisdom, feel are appropriate for them to consume.

One of the characteristics of today's world is that a large amount of time is devoted to consumption. Therefore, it is important to learn to be a critical consumer. A task for the school is to help consumers to learn to be critical in the things they consume. Even more importantly, the school must help young people to learn to be producers, to exercise creativity, problem solving and critical ability. It is not easy in a school with an overloaded curriculum, so there is little time to reflect, for digression, for critical debate, to discover, recognize and cultivate what is special with each student.

Much of the work that goes on today in the classroom of maturely modern societies, is consuming the curriculum, often an uncritical appropriation of pre-digested knowledge. Gaining knowledge often becomes a test of the student's memory, of things they can repeat, of what they have read or been told. A student can slide through school with relatively good results without understanding much and without having to reflect over what was presented or used in a creative way. The school itself is often the uncritical consumer of knowledge. There can be producers in many fields and in many ways. Production can be merely a mechanical and uncreative process, identified only with industrial processes. However, the term can be used in a much broader sense. Production is related to all activities of life that contribute to the welfare of society, activities that engage our minds, that draw us toward creation and contribution. Producers are not spectators watching others create and produce, but are engaged in acts of creation and production. Producers are not merely the passive recipients of TV messages, but the actors themselves. They do not simply listen to the radio, but engage directly in generating meaningful messages and discourse.

CREATIVE PROBLEM SOLVING

A close alliance exists between the ability to think systematically, to engage in what we have called learning to learn, to be motivated in work, to connect learning with participation and to practise assignments that require responsibility on the part of students. Problem solving that is connected to constructive assignments, can easily have a practical character that has long-range consequences.

Problem-based learning is a basic educational need. It is essential to connect school learning more tightly to situations that demand problem solving that goes beyond what a student knows. Learning must be centred on engagement with challenges, whose solution is not entirely clear.

It is not simple to find good problem-solving assignments in daily instruction, Therefore, the curriculum and time planning must not only be devoted to traditional subjects and their standard problems, but be related to concrete assignments in school and the local environment that demand both a theoretical and practical approach. In his book *Det musiske Menneske*, Bjørkvold (1993) focuses on the educational system of Norway and he demonstrates that the schools of Norway neglect certain important dimensions of human development, particularly the capacity for creativity. There is a close interdependence between the ability to compose music, choreograph a dance or the ability to express more general creativity and the ability to engage in independent activities, take responsibility for actions and engage in productive roles. It is by listening to their own sounding board, by going forward as producers, that people can make the greatest contribution to society and make their unique contributions to themselves and their community.

Bjørkvold points out the need for expanding the borders of each individual and the entire culture. Youth in their teens have a need to break the boundaries, move themselves out in the unknown, experience that which is exciting. In contrast to the youth environment where the boundary breaks are all too often connected with drug use and excitement, Bjørkvold recommends providing arenas that allow youth to play with behaviours and values that may be socially acceptable in quite different conditions. Otherwise, the passive and monotone reality that young find themselves, at least in most classrooms, does not facilitate growth and alternatives.

ACTIVE CHOICE OF VALUES

Future society might be even more characterized by a consumer orientation than is the case today. Steps should be taken to ensure that consumption is to be accompanied by the ability to make critical choices and to engage in choices from a vantage point of a clear set of values. Schools of the future must help students to develop an ethical orientation, and these ethics must be related to social reality. Students must join practice with theory so that their ethical orientations are meaningful. Without a practical and theoretical ethical connection, instruction will be an empty space in students' consciousness. They can easily become slaves of the consumer society, and of strong economic, political and ideological interests. In a pluralistic society, choice will be an important aspect of life, which can easily lead to a confused ethical orientation (Küng, 1990).

In the future society, to an increasing degree, religion, politics and economic interests will compete with one another for people's attention. Each of these spheres has strong self-serving motives. One of the critical assignments we feel schools must have shall be to prepare children and youth to participate actively in making sound choices, to be free and independent people in a complicated society. The school is, perhaps, the one institution that does not have economic, political or ideological interests. Therefore, the school is the most reliable institution we know that can prepare the students to make active and independent choices.

Chapter 6

Professional Standards

Schools ought to be centres of excellence, where professional standards define success. In this chapter, we shall concentrate on the meaning of professional standards, and how individuals can arrive at professional understanding. Our interest goes beyond questions such as 'How many cities there are in Belgium?', legitimate as opposed to illegitimate fields of study, or the extensive criticisms of teaching, all of which are a part of the current polemic regarding standards. We wish, rather, to give attention to more fundamental issues related to standards.

If schools are to survive the tasks being set in the coming century, educators must resolve the fundamental question regarding the nature of knowledge. What is authentic knowledge? How does everyday knowledge differ from school knowledge? How do people learn? Is it at all possible to learn how to reason – or even how to learn? We wish to promote a given perspective about what knowledge and learning is, as a basis for the discussion (in the final chapter) of what a good school is for the next century.

In Chapter 5, distinctions were drawn between knowledge and understanding. We argued that understanding is a primary task of education and instruction. In this context, we shall explore in greater detail the meaning of knowledge.

WHAT IS KNOWLEDGE?
Touko Voutilainen (1987) argues that knowledge, in contrast to delusion (which is untrue) or conjecture (which cannot be proven or verified) is a well-founded concept. He claims that knowledge is dynamic and not static. Consequently, learners must take an active rather than a passive role in relationship to learning knowledge. They must take a critical view toward knowledge, a view that knowledge is only understood in context, a view that knowledge, to be meaningful, must be put into practice, and must become part of the learner's own experience and reflection.

Gunilla Svingby (1993) distinguishes between *surface learning* and *deep learning*. Surface learning has to do with knowledge components or facts, while deep learning has to do with connections, relationships, wholeness and understanding. She argues that a concentration on facts alone can help a student to complete a test; however, that kind of knowledge is not what is demanded in life and in the job market. Svingby argues that knowledge, assumptions, and opinions will have meaning only through systematic reflection, connected to empathic understanding. She argues for a knowledge dimension, a proficiency dimension and a valuing dimension in deep learning.

This knowledge and learning cannot be obtained through subject-matter instruction alone. It is important to ask for knowledge that goes beyond the traditional and known, that helps us to problem-solve interdisciplinary problems. The philosopher, Jürgen Mittelstraß (1993), argues for a more creative, problem-oriented and general knowledge. He believes that:

> subject and discipline-oriented education, however important, has one great weakness, in that it thrives in isolation from other fields and knowledge spheres. Interdisciplinary learning is not something that should replace subject-based learning, but rather a complementary activity.

Mittelstraß recommends a clear subject-based instruction that is fundamental and exemplary. He feels free-standing facts are necessary, but they are meaningless unless understood in a context and understood as authentic. The goal of instruction ought to be that pupils be confronted with learning situations that are much like the learning situations of real life. To do this in the context of subject fields is usually difficult and the way the school day is organized does not make it easier. That may be one of the reasons why school learning is so different from everyday learning.

Newmann and Wehlage (1993) suggest that authentic learning is characterized by the following criteria

1 It requires the use of higher-order thinking skills, that give students the possibility of working with information, combining facts and ideas, synthesizing, generalizing, formulating hypotheses and arriving at tentative conclusions.

2 It develops deep knowledge, which gives students the possibility to develop arguments, solve problems, develop explanations, concentrate on a few issues and thereby provide a mindset that allows students to be problem-oriented and go into depth.

3 It encourages students to work with genuine problems in society and use their own experiences as points of departure. The task must have some meaning beyond the school situation and give students a real feeling that the work they do is important.

4 It is encountered in such a way that students are engaged in a genuine dialogue, exchanging ideas, breaking down and analysing ideas, related to the development of a culture of listening, developing understanding for other's points of view, and developing something new from common ideas.

5 It supports the work of students by setting high expectations for work, giving support where needed and developing a common understanding.

Authentic learning is close to concepts presented, some years ago, in *Learning by Participation* (Dalin and Skrindo, 1981). In that book, the concept of knowledge was drafted which formed the basis for learning by participation. The most important difference in that type of learning and authentic learning is that students must take personal responsibility for their own learning and for the work they do in regards to their community.

Learning is a deeply personal process. It is difficult to transmit knowledge, in the above sense of the word, from one person to another. What educators can do is stimulate the thinking processes that the student masters, to enable the student gradually to build a personal knowledge resource. Everyone has a unique learning frame of reference. Early in a person's life some basic thought processes are established. Later in life, the person depends on these basic structures and processes, but the person has the ability to develop and expand the ability to think. This brings us back to the question raised in the previous chapter: Can one learn to learn?

Two schools of thought dominate the discussion about learning to learn. One school of thought claims that thinking competence can be learned in isolation from a specific subject of study. Edward de Bono (e.g. 1994), of the Cognitive Research Trust at Cambridge University in Great Britain, is a major proponent of this point of view. He claims to have made a number of positive inroads in helping people learn how to learn within their frame of reference. The other school of thought is that learning to learn only takes place within the context of existing fields of study, that learning is related to grasping the basic structure and character of a particular field. Both ways of learning have proven to be effective and it is not sound to exclude either approach. It is possible to teach young people to learn how to learn within the context of their own maturational stage of development. This is the best investment possible in preparation for an uncertain future.

SCHOOL KNOWLEDGE AND EVERYDAY KNOWLEDGE

Success at school is rarely directly related with success in life. If a student is conscientious and solves the problems the school poses, that does not mean the student has an ability to solve problems in the school of life. In fact, everyday knowledge and assumptions may be wrong from a theoretical perspective – but they may function in practice. Scholars may have a highly sophisticated grasp of scientific knowledge, but that has little to do with their ability to cope with everyday issues in life. Teachers take for granted that the things they do in contemporary school are beneficial to life and they continually press students to engage in that type of learning. Attitudes towards schooling on the part of non-educators are perhaps less positive. Scepticism must be raised about what educators teach, how they teach, and how relevant and practical school knowledge really is. It is not even certain how relevant school learning is for success in the scientific world. That scepticism certainly is not reduced in thinking about preparation for a future, unknown world.

If the school is to survive as the primary learning institution for children and youth, it has to clarify its role versus other actors in the learning market. In addition, educators must further develop the quality of what schools do by attempting to arrive at greater consensus about what the primary tasks of schools are.

If school is to be transformed into an institution that deals with fundamental learning processes, educators must be clear about the kinds of qualities such processes ought to reflect. Standards of learning ought to be measured in terms of their capacity to help learners to engage in deep learning. A primary task of the school is to develop instructional programmes, curriculum resources and organizational structures that are geared to focus the school on competence regarding deep learning.

Children and youth are being confronted with a central developmental challenge that requires much more than conventional school programmes can provide. Schools must begin to attend to the requirements learners must master if schools are to survive. Schools must, among other things, help children and youth to learn to think. If the conventional fields of study help the young to learn to think, so much the better; if they do not, then these fields must either give way to other schooling activities or rise to meet this challenge.

There is a good deal of work on which appropriate schooling can build. Lauren B. Resnick (1983) has done remarkable work related to school knowledge and everyday knowledge. Research of J. Anderson, Ralph Tyler, James Brophy and R. Marzano (McRel Laboratories) is an example of this type of activity (Marzano and Dole, 1983). To understand the relative role of schools in the learning market a distinction must be drawn between school learning and everyday learning. Research has dealt with these phenomena. Some findings are given below:

Individual versus Group Learning

Schools focus mainly on individual learning, but learning outside the school is most often connected with group learning situations and is connected with the interplay between many people, who have access to unequal resources. New knowledge in a work unit can best be understood as a knowledge system, organized as a network of individuals or groups, who are dependent on each other as a knowledge community for accomplishing specific tasks. A single person cannot steer a ship into the harbour. That requires co-operation and association. Individual success in accomplishing tasks is dependent on what others in that association carry out and how they get together with the others in that setting. Knowledge alone is not enough.

Concepts versus Knowledge and Skills

Schools deal with the learning of concepts, while learning outside school has to do with knowledge and skills related to technology, tools or procedures. The school appreciates the thinking process unrelated to its application. In everyday life, tools have dramatically changed the need for knowledge (e.g. information technologies), and even redefined what may be defined as useful knowledge. Recent developments also indicate that the ordinary citizen can accomplish rather complex tasks without much detailed knowledge, if the knowledge system the individual works with is intelligent. Good practitioners have advantages, because they use practical problem-solving, intuition and decision-making with the use of advanced tools.

Theory versus Practice in Problem Solving

Schools are committed to symbol manipulation, while new knowledge outside the school is developed in a practical context. Schools teach rules that help to solve conventional problems. School problems follow known and well-defined frameworks and solutions. They help the young people to learn the existing paradigms of knowledge but give little training in independent thinking and problem solving in practical life. Outside school, people tend not to rely on the rules of the game that take place inside the school. Consequently, many people can be found, who are successful in solving problems in the world but who were not at all successful solving school problems. Take an example that Olivia de la Rocha has outlined. A young person, told to determine what three-quarters of two-thirds of a cup of cottage cheese would be, creates a round pancake of two-thirds of a cup of cottage cheese, cuts this into four quarters, then scoops three of the quarters into the cup. Arithmetic was not really used in the process, but most people would likely resort to some common-sense technique to solve such a problem. How much of what students learn in school do they ever use in everyday life? Should common-sense techniques be the criteria for school learning and if not, what should the criteria be (Marzano and Dole, 1983)?

Schools have a tendency to value generalized knowledge and theoretical principles. This form of learning can be useful if it can be applied to concrete situations. School learning is not often used in everyday life. What typically happens in everyday theory, practice-theory survives even though, by conventional standards, it may be wrong.

IN DEFENCE OF SCHOOL LEARNING

What do people need school learning for? To begin with, situation-specific knowledge limits possibilities. Research has demonstrated that persons who are successful in school but who are confronted with new problems rarely use general algorithms that were learned in school, but they are also more capable than others in developing methods that are useful in solving problems they confront. People can be innovative and creative. They can do things machines are unable to do in that they invent original ways to dealing with problems. Humans can take a position outside the problem and think about it!

Much research has demonstrated that people are more successful at solving complex problems when they have a clear mental model that can be applied to the problem situation. Kurt Lewin once remarked that there is nothing so practical as a good theory. However, most of what people know was probably not learned in school. One important reason for having schools is that they can provide good maps and models by which we can navigate our lives. Even though the maps and models are not always relevant, that does not negate the importance of using such models and maps. That is also the argument that fields of study make. They provide ways to deal with particular aspects of the world. They provide the basic structure for organizing information and sorting that information in a meaningful way. A broad, general education is more necessary today than ever before, and it is increasingly becoming more and more necessary for the world of work.

The point is not that conventional fields of study should be eliminated, but that they should begin to relate themselves to other fields of study and confront the challenge of dealing with a world that is largely unknown to specialists. The conventional school must transcend the tendency to be satisfied with competence in the conventional fields of study and turn these fields to the most important aspect of schooling: learning to think. Disciplines are basic, but mental processes are the ultimate aim.

EFFECTIVE LEARNING

The human brain is an incredibly complex organ with roughly 10 billion neurons, each one receiving messages from some 100 others and connecting to still 100 more. The web of interconnections is so complex that the whole cortex can be thought of as one entity of integrated activity (Pickover, 1990). When the brain is subjected to a rich sensory environment it grows. Modern brain research sees the brain as a single system, and it probably develops through a process of natural selection (Edelman, 1992). The brain can do many things at the same time, and process thoughts, emotions and imagination at the same time. It processes the Gestalt and the pieces simultaneously, it operates with a short-term memory and a vast long-term memory capacity simultaneously. It always tries to make sense out of disorder, out of the many stimuli that it encounters.

Learning and self-esteem are intricately connected and 'to frustrate the individual's capacity to learn is to destroy much of what it means to be a human' (Abbott, 1994, p. 66). The brain is capable of dealing with complex situations; it is always trying to discover the connections, map the known territory and identify what is new.

As learning is a complex activity that engages large parts of the brain, so is memory – the capacity to retrieve knowledge. It is likely that the memory function also uses multiple structures that can be found across the whole brain, and it is also clear that knowledge retrieval can be learned.

Effective learning happens when the learning activities are compatible with the way the brain works naturally. Learners must recognize why they are working on a learning task, since they usually motivate themselves by making sense out of their lives. They also learn best when they can identify with what they learn, by building on what they already know. Learners are also social and learn certain things easier when they learn together with others and when they receive concrete feedback and encouragement from others.

TOWARD A DISCIPLINE OF THINKING[1]

An important aspect of what we define as professional standards has to do with the thought processes connected with disciplines. We rely on the common distinction between:

1 factual understanding

2 process understanding

3 context understanding.

These, of course, are not entirely separate concepts. They hang together and in combination they constitute what is known as professional standards.

Factual Understanding

An understanding of facts focuses on who, what, when and where understanding. In order to think according to a discipline, it is central to have these fundamental understandings. An understanding of facts is presumed to be hierarchical in nature. At the lowest level is basic perception. At the next level, are the clusters of concepts that can determine correctness or incorrectness of declarations, such as 'apples are good'. Statements provide a means of expressing ideas. Individuals tend to organize information in statements. The important comparative element in any hierarchy is the relations between statements, such as 'apples are good, but pears are better.'. In order to understand, individuals must relate seemingly unrelated statements with each other. There are a number of ways that statements can be related to one another:

- He is tall and he is brave (addition).

---

[1] We have here used the general framework of the 'Thinking skills' programme of McRel.

- I was there, but I was not happy (contrast).
- I went to the ski jump; afterwards, I went home (time sequence).
- He waited in order to see the bull (cause).
- Astrid is my friend; I like Astrid (reference).

Finally, people organize relationships in knowledge structures. They make generalizations in order to understand information as a whole. They provide rules for individual students, so they can construct the necessary structure, and the more conscientious students become capable of establishing an effective knowledge structure. There are several effective ways to organize structures:

- *Sequences:* First I get up. Then I wash myself. Then I eat breakfast.
- *Topics:* Norway is Europe's richest resource.

    It has a free and undisturbed nature.

    It has much energy.

    It has a high level of scientific capacity.

People can rely on other principles in order to make generalizations or comparisons between specific relationships. The important issue is that individuals find methods to organize sets of information. These provide the best possibilities to organize and make practical use of knowledge in unusual contexts.

Good teachers know that they must communicate understanding of facts within the context of a field of study, and they systematically help students with various approaches to work through bodies of information. This helps students to build pictures of concepts in such a way that both hemispheres of the brain are activated. It helps students to describe concepts in their own words, to develop taxonomies, to develop understanding for the situations and problems for which these concepts have some utility, and it helps them to develop structures that illuminate the meaning of concepts.

Process Understanding

Understanding of procedures is the ability to understand how things work. This understanding assumes factual understanding; it is not a new form of understanding, but is a new dimension of disciplined thinking. A person who wishes to sail ought to know much about boats, rain and wind. But that is not enough. Sailors must also know why they are going to sail and how to put all of the processes together in applied form. To become competent with this type of understanding, they must begin with an understanding of facts. Many teachers work systematically helping students to understand procedures. In geography, teachers have techniques for teaching how to use a map. In language, teachers help students to learn how to find citations and references. In mathematics, they teach students how to solve practical calculation problems, etc. In spite of this, researchers have demonstrated that schools generally do a poor job with this type of learning. One of the reasons for this is that procedures often entail hidden assumptions which are difficult to detect. To understand procedures, students must go through a number of steps and levels of understanding. Even then they must have a critical eye to procedures, not simply accepting guidelines in a rote and automatic way. The problem many students have is that they learn rules of behaviour but do not understand the principles on which these rules are based. If successful, students will have synthesized a great deal into a meaningful whole.

Students seldom simply copy procedures from their teachers. They inevitably adjust and manoeuvre processes until they fit the individual learning style and experience of the student. Consequently, procedure learning requires long periods of tinkering, trial and error, and practice. That is one of the most important tools of the students as they learn to make use of individual facts. Such learning is always experimental and depends on the ability and willingness of the student to consider traditions, use reason and play with ideas.

Contextual Understanding

Contextual understanding is the knowledge people bring to bear that dictates what procedure to use. Some people tend always to take context for granted. They assume similar conditions will always hold and attempt to apply the same processes without regard to the shifting context. It is critical to help students to see how changes in context demand changes in the procedures that are to be used. They must be able to identify the more important context variables that are connected with the specific problems and ways to deal with them. Linguists, for example, recognize that language is highly context specific. Its proper use and meaning are deeply imbedded in the context in which language is being used. It is not appropriate simply to apply rules of language without regard to the situation at hand. Attempts to develop computerized programs that use language have long demonstrated that non-contextual rule application leads to meaningless and nonsensical language. Language use is only one of a host of knowledge uses that require context. Gestalt psychologist Max Wertheimer (1959) attempted a number of experiments with students regarding the way they figure out the area of a parallelogram. As long as the students were receiving the task in the usual way, most students were able to find the right answer. When the parallelogram was presented upside down, few students were able to solve the problem. They reacted by saying, 'we have not been taught this yet' or the 'problem cannot be resolved'. Their understanding of the procedure was closely related to context.

We have previously written that teachers often fail to appreciate the difficulties students have in integrating facts, working out appropriate processes and accounting for context factors. They assume far too much. They give problems that students have no connection with. Productive teachers take the psychological and contextual situation of students into account and help them to develop their problem-solving skills. They learn how to think in a disciplined way!

Researchers have begun to analyse how specialists think in the framework of a discipline. That type of thinking must be brought into touch with the world of the learner, the way the student handles everyday life, and attempts to connect individual learning styles with the discipline in question.

TO REASON

How are people to integrate the three types of understanding outlined above: factual understanding, process understanding and context understanding? We shall deal initially with this question at a theoretical level. If a picture of how people reason is drawn, there must be some notion of how the brain works. Two processes at work in the brain are short-term and long-term memory. Short-term memory processes can only handle a small number of variables, five to seven bits, at a time, but long-term memory can handle a hundred-trillion bits of information at once. That is significant in terms of how the brain works, and it has great implications for the way educators ought to try to stimulate the reasoning process.

Three distinct processes are to be considered:

1 *Transferring of specific information*: The process takes place in long-term memory. People process information when they bring it back to the short-term memory. Educators usually call this process one of recalling or remembering.

2 *Comparison of memory* in the short-term with the information in the long-range sphere: This takes place in many ways and is a central activity in the process of reasoning.

3 *Restructuring* as individuals create new understanding of knowledge or modify old knowledge: Through this process individuals attempt to reorder their picture of reality, give space for creativity and new insights, and evaluate new information being added to an understanding of reality.

Transferring

Transferring is critical in processing information. Factual, process, and context understanding gives people structures which help them to work with new information, although there are some who claim that structures can hinder the creation of new insights. We come back to that issue in a short time.

Transferring techniques can be learned. It is not possible to remember everything; an individual must identify that which the individual wishes to remember. Students understand that facts, procedures and contexts are good aids in remembering. In addition, teachers can help students to create pictures that contain elements that stir recall. They are lodged in long-term memory as visual, auditory, movement, feelings and verbal expressions. If a person develops good pictures, that person can recall things that do not even fit together. This is a well-proven technique for recall. The use of memory frameworks or rules is another effective method; it provides a mechanism to recall a word or pictorial experience. It helps students to appreciate what power the brain has, which in turn stimulates self-confidence and motivation for further work. There are some teachers today, who resort to such techniques as a means of helping students cram for tests. That is one way to cram, but it is also a means of helping people learn to reason. It can help students to organize and store information and then begin to reason from that base. In the end, each student must experiment with various styles of recall and find one which works for them.

Comparison

Comparison means to determine to what extent new information is like or unlike information individuals already know. There are five comparative competencies:

1 *Categorizing* is valuable with regard to concepts. One technique is to

establish likeness/unlikeness with concepts. This technique can begin even in nursery school, and it can extend to the most sophisticated research projects.

2 *Analogical reasoning* can be constructed in statements such as 'the ratio of A to B is the same as the ratio of C to D'. There are a number of techniques for training in analogical thinking and the ability to identify various types of relationships between similar/different concepts, classifications, derivations, functions and magnitudes. Analogical reasoning is a fundamental comparative method that is applied intuitively in almost all spheres of experience.

3 *Extrapolation* means to extend an existing model or structure into the future. The factual structure discussed above does not require students to go beyond the information that is presented. Extrapolation, to the contrary, is the process of taking an existing structure and extending its meaning into quite a different structural situation. Extrapolation is the capacity to engage in *divergent thinking*. It is similar to the development of metaphors, and has great potential for weaker students.

4 *Evaluative assertions* are similar to what educators typically call critical thinking and involve relating information in a set to specific criteria. Learning how to make evaluative assertions is similar to learning logic. It is based on proven procedures and there are well-known methods to teach this, such as helping students to identify an unusual statement, deciding if that statement falls within proven knowledge and, if not, investigating if the statement is based on valid information. Students learn how to assess statements, for example, if a statement includes no proven over-simplifications, generalizations or false conclusions.

5 *Evaluation of values* is the capacity to determine if information ought to be viewed as positive or negative. As a general rule, people must be able to relate feelings and emotions to the judgments being made. They must be able to understand the underlying premises of a person's own value orientation. Those who engage in this process are usually engaged in so-called *dialectical thinking*.

Restructuring

These five methods (selected from Marzano and Dole's work) assist in comparing new information with established experiences, a central process that can be applied to new knowledge at any time. In this connection, it seems appropriate to discuss briefly a number of processes involved in reasoning. These are closely connected with so-called restructuring in that they all involve the drafting and developing of a certain level of new understanding. Restructuring processes are intended, by and large, to create new knowledge in the long-term memory. This occurs through three main processes.

1 *Further development* occurs when people make connections with information that is not directly transmitted. A person, for example, who hears of an airline accident, automatically recalls experiences of similar

accidents, even though that information was not transmitted in the report of the accident. People attribute the characteristics, cause and consequences to things that were never in the original report. This is an entirely appropriate and natural human tendency. The understanding of such a process is important for students to become more creative and critical in their analysis of events.

2 *Problem solving* is a process people apply when aims are relatively clear, the problem is defined but the relevant information or ideas to solve the task are not at hand. There are today a series of more or less creative methods for solving both everyday and academic problems. These are just beginning to become a part of the learning activities of young people. They are becoming more and more available on the open market. However, they have not yet become a part of conventional programmes of study that ensure problem-solving competence on the part of all youth. Because problem solving ranges across such a large sphere of learning and competence, the educator's main task is likely to provide students with a sense of the alternatives available and the broad range of methods available, so they might develop their own way of problem solving with regard to educational problems.

3 *To create* is the ability to develop new information or products. When this occurs in connection with the school, it usually is done with written presentations of some sort. Writing remains today an important means of expressing thoughts and ought to remain high on the educational agenda of the future. To create, in connection with problem solving, demands that the problem situation require a single outcome. In life situations, outcomes and goals are usually general and even unclear; at times this can be an asset. Einstein once explained: 'The primary gift I possess is what some people call fantasy, and that has been much more critical to my own development than the absorption of information.' It is possible to develop the capacity to fantasize. There are a number of methods available to help learn how to fantasize, and that is surely necessary for the creative act.

LEARNING TO LEARN

The third dimension, which we call professional standards is connected with the ability to control and stimulate the first two dimensions, because of an ability to 'think about our thinking'. Learning to learn is a competence that has always been necessary in the schooling situation and it will become ever more important than in future schooling.

Study techniques have been stressed from time to time in school reform debates. There was a time in Europe in the 1960s, for example, when schools engaged in systematic processes to help students to deal more effectively with their learning situations in school. All students were given hints about study habits and ways to improve their performance, and some students learned their lessons well. However, most of these hints were intuitive in nature and were directed toward satisfying the teacher's demands. Our interest here is more student-oriented in that we wish to suggest that students learn how to understand their own learning styles and how to take advantage of that style. Four main spheres shall be discussed:

1 the ability to focus attention;

2 setting objectives;

3 developing self-discipline; and

4 self-valuing.

The Ability to Focus Attention

If students are to make productive use of their resources, they must have the capacity to focus. That usually happens automatically in reaction to external stimuli. In a learning situation, educators cannot rely on the assumption that all students will automatically focus their attention on the learning situation. Educators must ensure that students' attention will be focused, that they will be on task, in a specified learning activity. In today's schools, it is difficult to help students and even teachers to become focused. The necessary social capital is simply no longer available to ensure that students bring this capacity with them.

Many classes have a minimal capacity to attend to the processes going on, and many teachers have difficulty knowing how to direct the attention of the students. Research on classrooms has shown that the time spent on task may vary as much 40–80 per cent. There is growing evidence that a high correlation exists between so-called *time on task* and student achievement.

A number of techniques are available to help students to exercise greater control over attention, from purely physical constraints to mental exercises that bring about greater focus. Probably the most promising are those that involve the student, engage the student in the instructional process and use group-dynamics methods intending to develop a working group in the classroom.

Setting Objectives

Conscientious students set clear and demanding goals. Research on effective schools has demonstrated that good schools not only have high expectations of students but also they do a great deal for the individual learner. Productive schools have high expectations and the kind of support that produces positive results. It is an illusion to believe that poor students are helped if teachers do not set difficult goals for them. Students know what is expected of them and they will raise the standards if resources and personal attention are given to them. A problem is that many students go for years without experiencing success and they slowly develop such a negative self-image that they are afraid to try and their energies are blocked. The setting of goals is not a technical question but a psychological question. It must be done in such a way that students can be challenged but also receive the resources and support to meet that challenge.

How can educators help the individual student to establish reasonable goals? Initially, goals must be short-ranged and realistic, which is accompanied by support, encouragement and reinforcement. Second, students must be given concrete goals. Third, students must be able to change goals during the process. Goals are not something set in concrete, they are guides toward more general objectives. There are a number of practical guides that give students practice in defining and working toward goals.

Developing Self-Discipline

It helps little if specialists develop techniques but are unable to carry them through. Values and feelings must be consistent. Some brain researchers claim people have a decision-making centre in their brain, a special form of memory, that leads the thinking processes. General attitudes toward work, attitudes that encourage innovative thinking and accept new perspectives, are important.

General discipline to work Persons who are in a position effectively to carry out tasks are able to engage themselves in tasks. They are committed to quality work; they are sensitive to the way tasks unfold and they are ready to change their behaviour under way. These characteristics to problem solving are common of good problem solvers, independent of their other talents.

Discipline to stimulate new thinking Many students think that the control of a situation is outside themselves, i.e. beyond their personal control. Maslow (1971) believed, for example, that we are trained not to trust ourselves or to be confident in the general laws of life. Research on student motivation has shown that an important factor for positive self-esteem is that students have confidence that conditions outside themselves will not hinder them in achieving good results. If students generally find that they can trust life as it is, they will be more inclined to take chances, to seek new ways and to be creative.

Attitudes that expand perspectives Perceptions are subjective; they are based on the way a person looks at things more than the way things are in some objective condition. Each person has theories about 'how things are related in this world'. There is a theory that the things one learns must be connected with that which one already knows. If new impulses give new understanding, they must be compatible with one's existing theory about 'how all things hang together'. Does that mean that people, in fact, are not able to learn anything fundamentally new? We think not.

A number of school critics claim that schools restrict creativity, arguing that the disciplines themselves prevent expansion of learning. That can be the case, if the discipline is taught as a collection of facts rather than as training in reasoning ability. A discipline is restrictive if it is taught in such a way that rigid perspectives are gained. Any subject must include a creative dimension and must stimulate creativity.

It is possible for people to shift their perspective, and to freely alter their paradigms. It is even possible to help someone to learn to make such transformations. To do so requires that one accepts the assumption that all perspectives are subjective, that they are controllable and that they can allow one to see the world from different vantage points.

Does the learning of a field of study, a discipline, hinder a student or facilitate such a quest? Does it put blinkers on students so that they can only see the world according to the structure that was imposed on them? Does it hinder their creativity? If that were the case, the entire concept of professional standards would be suspect. We feel it has the potential to help learners to understand themselves, to change their perspectives, to understand the connections things have with each other and to assist them in their quest to discover something new. If learners do not master the fundamentals, they will most likely be insecure about the unknown.

It is possible to help students to understand that self-discipline is important to them. Through role-plays, simulation and psychodrama, they can find new roles. Students must first find their own perspectives and self-discipline, and then appreciate those of their teachers and fellow students.

Self-valuing

To work with one's self, in an attempt to become centred and develop self-discipline, is difficult. Methods of focusing on personal development and the ability to exercise self-discipline must again be developed. Those who do not value themselves find difficulty in learning to learn. Fortunately, there are a number of programmes available that help students to assess their own values and gain a higher sense of self. Students are taught to practise positive thinking and they are taught to work co-operatively with other students. A combination of three factors appears to be evident in most effective programmes:

1 students learn to set realistic and concrete goals;

2 they practice assessment of their own work; and

3 they receive external help from classmates and teachers through group work and/or classroom instruction that helps to repeat important elements in the thinking process.

Many students appear regularly to fall between the cracks. They are on the margins of the world of schooling. They find themselves in a school world that overloads them with facts, relies on mechanistic rules, engages the students rarely in reasoning and fails to teach them how to learn. And these students feel that their teachers are not helping them in any significant way. Outside the school, these same students likely find themselves bombarded by isolated bits of information. They have little systematic exposure to structures that help them to organize and make all of this information meaningful. If no commitment exists to establish professional standards, one thing would be certain: those who are the weakest in the school do not have the resources and support outside the school to ensure that they will have a stable and secure life.

Research information is available today about the importance of the school becoming a place where students learn to think. People work better in complex situations if they have a mental map by which to operate and if they understand why the tasks they are expected to engage in are crucial. All young people today face an unknown world. In the future years, people must be capable of mastering change. It will not be enough to expect the experts to resolve problems. All people must be capable of adjusting their lives, making decisions and using all available information. Otherwise they will find themselves manipulated by the situation and even the information around them.

What does the future hold for the school? This is problematic. We have outlined in this chapter what the potential is for the school. It must recognize its isolated character and begin to help young people to learn to deal with the real world rather than dealing with artificial learning tasks that have come to be called lessons. The school of the modern age was centred around fields of study. These will likely constitute the main ways knowledge is organized in the future, but these fields must cease focusing only on conventional problems of the field itself and begin to demonstrate a capacity to help learners to deal with everyday life. They must help learners to cope more adequately with authentic learning situations.

Schools generally do not help students to discover the structure of fields of study, nor do they help students to learn. It is important to stimulate the processes that lead to systematic reasoning. It is through co-operation and dialogue that people are able to shift from situation-specific to more general understanding.

Chapter 7

Contemporary Educational Models for the Future

LIMITATIONS OF CONTEMPORARY EDUCATIONAL MODELS

Most contemporary models of education are limited by their singular focus. That focus may be the democratization process of school, multiculturalism, the impact of the information society on education, or the establishing of closer relationships between the school and the world of work. But each of these models has only one dimension. Instead, we should have a broader model of schooling which includes all of these inputs. Of course, there will be contradictions and conflicts between the one-dimensional perspectives, but perhaps there is some way to bring harmony between them, forming what should be a general model of schooling for the year 2020.

SCHOOLS IN THE SERVICE OF DEMOCRACY

If future societies are to be characterized by democracy, democratic attitudes and values should be instilled in younger members of society. Further, young people should be given practice in democratic behaviours. Many of the institutions that traditionally serve youth are not always democratic. Clearly, many families and religious institutions are characterized by hierarchy, authoritarianism, and patriarchy, usually antithetical to democratic expression (Levin, 1993, p. 2). Amy Gutmann (1987, pp. 282–3) also points out that most work places do not reflect the characteristics of democracy. Employers often expect workers to practise absolute obedience to arbitrary rules. Those at the higher levels of an authority pyramid in firms may expect workers to perform a limited number of operations, to be uninventive in their work practices and to accept mandates without question.

Even though institutional patterns are changing, it is risky to rely on families, churches and the workplace to help youth to learn democratic values and practise democratic behaviours. Unfortunately, we could make a similar indictment of the school. It has not been an exemplary institution for instilling democratic values in its youth. Most schools are organized in an authoritarian and hierarchical fashion. Important decisions are typically made at the upper levels of this hierarchy and passed down to lower levels of the structure, where teachers and students form the lowest tier. Even so, as humankind faces the future, its greatest hope for developing democracy among the youth ought to be the schools.

Those measures taken by parliamentary democracies to ensure that schools instil democratic values, attitudes and behaviours have, to this point, been disappointing (Jennings and Niemi, 1974). Typically, schools have adopted formal curriculum units to teach youth about the struggle for democracy, about the democratic processes in government, including laws and governance practices, and about the role of the general citizen. However, empirical evidence concerning political and civic knowledge has not been positive. Central and Eastern Europeans, who are attempting to democratize their societies through education, are acutely aware that preparation for democracy is more than teaching about democracy. Of course, it includes having knowledge about the rights and obligations of citizens, but it also includes competence about human relationships and a mode of behaviour. Democratic education may best occur through democratic practice (Loránd 1993, p. 2). Democratic practice occurs at many levels in education. We shall touch here on choice of schools, administration of schools, and school programmes.

Choice as a Democratic Value in Education

For many, choice of schooling for children through some sort of voucher initiative, is consistent with democracy, because it empowers parents to define which school is most appropriate for the child and provides public resources to support these choices. For many others, the community and state are thought to be the agents best suited to make decisions about the type of school most appropriate for the child. There are strong arguments for both views. John I. Goodlad argues, for example, that the unique role the school must play is to provide a set of common, national values, while the family and church provide the unique value orientations of society (Goodlad, 1975). Arthur Schlesinger, Jr (1995) has also decried the practical recommendations of the New York State Social Studies syllabus Review Committee of 1991, because it 'reverses the history theory of America'. He argues that the US has been the most successful large multi-ethnic nation 'precisely because, instead of emphasizing the perpetuating ethnic separatism, it has assimilated immigrant cultures into a new American culture' (p. 631). Schlesinger feels family, church, and community are sufficiently vital to provide for the ethnic subcultures, but 'it is surely not the office of the public school to promote ethnic separatism and heighten ethnic tensions' (p. 632). Rather, he feels the schools must dedicate themselves to a general, common programme, a common base and value system. They must provide the glue holding society together. They must be the arena where different children learn to get along, resolve differences and debate points of view.

The history of modern European education has been the story of overcoming separation of children according to their social class backgrounds. Some European countries have been more successful than others in their quest for a common school. Scandinavia has generally been the model for Western Europeans in that all children are mandated to attend the same school for at least nine years. In addition, almost all children in Scandinavia have participated in the same curriculum. Of course, significant difference remains, both in social class terms and in geographic terms. Children of lower class origins do not succeed at the same rate as children of the upper social classes. And children in large urban areas succeed at a much higher rate than children from rural and isolated areas, even when social class is held constant (Rust, 1989, Ch. 18).

The argument proponents of common schooling give, however, is that in spite of continuing inequities, schools are considerably more equal than political rights and income in the larger society. Common school proponents argue that education is less unequal than the rest of society. Even if schools are less unequal, Gutmann points out that, in America at least, schools continue to engage in educationally unnecessary tracking; they have presided over racial segregation and they have instituted some of the most intellectually deadening methods of teaching democratic values and concepts one might imagine (Gutmann, 1987, p. 65). And Europe is clearly more extreme in these respects than the US.

Recent developments in Central and Eastern Europe can only contribute to a sense of unease about the dangers of fragmenting tendencies. Without question, one of the major disintegrative forces in the Russian Republic today is the insistence of local groups that they have autonomy. It is little wonder that, with *perestroika*, the strong currents of nationality interests came to the fore as minority groups protested against Russification and normative socialist ideals.

The developments in Central and Eastern Europe are sobering, but they must not be construed as prototypes of things to come in the West. The reason it is highly unlikely that young people in Western Europe and North America will fall into isolated cells is because the various institutions that serve them have highly dissimilar memberships. The small, fragmented workplaces have no overlapping membership connection with the small, fragmented churches, families, schools and youth associations. The small, fragmented churches have no overlapping membership connection with workplace, families, schools and youth associations. Even institutions that in the past had overlapping memberships, such as churches and family type are increasingly unconnected. That is, gay, single parent and childless families are found in every church group and do not cluster according to family type. Consequently, even though institutions have similar characteristics in terms of size and structure, they have little in common across different types of institutions. It is even difficult to distil cultural groups into isolated groups in postmodern societies. For example, American Indians are thought to be groups that live in isolation on reservations, when in fact the greater numbers of American Indians are located in large urban areas, such as Los Angeles, and they often have little to do with other American Indians in the urban settings. And American Indians are not the exception. The segmentation and fragmentation of groups in Los Angeles have created a geographic landscape that has become so kaleidoscopic, so filled with unsettling contrariety, that it defies interpretation (Soja, 1989). Given these developments, it is imperative that some mechanism be in place to ensure multiculturalism does not result in general fragmentation of society.

Even if we were to argue for the continuation of some form of common schooling, we anticipate that the future will bring greater fragmentation and choice into the school arena, and that must be prepared for. Probably, an environment providing family-choice will override common schooling interests and by the next century some form of family-choice or voucher system will become common. On democratic grounds, there may be reason to support the development; a family-choice system implicitly exemplifies democratic values of choice. Families who are given an opportunity to choose among schools and programmes are making democratic decisions that are not available where everyone is forced to attend the same school. We have noted that private schools may have been able to do better than public schools, and family choice options open these opportunities to a broader spectrum of families (Coleman, 1988). That is, whereas private schooling has been the domain of the rich, family-choice programmes would also provide resources for poorer families to take advantage of these options.

In Europe, some countries have long maintained a school tradition that supports the notion of choice. For example, a feature of Dutch society is a segmented system. The Dutch are highly individualistic in temperament and, in 1920, they established a school law which allowed three systems of education to exist: neutral (28 per cent of students in 1990), Protestant (27 per cent of students) and Catholic (40 per cent of students). There is greater variation than this because some non-religious private schools also exist (6 per cent of students), and Protestant schools are not unified in their schooling orientations but reflect the political and religious orientations of their sponsors.

The Dutch practice free choice, as the constitution declares the government responsible to provide parents with the type of education which best suits their way of life, their outlook, or the teaching method they prefer. If 50–125 people, depending on size of the community, petition the government for a school, it is obliged to see if such an undertaking is feasible, and if a school is established, the government pays all running expenses according to a formula, which includes paying for teacher salaries based on a teacher/student ratio of 31–1. Private schools are able to charge a small fee to cover some nonpersonnel costs, which is usually about 10–20 per cent of the budget. A private school need only raise 15 per cent of the estimated building costs of a proposed school and must demonstrate to authorities that a minimum number of children will attend, 6 children for a primary school in a rural area. The government and municipality are required to provide the remainder of the building costs and all other costs. Recent school laws in the Netherlands are intended to increase even more than before the possibility for choice (Liket, 1991).

The Netherlands is a prime example of why Western Europe and North America may be quite different from Central and Eastern Europe. Even though the fragmentation process is dramatic in the West, the developments are toward intermixing of groups rather than the isolation and separation of groups. Even in the Netherlands, where public policy has been toward a so-called 'pillarized' social structure, that has encouraged the people to exist separately in many phases of Dutch life, including places of residence, jobs, friendship circles, political parties and schools, that public policy has become almost irrelevant, because the personal choices the Dutch are making have obliterated the pillarized nature of Dutch society.

The issue of choice has also driven the reform discourse in the UK in the past two decades. The UK retains close ties to its historical tradition in that it relies on the private sector to satisfy some of its educational needs. However, through most of the twentieth century, the private sector had been reduced in size, if not importance, due to gradual improvements in the quality of state education (Papadakis and Taylor-Gooby, 1987). Recently, the proportion of children in private schools has been little over 5 per cent and the overwhelming majority (85 per cent) are in schools wholly maintained by the state (p. 76).

The Conservative government of the UK has been trying to reverse the trends of this past century. Its recent reforms might be seen partly as an attempt to address discontent among parents, particularly among the middle classes, who are dissatisfied with the recent impoverishment of state-provided education (Newton, 1986), but who are unable to gain access to the current private system. In 1981, the Conservatives introduced an Assisted Place Scheme, providing a state subsidy to poorer parents, whose children were able to gain entry to private schools.

The government has also introduced a type of privatization within the public sector itself. The 1988 Education Reform Act gives all schools a much greater voice with regard to recurrent expenditures and school policy. In addition, parents have been given the right to enrol their children in schools of their choice regardless of community boundaries, as long as those schools have room for additional students. Central government in England and Wales, far from following the permissive or *laissez-faire* approach it has followed previously, has attempted to gain from the diminution of local education authority (LEA) control.

The government has also systematically moved the sponsorship of government schools away from the Department of Education and Science. Some state schools run by local authorities have opted out. Thus, the private schools are part of a wider market and the government's aims are, above all, to encourage the development of market principles and competitive institutions throughout the education system (Williams and Heritage, 1988).

In the coming age, the current voucher notions may prove to be too restrictive and limiting, in that they are related only to school choice. Instead, specific aspects of the educational process probably will fragment so that young people will be able to take advantage of the best of several programmes within the context of the general voucher provision. For example, the best music programme of a community might be sponsored by a single group, that satisfies the needs of a wide range of students from various schools. The best computer education programmes of a community might be offered by a national centre offering interactive instruction through electronic means to young people all over the nation. The best mathematics programme might be offered by a local aerospace firm, whose staff wish to be involved in teaching. There is no reason why a student should not be able to take advantage of all of these options, in addition to one of the local public/private schools that serve as the home-base for the student and fills out the remainder of the school programme.

The school's capacity to take advantage of the latest technology has been found to be limited. Developments outside the school only gradually impact it, so the school is rarely on the forefront of informational technology. The possibilities exist to learn in the context of informational technology, but that process will always occur on a broken front. The use of CD-ROMs, databases, information networks, and *edutainment* (a kind of learning through play and entertainment) are examples of developments that are occurring as rapidly as they ever have occurred.

People experience a similar dissonance in the general schools as is occurring in vocational schools. It may be that all schools should not attempt to be on the forefront of movements but should concentrate on more general learnings and issues related to the home and to free time.

There are a number of examples of unusual schooling arrangements. In the Soviet period, for example, most children attended at least two different schools. All children attended a general school, where they were exposed to a common curriculum. Then they also were channelled into specialized schools for art, languages, mathematics, sport, etc. In the West, such opportunities have also existed, but typically only in the private sector. That is, after school, parents would have their children take piano lessons, participate in sports clubs or attend dance classes, as a supplement to general schooling.

Such diverse arrangements would likely require a radical restructuring of educational programmes, because they would not allow for a series of 50-minute class sessions to constitute the school day. One of the most likely innovations would be a modular-type structure similar to that in vocational education found in the Netherlands, because it allows for much greater flexibility in curriculum design. A module is a small compact curricular unit with a clearly defined set of objectives, contents and processes (Weugelers, 1988). These would allow a student to work intensively on a single course for, say, two to four weeks, or in combination with other modules that would allow for travel and extended instruction.

There will also likely be great changes in administrative arrangements. In the US, the local school district has traditionally been the seat of authority and power, but the school district is quickly losing its authority, part of which is moving to the local school itself. For example, the local school is playing a growing role in school finance. In Chicago, for example, funds coming from the central state are bypassing the school district office and are being channelled directly to the school itself. The school is taking on the responsibility of hiring its own teachers and deciding what the teachers shall earn (Williams and Heritage, 1988). Schools are not allowed to participate in certain funding options provided by the state unless they agree to establish a local school commission. The local school is defining what its programme shall be, at least within the limits allowed by the centralized state programmes.

In America, schools are traditionally neighbourhood schools. That is, children are expected to attend the school that exists in the neighbourhood where they live. A consequence of this tradition has been that every school – primary, junior high, and senior high – was seen as a comprehensive school, i.e. a school that would attempt to satisfy every talent, every interest, every academic and vocational competence. The school could not focus on one stratum of its population, but it would address every need and satisfy every desire. How would it do this? Schooling in America adopted what has been describe as a cafeteria style, where each child was given great latitude in deciding what his or her programme would look like.

With bussing and integration, which developed mainly during the 1970s, the tradition of the neighbourhood school was somewhat modified. The Supreme Court of the US ruled in 1954 that segregation was illegal and it ruled that schools must maintain some racial balance (Brown vs Board of Education, 1954). A few creative solutions developed out of this movement, including home study, magnet schools and regional occupation programmes. However, bussing and integration were programmes of the late 1960s and 1970s. With the rise of conservative politics, exemplified by Ronald Reagan and George Bush, these programmes have been counted as historical elements of a liberal past.

The contemporary reform movement has clear conservative roots and is economically driven. Its leaders have little interest in social welfare issues such as racial integration. They wish to create schools that prepare youth for a free market economy. Significantly, just as in the UK, they have also adopted a free market model for schools, claiming that schools themselves must be subjected to a competitive format. This competitive format allows parents to make choices about where they may send their children to be schooled. The notion behind this is that competition will strengthen the quality of schools. They maintain that when a school has a monopoly, it experiences no competition so it has no incentive to improve itself or make itself more attractive to the students. If schools are in competition with each other for resources and students, then the good schools will attract pupils and the poor schools will decline and eventually die. This notion means, however, that the leaders of the movement today must destroy the idea of the neighbourhood school, in order to give parents the opportunity to choose between schools. They maintain that parents are the best judges about which schools serve the needs of their children, parents know best what is necessary for their children to receive the best education; see, for example, the discussion on New Zealand reforms in Chapters 4 and 5.

There are three levels of activity regarding parental choice in America. At the first level, parents are given the opportunity to decide which school within a school district their children will attend. At the second level of activity, parents may place their child in a school outside the school district boundary, if they can demonstrate that a particular school is important for the child's talents and interests. At the third level of activity, parents are working to obtain the right to enrol their children in private schools using public funds to pay most of the tuition costs. This is a radical departure from the historical tradition of countries such as the US. America has a strong tradition of separation of church and state, and because almost all of its private schools are religiously sponsored, they have never been allowed to use public funds. This split came at the time primary schools were being established in America in the 1800s. At the time, most states of America were based on some form of Protestant religion. At about the same time a rather large influx of Catholics from Europe began to arrive in America. In an effort to curb the influence of the Catholic Church, American public schools took on a Protestant Church value system. The Catholics eventually were forced to establish their own private system of schooling, to provide a place where their children could receive an education that was not Protestant in orientation. Today, about 12 per cent of all pupils attend private schools, most of which are Catholic Church sponsored schools. However, recent studies have demonstrated that children who attend private schools usually perform better than those who attend public schools, so leaders of the present movement wish to make private school available, without great cost, to greater numbers of parents (Coleman, 1988).

The three examples given above of the Netherlands, the UK and the US are of countries that already possess a long tradition of local autonomy. One of the remarkable developments of recent years has been the decision to decentralize programmes that have heretofore been highly centralized. Norway, for example, moved quickly toward decentralization in the 1970s and 1980s, and more recently Sweden has moved to rid itself of the tradition of highly centralized state regulation. The argument has been that while the state reform activities of the past half century have been instrumental in establishing a homogeneous system where equity is ensured throughout the country, the system itself has become so institutionalized that it has choked creativity and humanity out of the schools. Since the 1990s, a new direction has begun to take form with initiative coming from central authorities. One example of new developments has been the Uppsala Project, which has turned almost all authority over to the individual schools. The higher authorities have shifted their roles so that they now act as a support element and sounding board for the schools. The consequence appears to be positive on the school level, the main difficulty appears the ambiguous role of the local politicians, who at times begin to act like central authorities in that they tend to lay a heavy hand on school affairs. In spite of this, the trend appears to have great potential (Odmark, 1993).

School Governance

One of the prominent features of education is the trend toward school-level decision making with regard to most aspects of the educational process. Throughout the modern age, regardless of centralized or decentralized systems, the individual schools have had little discretion in determining the way they have been organized and how they run their educational programmes. Curriculum, teaching practices, textbooks, school schedules, examinations, etc. have typically been set at the district, regional, or national levels. In recent years, there has been a radical departure from this tradition in Scandinavia, the US, Germany and many other countries, in that schools and local authorities have been empowered to make more and more decisions about the nature of the institutions where they work.

The attention being given to democratizing educational decision making in Central and Eastern Europe is dramatic. Democratic education has been on the agenda of every country and republic that was formerly within the Soviet sphere (Rust et al., 1994). Significantly, much of the attention given to democratization has focused on administrative restructuring, including school-based management (Loránd, 1993). In Poland, school-based management is being developed through a close relationship between university centres and individual schools (Niemozynaski et al., 1993). The Russians have proclaimed school-based management as the 'most rewarding strategy of educational management'. In this context, school-based management relies on a number of groups participating in the decision-making process. The highest organ of management in Russia is the so-called School Conference, in which teachers, pupils, parents and interested community members participate. Delegates are elected and they are charged with the responsibility of establishing the rules of the individual school. In addition, there is a School Council, which is an executive group elected by the School Conference. There is also a Teachers' Council, that decides professional aspects of the school, such as the school class schedule. The School Council enforces the rules laid down by the School Conference, implements the school curriculum, controls the school budget, seeks extramural resources, outlines the school profile, etc. (Gazman, 1991).

Those engaged in democratizing the governance system have been trying to include the teacher as a central player in school administration. The project *Education for a Democratic Future*, in Melbourne, Australia, illustrates the type of activities being undertaken. In that project, teachers begin to work with formal administrators in in-service courses that attempt to move them toward being more centrally involved in curriculum development and school change. In the process, teachers are sensitized to the need to break away from conventional content areas of their school curricula and include critical content areas that have not received the attention these will likely require in tomorrow's world. These include issues such as war, poverty, injustice, ecological imbalance and dehumanized social institutions (Knight, 1987).

Another major interest is the involvement of parents in the life of the school. In the past, parental relationships with the school have too often been seen as a mechanism to make the pupils do what the school wants them to do. More and more, parental involvement includes participation of parents in defining where the school ought to be going, defining appropriate pupil behaviour, working to enhance self-esteem of pupils, etc. (Meadows, 1993).

Learning to be Democratic

While attempts to democratize the schools as organizations and to provide greater flexibility in choosing educational programmes on the part of parents is growing, a relatively small amount of attention is being given to concrete programmes of study for students. And yet, youth must learn democratic values and how to behave democratically. This might involve such simple arrangements as student government, where the youth begin to practise group decision-making processes (Dixon, 1994). Or it might include attending to the development of empathy, gaining respect for other children, co-operating and making ethical choices. For example, Polly Greenberg has developed a programme which includes group exercises and the processes for identifying children in the group who may have the talent to contribute unique and valuable skills to the accomplishment of specific tasks. In this respect, the children learn to engage in productive group formation and rely on each other in the accomplishment of tasks (Greenberg, 1992).

A number of case-studies have been engaged in to illustrate democratic education in schools and classrooms. One programme has been instituted in Australia that attempts to provide an apprenticeship in democratic practice to young primary children (Knight, 1988). The programme is based on the belief that learning to be democratic is evolutionary and gradual. In fact, we maintain democracy is never completely learned but is a lifelong process and struggle. The programme focuses on primary education and has two stages. In the first stage, lower primary school pupils (grades 1–3) devote considerable time to the rationale of the programme. Emphasis is given to the need that democracy only functions when a rational social order exists. Consequently, the social order of a school must also be rational. At the lower level, teachers are in full control of the classroom, but the initial emphasis is that the young children learn why there is a need for rules of behaviour and the consequences of rule breaking. This quickly turns to an exploration of student rights, in the context of individual rights and social responsibility. At this level, the model of democracy is imposed on the pupils, in that the teacher sets clear standards and consequences for breaking the rules. Pupils are continually reminded that they are making choices to observe the rules or break the rules, and they are reminded when they are working within the parameters of the classroom rules and when they are working outside them. Their decisions bring consequences that can be predicted. The professional educator will see the relevance of Canter's Assertive Discipline model in this programme (Canter, 1976).

At the next level (grades 4–6), students begin to experiment with their own self-management, although this is done in the context of shadow leadership on the part of adults. Students begin to participate in a process of rule establishment and take responsibility to decide on the consequences of rule breaking. Such a process involves surveying opinions, learning how to conduct meetings where possibilities are explored, electing representatives, resolving conflicts, etc. All of

111

this is done within a controlled context where freedom is not seen as licence but as shared responsibility.

In the US, Mary Hepburn has compiled a series of cases for the National Council for Social Studies, which illustrate democracy in action in specific schools and classrooms. Illustrative of these would be Parker High School, Minnesota, which attempts to expose students to issues surrounding representative democracy in developing a school constitution, defining rights and privileges, defining school budgets, etc. St Paul Open School, also in Minnesota, includes pupils in deliberations of school governance arrangements, curriculum development and even such specific activities as school graduation. Northport Union Free School District in New York has adopted an ombudsperson to help pupils to resolve conflicts and address grievances (Hepburn, 1983). These and other cases help to illustrate how democratic principles might be learned as a part of school practices. One of the most inspiring institutions we have found has been the Experimental Gymnasium (Forsøksgymnasiet) in Oslo, Norway, which has helped young people to begin to learn in a milieu that encourages personal initiative and mutual respect. It has served as a model for other alternative schools in Denmark and Sweden, where democratic principles are practised in the daily life of the school.

SCHOOLS IN THE SERVICE OF MULTICULTURALISM

At this point in the evolution of most countries, multicultural education is only something to be anticipated; however, in some countries and major cities it is already a reality. German schools now offer elite secondary school certificates in the Turkish language. In California, one of every six pupils in the schools was born outside the US, and two-thirds of the pupils speak a language at home other than English (Gray, 1993, p. 69). As mobility increases in the world, a large number of places will begin to reflect a demographic profile similar to California. In other words, the schools will become multicultural in terms of their student populations. The question is, will the schools hinder multicultural developments or will they only contribute to the problems such a world brings? In California, many teachers have already given their answers. Schools must turn ethnic diversity in classrooms to an educational advantage. The children and teachers themselves can serve as vehicles to geography, language and history awareness that reflect multiple cultures. The school can become a polyglot of different nationalities in their school lunches, their library selections, their recess games, their interschool athletic programmes, and their dress styles. Counselling, courses of study, teaching styles, learning styles, community input and assessment procedures can all begin to reflect a multicultural orientation.

It was not an easy process to arrive at the point of multicultural schooling. Indeed, much remains to be done. According to James Banks (1988), the US has evolved through at least four phases before reaching genuine multicultural education. In the first phase, as Mexican Americans, Blacks and others began to make demands for recognition in the schools; the schools responded by instituting what Banks calls monoethnic courses. That is, they began providing small courses and workshops to these ethnic minorities about their own backgrounds. At the Victor Berger Preschool, for example, which is predominantly populated by African-American children, the entire curriculum is oriented towards African-American content (Scherer, 1992). As more and more groups began to press for recognition in the school curricula, it became impossible to satisfy the demands by multiplying separate courses, so a second phase was initiated. Courses came into being that look at more general concerns of ethnic groups. However, these courses continued to be directed towards the ethnic populations themselves.

The third phase witnessed the development of programmes that went beyond an ethnic studies focus. Achievement studies indicated that ethnic studies could help in terms of self-respect and self-esteem, but they were not sufficient to help many young people to achieve at a respectable level in schools. It would be necessary to conceptualize education more broadly, to deal with the total school environment and to deal with many facets of schooling if the young were to be successful in school. At the Shoreham-Waking School District, for example, students focus on human rights in the context of understanding the achievements and experiences of their own culture. At the same time, the school attempts to help young people to understand and appreciate certain other cultures (Adames *et al.*, 1992)

The final phase of development came when educators began calling for more than multi-ethnic studies. They demanded that ethnic groups were suffering a plight in schools similar to many other cultural groups, including females, handicapped persons, religious groups, many poor white groups. This label has come to be known generally as multicultural education in that it deals with various types of cultures including ethnic cultures (Banks, 1988, Ch. 2).

In Europe, two models of multicultural education appear to be taking shape (Roosens, 1994). First, the *European School* model has taken root with 15,000 pupils and 1000 teachers working and enrolled in schools that focus on Europe rather than a single nationality. The European movement issues its own European school-leaving certificate, known generally as the *European Baccalaureate*, which gives access to all universities of the European Community as well as institutions in Austria, Switzerland and the US. Second, a number of schools specifically target children of immigrant labourers and refugees. The so-called Foyer Model in Brussels, is a good example of this approach. In that school model, children are engaged in a process of identification with their own culture as well as other cultures. In kindergarten, the time devoted to their own ethnic group is equal to the time devoted to children of other cultures. At the primary school level, about 60 per cent of the first-year programme (language, culture and mathematics) is given as a part of their own ethnic or cultural group, while 30 per cent is provided in a new language and 10 per cent is devoted to integrated activities. In the second year, the separate programme is reduced to 50 per cent and in the third year about 90 per cent of the time children are taught as an integrated group, while they continue a small part of their programme in their mother tongue.

One of the *Schoolyear 2020* representatives, Prentice Baptiste, Jr, has been an advocate of multicultural education. He and Karen Hughes, a colleague in Houston, claim that the goals of multicultural education should include:

1 appreciation and respect for cultural diversity;
2 promotion of the understanding of unique cultural and ethnic heritages;
3 promotion of culturally responsible and responsive curriculum in all areas;
4 acquisition of attitudes, skills and knowledge to function beside and co-operate with various cultures;

5 reduction of racism and discrimination in all areas of the organization as
   well as society.

Baptiste has developed a typology of multicultural evolution consisting of three
levels. He suggests that people and groups progress through three levels of inquiry
as they become more and more sophisticated with multicultural education programmes. Significantly, these levels replicate in some ways Banks' historical phases
mentioned above, but Baptiste goes beyond Banks. At level one, programmes are
additive in that they are tacked on to the regular programme of studies and focused
on specific ethnic groups. They target specific ethnic groups and are intended to
help ethnic group members to become more competent and develop a sense of pride
in their own culture. They are ameliorative in that they try to help ethnic minority
groups to deal more adequately with the expectations of the dominant culture. At
this level, no changes in the dominant culture are suggested or anticipated.

At level two, there is a shift toward more general multicultural concerns, in
that various cultural and ethnic perspectives are included in topics, units of study,
concepts and events. Programmes are incorporated into the regular programme of
study. Most programmes attempt to transmit information about a variety of
cultures and their contribution to the broader development of society. The
programmes also go beyond ethnicity and include gender, handicapped and social
class issues.

Level three is only reached after the first two levels have been achieved. It
involves a process whereby positive attitudes toward a pluralistic society are being
internalized. The legitimacy of multiculturalism is no longer in question, only strategies for attaining the best from a multicultural society. There is no intention, within
this framework, to expect young people to become multicultural in that the young
would be expected to be competent in more than one culture. Rather, the focus is
on being able to understand more than one culture. There are many people who
have competence in a culture without understanding it. Likewise, it is not necessary
to practise cultural behaviours in order to be sensitive to them and understand their
form and importance (Feinberg, 1993).

Baptiste's conceptual framework has been applied in many different types of
institutions. His colleague, Karen Hughes, has been particularly active in developing
such a programme at preschools in Houston, Texas. Very young children are taken
through a series of experiences, beginning with celebrations of ethnic holidays and
ethnic dances, stereotypical portrayals of cultural groups, etc. Then they are expo-
sured to culturally diverse resources and materials that highlight multiculturalism.
Finally, they deal with experiences that enable them to express empowerment and
positive group identity. Included in this exposure is material that expresses prejudice and bias, and the young people learn to counteract such materials. They learn
that cultural diversity is an asset and that all children ought to be valued (Baptiste
and Hughes, 1993, p. 41).

Empowerment is a central facet of multicultural education. A number of programmes exist which attempt to help those who are traditionally marginalized come
to terms with their location in society and these programmes are intended to help
the young to gain the sense of self-respect and recognition necessary for them to
play a role in a multicultural society (Sleeter, 1991).

Multicultural education has progressed to the point that it is now credited with being an academic discipline by some members of the community (Banks, 1993). This means that a cadre of academic leaders are emerging who identify themselves as specialists in multicultural education. There are groups that are formulating standards for the field. As yet, no such standards exist, even while a number of excellent programmes for the schools are in existence. This is most evident in places such as Los Angeles, which are truly multicultural in nature and must deal with the situation in a positive and direct way. Essentially, every secondary school in the city has a wide range of diverse activities specifically targeting their diverse populations. These include celebration of days special to various racial and ethnic groups, such as Cinco de Mayo and Martin Luther King's birthday. They include student assemblies where ethnic music and dance are presented, global village celebrations are engaged in, etc.

Special training programmes are widespread. Students and staff alike engage in conflict resolution training and multicultural literature units in language courses. Teachers develop modules intending to supplement textbooks that fail to provide adequate perspectives of events and peoples. Most schools have a wide variety of student-run clubs and organizations such as Hebrew, Korean and Persian culture clubs, Amnesty International and WISH (world in search of harmony). A number of specific programmes exist at various schools. One programme developed in Los Angeles, known as *Hands across the Campus*, focuses on a humanities approach to culture. The developers claim it is humanities-oriented because it falls in the humanities section of courses offered by the school district and relies heavily on anthropological concepts, such as culture, race and ethnicity. If successful, students would gain some appreciation of their own backgrounds, they would appreciate and understand the roles and contributions of various cultural, racial, and ethnic groups, they would make progress in the English language and basic communications skills, and they would learn to clarify their own values and to participate as members of a self-governing society (LAUSD, 1993). The programme relies on a large number of learning approaches to achieve its aims, including a number of language development approaches, such as journals, panel discussions, buzz groups, oral reports, dramatizations, talk show simulations, newscast simulations, role-plays, learning games and other experiential exercises. In the Bay Area (San Francisco), a so-called DARE programme (diversity awareness resource education) has been developed and many teachers in cities such as Los Angeles have adapted it. The main focus of DARE is to facilitate communication between different ethnic groups, to challenge stereotypes about different races, religions and nationalities, and to encourage personal relationships between groups. Many schools have a so-called big-brother/sister programme, where experienced students and staff members adopt a new immigrant as a brother or sister in an attempt to establish a long-range relationship with someone. Where ethnic tensions may be quite high, a Blue and Red Ribbon programme may exist, which is intended to enhance a greater sense of community in the school and create a student crisis management team that works to prevent or stifle racial and ethnic strife.

SCHOOLS RESPOND TO THE MEDIA

Schools must help young people to learn how to take advantage of information media and the new communications technology for their own learning. Technology has moved so quickly that it promises soon to give learners access to information, wherever and whenever the learner wishes to access that knowledge. Already, major projects exist with the intention of making that promise a reality. The European Community, for example, has taken the initiative to develop the DELTA project, which attempts to provide direct and remote access throughout Europe to learning resources. With a budget of 100 million dollars in 1994 alone, it draws 174 organizations together to focus on more than 300 sub-projects intending to facilitate networks of information (Collis and de Vries, 1994).

While the DELTA project is marvellous, the new technology promises to engulf the entire world. One of the major breakthroughs in telecommunications work has been the so-called Internet, which at the time of this writing was a network of over 5000 networks on all seven continents around the globe. In 1993, up to 10 million people had addresses on this network, including more than 50,000 teachers. One of the services this network provides, is that a person may have contact with a particular computer system anywhere in the world as easily as if that person were sitting directly in front of the machine. Finland, for example, has incorporated e-mail into its foreign language education programmes, so that students might interact directly with young people whose mother tongue is the language being studied (Tella, 1994). The implications for education are monumental. Educators are finally able to talk about genuine equality of educational opportunity, at least in terms of accessibility. Those who have long been disadvantaged because they were living far removed from centres of learning now have direct access to those centres. In New Mexico, for example, remote high schools are engaged in interactive instruction through two-way video hook-ups with community colleges, which provide instruction in the most current courses available anywhere (Technology in Education Act, 1993). Already some school districts exist in America, which allow a child, who is at home, ill, to take part in school classes from the sickbed at home (Dyrli, 1993). One of the major breakthroughs in education is that institutions of higher learning are no longer some distant place of advanced learning. They are becoming increasingly integrated into the everyday life of school children. In North Carolina, for example, Appalachian State University has joined with private enterprises such as AT&T and Southern Bell to provide rural high schools with the most current concepts and information (Riedl and Carroll, 1993).

At the same time, computers have become so pervasive in classrooms that they are now a common part of language, mathematics, natural science, social science, music, art and technology classes. With telecommunications developments, the necessity of schools remaining in large complexes is quickly becoming obsolete. It is possible to bring people from everywhere together in face-to-face meetings from almost anywhere on the globe. The local school appears to be much too confining in face of a world open to all. Already people can communicate through electronic mail as readily with people on the other side of the globe as with a friend across the street, and almost as inexpensively.

Neil Postman (1987) suggests that Americans have fallen in love with technology. To fall in love suggests that they so adore their love that they see no faults in it. Technology is dazzling and alluring and Americans are captivated by its seductive attraction, so much so that they are incapable of distancing themselves from new and exciting technologies.

To the first issue, there is a growing attention to electronic technology in education. Here we shall focus our attention only on the computer. A number of projects have recently been under way that have explored how the computer can be integrated into the school programme. Ragsdale (1987) points out that the three major areas of competence schools concentrate on is on the study of the computer itself, the computer as a teacher, and the computer as a tool to be used. The largest developments in instruction are probably based on the fact that many teachers are behind their students in terms of understanding the latest technology. San Marcos, Texas has demonstrated it is possible to overcome this obstacle as a number of institutions, including the local school district, Southwest State University, Region XIII Educational Service Center, and Century Telephone Company have formed a consortium that provides each classroom with extensive, interconnected hardware, equipped with the most current software. Classrooms are fully equipped with full motion interactive TV, with video cameras, videotapes and laser discs. All teachers, teacher candidates, parents and pupils can take introductory courses in the entire system and teachers then have an additional two hours a week of ongoing training. The project has led to a striking sense of confidence and enthusiasm, greater student-centred learning and increased community involvement in the schools (Curtin et al., 1994).

In Finland, a wide variety of activities has been under way for many years. The University of Jyväskylä (Konttinen, 1987), for example, has conducted a project in the use of the computer as a tool in schools. This project has included the study of the mother tongue through word processing, the enhancement of Finnish literature, French language and history courses by developing relevant databases, the incorporation into art courses of drawings and digitized pictures by computer, the enhancement of music courses by computerized composition and harmonization, the incorporation into mathematics classes of spreadsheet programs, etc. And the University of Joensuu (Enkenberg, 1987) has engaged in a novel experiment, called the KONTI Project, to bring advanced computer technology into small country villages. This project uses the village school as the centre for training in information technology, but it goes far beyond that; it collects databases of jobs that exist and jobs that are open in the area, so the school becomes a partner with the entire rural economy and serves as a clearing house for employment. Such a partnership keeps the school up to date in terms of the jobs available and the training necessary to fill these jobs.

In Canada, a project has been under way to establish a network to help individual teachers function more creatively with regard to the use of data technology in training, mutual experiences and support, and the development of instructional options. A major outcome of this project is that teacher-directed programmes can lead to striking advances in student participation and learning with regard to technology and computers (Ragsdale and Durell, 1994).

One of the important features of computer education has been the involvement of private firms in the development of viable programmes. Some of these firms target their efforts almost completely to their own industrial or commercial staff, such as the Noika hi-technology company in Finland (Laaksonen, 1987). The value of such efforts may be in the availability of a training package for schools to emulate. One company that has targeted its efforts toward schools has been the Apple

Classroom of Tomorrow projects (ACOT, 1987). One of ACOT's beacon projects has been at a rural Blue Earth School District, in Minnesota. All grades participate to some extent, but the main focus has been on the upper grades of primary school. For example, each sixth grader shares a computer at school with one other student, and every student has a computer at home for the entire school year. The impact has been impressive. For example, entirely new mathematics and language arts programmes have been instituted that allow students to move ahead as quickly as their ability and motivation permits. A problem-solving course has been developed that compels students to become globally aware as they attack local problems. The base of this course is a rich, global database that allows students to access information about those problems on a global level. Creativity is stressed through the use of graphics and sound capabilities by the computer. Such innovations required a whole set of new skills, including keyboarding skills, knowledge of wordprocessing programmes, use of databases and graphics packages. At West High School, in an urban slum area of Ohio, the level of absenteeism was dramatically reduced over a four-year period of the ACOT programme.

Because of the seductiveness of computers, there may be some tendency to adopt all of these needs into the curriculum by squeezing out other components of the school curriculum. Such an unreflective course of action is dangerous. The second issue stressed by Postman (1987) and Ellul (1981) is that new technology must be approached with a critical eye. We shall paraphrase seven critical ideas suggested by Postman, that youth ought to learn regarding technology.

1 For every advantage that technology brings, there are corresponding disadvantages. A culture always pays a price for a technological innovation.

2 New technologies are never distributed evenly in a population and so some benefit from them while others may suffer. New media tend to break up monopolies of old media. For example, TV may well be detrimental to schooling, because schooling is an institution based on the printed word.

3 Embedded in every technology are powerful ideas and philosophies, which reflect some kind of prejudice or perspective that is detrimental to other perspectives. Writing favours logical organization and systematic analysis, while TV focuses on immediacy and speed rather than introspection. The computer favours calculation rather than introspection.

4 The philosophy in a new technology makes war with the philosophy embedded in an old technology. In schools, the philosophy of the new emphasizes imagery, narrative, presentness, simultaneity, immediate gratification and emotional response; this philosophy wages war against the old emphasis on logic, sequence, history, exposition, objectivity, and discipline.

5 Technology is not additive; it is ecological. It does not just add something; it changes everything. Printing brought about a different Europe. TV has transformed the modern world. It has had a greater impact than the philosophers and social critics of our day.

6 The media tends to become mystic. It tends to settle into our consciousness as something that has always been there, as if it were God

given. It has already become natural to Americans to have 60 TV channels at their disposal. It would be inconceivable that it should be otherwise.

7 Technology and the media are two different things but have become synonyms. Media are seen as tools, and technology has come to be seen as a tool, but it is much more. It tends to take control of our lives and to dictate its own imperatives. But if we separate the two things, we can once again gain control over our social change.

The great challenge, from Postman's vantage point, is that schools must not serve technology, they must help young people to become critical of technology, to understand its nature and its negative elements, and to use it in a constructive manner. Few examples of that type of orientation exist at present, related specifically to computers education. An innovative project at Helsinki University, the Utopia Project, begun in 1992, uses the attractiveness of computers and data technology as a type of change agent, where teachers are encouraged to create a more open instructional environment while they introduce the use of technology (Tella, 1994).

If the young are to be educated to be critically aware, they must be in educational environments that emphasize higher-order thinking and critical evaluation skills that extend across curriculum fields. Such demands can take place at every level. Preschoolers at the Perry Preschool project in Ypsilanti, Michigan, for example, begin their days by making decisions about what they would like to do during the day. They are given skills to monitor what they do, they think through what they must do to accomplish their aims and, at the end of the day, they evaluate what has happened and decide what modifications are in order if they are to do it again (Jones, 1988).

SCHOOLS IN THE SERVICE OF SURVIVAL

There are a number of issues that merit special consideration as humanity faces the new century. The emerging role of women is of vital importance, as are containing violence and the growth of gangs and disaffected subcultures. Four issues relate to our survival as human beings on planet earth:

1 environmental education,
2 peace education,
3 health education, and
4 poverty.

We will focus on the educational dimensions of these issues. Environmental education is crucial because it deals with the possibility that humankind might destroy the natural environment that has sustained our globe. Peace education is crucial because it deals with ways to prevent us from destroying each other through physical arms. Health education provides a major corrective to the destructive life-styles of mature modern states. Poverty issues are crucial because we recognize that while some people may satisfy their basic human needs in this world, others are not so fortunate. They too deserve to have their minimal basic needs addressed through education.

Environmental Education

According to Al Gore, the world must become engaged in a global Marshall Plan, if it is to survive economic and technological development (Gore, 1993). Each individual must ultimately become ecologically conscious, so the educational process can begin with single classrooms, schools and administrative districts. Environmental education must become a part of education and school programmes. These programmes may be as simple as the Coombes Infant School near Reading, Berkshire, England, where pupils as young as five years of age are actively engaged in maintaining a healthy natural school environment. Naturally occurring plants are supplemented by judicious planting and imaginative efforts to add species and variety to the environment. The children learn not only that everything comes from the earth, but that they must work to maintain and cultivate life. They learn about the cycles of planting, caring and harvesting. They learn they cannot just take from the earth, but must return what is taken. The school attempts to maintain harmony with its environment and to be a centre for environmental awareness.

There appear to be some exemplary programmes. Many of these exemplify the melding of formal, nonformal and informal education, though they usually have a base in one or another of these types of education. Some activities are taking place in terms of thematic instruction about ecology in formal disciplines and courses of study at the schools. Across the Western US, for example, in the late winter and spring students in hundreds of schools monitor the immigration of Monarch butterflies from their winter homes in Mexico to northern parts of the US. As Monarchs arrive in a community, its students chart their numbers and progress and feed this information to other schools. Computer software maps the progress of the Monarchs and feeds this information back to the millions of computers plugged into the project. This is not only a remarkable educational activity, it also has environmental significance in that it is helping to save a species from extinction (Brandt, 1994). It also plays a significant role in helping to overcome a major obstacle facing our present capacity to generate information.

One of the problems humankind faces in the future is the prospect of information overload. The Landsat satellite, for example, is able to photograph every inch of the earth's surface every 18 days. Almost all of that information is never seen by human beings, because it is too vast; consequently, it never contributes to vital information about the environment. The world may reach a point of information pollution unless there is some mechanism for processing this information. The education world must become a part of this information processing activity. In the past, educators have thought of education too often as recycling information, of passing on the known wisdom of mankind. Education as an ecological activity must become more attuned to actual investigation and production of raw data. The Monarch project is one example of how information overload might be contained and made useful.

In Finland, OKO project has been running since 1986. It began when a small number of teachers from primary, lower secondary and upper secondary schools in Finnish Lapland joined together to develop a programme that would help students to gain 'the skills necessary for understanding and controlling the concrete environment in which we must function daily and for dealing the problems posed by it' (Kurtakko, 1988, p. 1). As they developed the programme it became clear that the schools must shift away from a subject-centred instruction toward a problem-centred and people-centred approach to education. Such a shift is consistent with recent environmental education literature, that makes a distinction between environmental instruction and environmental education. Instruction may sensitize or provide knowhow, whereas education helps people to act wisely in difficult situations (Hungerford and Volk, 1990).

There is a place for environmentally oriented experiences in nonformal contexts, which place young people in various types of settings that inspire inquiry concerning ecology. These often take place in the context of summer camps, nature parks, one-day workshops and field trips. For example, Camp Earth Options (EO) is a special day camp and summer camp in Southern California for upper primary school children that provides recreation and play opportunities intended to awaken awareness of children to their environment. At the ten-week summer camp, inner-city children engage in hands-on activities connected with nature. They play games, sing songs and do other things that awaken interest in their surroundings. In addition, they participate in team building, lectures and study of nature (Clendon, 1993).

In terms of informal education, a number of initiatives can be identified that might be described as action projects involving students in responsible community development endeavours. In fact, certain schools have already begun to take on the mission of being environmental watchdogs of the local world. An ordinary teacher may discover a toxic dump near the school and she begins to worry about the health and safety of the children for whom she is responsible, so she begins to help the children to become sensitive to the threat of the environment to their wellbeing. That teacher has recognized the need for ordinary citizens to move society and improve it, however imperfectly and unsteadily. A study of the environmental movement itself is evidence of the capacity of a small number of people to influence decisions among power brokers that often appear to be intractable. Some schools will make ecology one of their prime missions.

World Peace

One of the most vital issues facing the world community is that of maintaining world peace, and one of the challenges of schools will be to run programmes that will give greater assurance that future generations will work toward a more peaceful world. Even though the East–West tensions appear to have been eclipsed, the threat of war remains a major problem. The former Soviet Union is reducing its nuclear bomb arsenal, but the US continues to maintain a stockpile sufficient to destroy all life on earth many times over.

A number of educational programmes have been instituted that have peace education as a major goal. In the US, peace education has become a part of most higher education programmes, especially as subdisciplines of political science, history, sociology and psychology. In the most recent edition of *Peace and World Order Studies: A Curriculum Guide* (Thomas and Klaare, 1989), no less than 93 university and college course syllabi were discussed. Such a wide range of interest has not filtered down to the schools as fully as necessary. In fact, most peace education in the schools remains peripheral. It is seen as a side issue, but we anticipate that in time it can become a core element of most school programmes (Sloan, 1982).

In Europe, some excellent work is under way. Hermann Röhrs has developed a programme to help preschoolers become more sensitive to the dangers of war and violence (Röhrs, 1994). Magnus Haavelsrud (1981, pp. 100–13), at Tromsø University in Norway, explains that four different approaches to peace studies have been identified: the idealistic, scientific, ideological and politicization approaches. Each of these have different orientations.

- The *idealistic approach* claims that war is in the minds of people and the only way to ensure peace is to create a more rational and reflective society, a society where people learn to tolerate and accept each other.

- The *scientific approach* focuses on peace research at the macro or international level, and the curriculum would emerge out of the research findings of the academic community concerning the arms race in the orld.

- The *ideological approach* claims the school must mediate the interests of powerful groups that encourage conflict for their own self-serving purposes. The school consequently acts as a counteractive force in society against war.

- The *politicization approach* is somewhat unique. Whereas the other three approaches focus mainly on information and content to be transmitted to the learner, the politicization approach provides strategies for achieving desirable goals. Even though people know what ought to be done, they must have the skills to act on that knowledge and bring about desired ends.

As has been mentioned, the major thrust in peace education has taken place outside the schools themselves. Churches, physicians, scientific organizations, women's groups and others have long organized efforts to warn about the dangers of nuclear proliferation and expanding military conflicts. Significantly, the first individuals who really taught seriously about the threat of nuclear war were those scientists who helped to develop the atomic bomb (Totten, 1982, p. 200). Feminist groups maintain that male domination is at the root of much violence and that female orientations must begin to dominate institutions such as the school (Brock-Utne, 1985). In the nonformal education sector, a number of initiatives are taking place around the world. In Israel, for example, socalled Buberian Learning Groups have been running since 1979 attempting to bring about dialogue between Jews and Arabs. These groups found quickly that it would not be enough to remain at the level of dialogue. They must begin to translate insight into active responsibility for furthering peace in their region (Gordon and Demarest 1982). In the US, religious groups, such as that at Old Pine Presbyterian Church, have conducted extensive peace-education activities. At Old Pine, the focus has been on the home, with the notion that peace begins with the single individual and positive, healthy relationships in the most basic of social institutions: the home. A nonviolent society is seen as a multiple extension of local, intimate institutions (Glass, 1982).

There are schools that have taken the challenge, though examples are not plentiful. Immediately after the collapse of the East German regime in 1989, educators began work to organize a completely new type of educational programme. Blenheim Street School in East Berlin, recognizing the terrible tensions that had existed between East and West, developed a full school programme for its ten-year school having the label: European Peace School. The school intended to provide various language options for its students. It wished to provide students with an appreciation of being European rather than a part of some nationality-oriented institution. It intended to focus its curriculum on harmonious life between various cultures of the world, and this curriculum included various mechanisms for teaching how to resolve conflicts (Rust, 1993).

Health Education

Health education is something that must be a part of formal schooling in preschools, primary schools, and secondary schools. Attention is vital even in tertiary and adult education programmes. Of course, these programmes must be supplemented by family and institutional programmes serving youth, including clubs, churches and community agencies.

Even though health-education programmes of the past have not been successful, a number of recent programmes show some promise. The older programmes that relied heavily on scare tactics about the link between cancer and smoking, the link between homosexual behaviour and AIDS, etc., gave way to health programmes that not only showed consequences of destructive behaviours but provided strategies for avoiding temptation and refusing invitations to participate. Newer programmes recognize that people must be sustained and provide individuals with life-skill training that is comprehensive in nature. A good example of this type of programme is a so-called Life Skills Training introduced by Botvin and Eng (1982), who were interested in the issue of smoking. It is a multi-component programme including the types of motivation of clients, knowledge (human biology), and social competence (body image and body integrity) that are beneficial, as well as how the socio-environmental context affects behaviour, social skills (communication, body language, empathy, etc.) and what effects assertiveness training can have on behaviour. Another example focuses on cognitive skills, including higher-order reasoning and critical thinking skills. Spivack and Shure (1982) introduced such a programme, which relies on a question and answer technique called dialoguing that attempts to make the learner consider various options and reject the single-answer mode of thinking. Still another example of various approaches is a health education programme with a decision-making component. The Midwestern Prevention Project in America relies on a comprehensive school and community approach involving TV, newspapers, health policy investigations, community organization and parents (Pentz et al., 1989).

One programme that shows great promise is in human biology and comes out of Stanford University, in California (Heller and Kiely, 1994); it is aimed at lower secondary students, though the programme could easily be modified to address other age groups. This programme relies on teaching young people biological sciences in quite a new way, in that the context for biology is the biological, behavioural, and social transformations that adolescents are undergoing. From this base, students are encouraged to make better informed choices about their lives and bodies, to attain a useful level of scientific literacy, to become more motivated to learn, and ultimately to begin making wise career choices.

Coping with Poverty

It is difficult even to begin thinking about coping with poverty on a global level. A billion people are unable to meet their basic physical needs, almost a billion people cannot read and write, 14 million babies die of starvation each year and 100 million have no shelter at all (Sivard, 1987). The educational enterprise must at least explore some ways in which it can respond more adequately to the poor youth of world society, and yet support for youth is in a world-wide state of decline. Since 1983, UNICEF (1988) has been collecting data on the developing world and it reports that the well being of the young in at least thirty countries of the developing world had deteriorated during the 1980s. For example, from a sample of ten countries, it was found that malnutrition had risen in half the countries, child death rates had risen in a third of the countries, and school attendance had declined in eight of the ten countries.

One of the hallmarks of modernity was a commitment on the part of nations to provide an equal chance on the part of youth to share in the political, economic and social opportunities available, and the school has typically been given the responsibility to ensure some level of equal educational opportunity. According to Levin (1976), four different types of equal opportunity are in question:

1 The more conventional notion of equity has to do with *equal access* to the educational system.

2 A second level of consideration usually has to do with ensuring that there is *equal participation* in the educational system.

3 A third level is to attempt to produce *equal educational results* or outcomes.

4 Finally, there is some consideration given to *equal life chances*.

In the US, recent interventions for the poor and disadvantaged have been at the first level noted above: to ensure equal access to all schools, through forced bussing and open access provisions. Once the children are in school, the second level of equity has been dealt with by instituting smaller classroom sizes and remedial specialists for those not achieving at a sufficient level (Levin, 1993, p. 6). The Scandinavian countries have probably been the most exemplary in Europe in terms of equity provisions. The Scandinavians have maintained, until recently, that equality of opportunity could only be achieved by creating an extensive schooled society. By the early 1980s, for example, the average adult in Norway had attended almost thirteen years of school (Rust, 1989, p. 250). A second provision of the Scandinavians has been that everyone participates in the same school for an extended period of time and be engaged in a similar course of studies. Equality, in this respect has had a special meaning: sameness. However, the schools have not been able to overcome differential outcomes in terms of males and females. Girls now achieve at a much higher level than boys during the common, basic school period, but that advantage drops off quickly at higher levels of education.

Even though schools have fallen far short of the intentions of policy makers, they generally reflect greater equity than other institutions. It is certainly not clear what schooling in the post-comprehensive schooling era will bring. As schools fragment organizationally, they may tend to reinforce social distinctions more than has recently been the case. In spite of this, by their very nature, educational institutions are capable of enhancing each person engaged in the educational process. If schools are successful in enhancing a positive sense of self on the part of the students, if they expand each child's notion of what the world is and provide a wider range of options for that child, it may not be possible to ask much more of them. However, future schools must see themselves as being in the service of greater social opportunity.

SCHOOLS IN THE SERVICE OF WORK

In the beginning of this volume, it was argued that the concept of work will undergo a radical change. In postmodern society, work will include three main kinds of activity: there will be work as it is present understood and defined; at the same time, community involvement and participation will be counted as legitimate work; there will also be personal activities and development in the home. It is even conceivable that people will begin to receive an income from such activities. It will be necessary to provide educational options in connection with each of the three definitions of work and, in the following sections, we shall explore various ways in which such education may be organized.

Education for Conventional Work

An obvious way in which schools can better serve the conventional work world would be to train young people better. This appears to be a reasoned response. If someone is not able to find a job, then that person ought to be given a job skill in order to find work. This happens to be a typical governmental response to unemployment. It is the foundation of President William Clinton's employment policy. Even though German experts maintain that approximately one quarter of jobs will be of an unskilled nature, the government maintains that everyone should be given a full skills training of some kind (Solmon, 1992). Knight (1993, p.4) has summarized various job creation schemes in the following way:

1 direct wage subsidy payments to employers;
2 assistance to employers who offer apprenticeships;
3 improving jobs skills and life skills of unemployed youth;
4 short-term employment programmes in local communities; and
5 job search, job training and traineeship pathways programmes.

Almost all of these programmes are based on the assumption that if young people have certain skills, there will be a job available for them. A number of comparative efforts have been made to project what kind of training experts in various countries think will be most appropriate for the worker of the future. In one study, Knight (1993) summarized the training of three programmes in Australia, the UK, and the US, where he found a consensus as to the type of general education necessary to prepare young people for the work world of the future. All programmes included communications competencies, planning and organizational skills, interpersonal skills, foundational competencies (mathematics, reading and writing), problem-solving skills and evaluation and technological skills. We anticipate that those types of competencies will characterize the training and vocational programmes of the future. At the same time, we anticipate that different educational systems will opt for various ways to convey these skills. In America, for example, we expect vocational pro-grammes to continue to be on the fringes of the formal educational system, with gen-uine vocational programmes being conducted mainly in the private sector and not in direct competition with the general educational programme. At the same time, how-ever, Americans will find growing engagement with the so-called dual system of German vocational education (Hamilton and Hamilton, 1992)

Germany has maintained a long tradition of exemplary vocational education, which is central to its educational system. It can justifiably claim to have established a model which will influence vocational models throughout the world. The dual sys-tem is at the heart of German vocational training; it is based on the idea that young people who have satisfied ten years of general education can move directly into vocational training. Approximately 60 per cent of all present-day German youth select this option rather than continuing in full-time general education. Admission to a vocational place is based on a written application and a follow-up interview. Actual training is two-sided in that it consists of on-the-job training (75–80 per cent of the time) in the workplace as well as formal education in educational institutions (20–25 per cent of the time). The workplace ranges from a small local firm to a large industrial complex. Training is tightly prescribed by central authorities, but the training plan is defined by a consultative process that includes representatives from industry, political authorities and vocational educators. The youth are paid a salary for the work they perform for the firm, but that work is closely supervised and mon-itored during the training period.

Through the generations, German firms have developed a work culture that lays great stress on the training of apprentices. A young person seeking an apprentice-ship signs a contract with an appropriate firm and then seeks a place at a vocational school. The importance of apprentices to firms cannot be underestimated. The three-year training process can cost a firm around $80,000. It has also contributed to the development of specialized vocational educational programmes located within large firms and ensures a continuous flow of young talent into the firm. Small firms rely mainly on vocational education centres that draw from a wide range of appren-tice placements for their students.

The most important advantages of this system are that training takes place at the workplace, that training is continuously updated and that students participate directly in the world of work. At the same time, employers in industry and the com-munity are ensured a relevant and highly valued general education of their workers.

The German system probably will serve as a model for the next decades and its basic structure will be adopted by a wide variety of countries. Even in countries where such programmes are foreign, some interest is already being shown. In the US, experiments are already under way to see if certain aspects of the dual system can be adopted. In Broome County, New York State, for example, Cornell University has initiated a 'Youth Apprenticeship Demonstration Project'. A small group of eigh-teen-year-olds from different schools are being placed in four different work envi-ronments: a garment shop, two health institutions and an insurance firm. The programme does not attempt to prepare apprentices for a specific job but for a gen-eral vocational training. It is based on the assumption that the employer will design a learning milieu at the workplace. It is also based on the assumption that the apprentice will be seen as a legitimate member of the workforce, who will receive a regular salary, while at the same time receiving training and supervision. It is a four-year programme, where two years include regular schooling and completion includes a formal certificate of further education and worker qualification (Hamilton and Hamilton, 1992).

Even if there are good examples of relevant and highly valued vocational training, one of the major challenges of the future will be the identification and development of training programmes that can prepare people for work that is not related to conventional vocations, particularly training for the service sector.

Training for the Service Sector

Whereas technology and innovation have reduced the need for farmers and industrial workers, even while farm and industrial productivity has increased, this is not the case with regard to knowledge and service workers. In fact, as workers become more proficient, more are needed to satisfy growing productivity requirements. For example, as today's hospitals have invested growing sums of money in new, more efficient facilities and equipment, these investments have brought with them the need for expensive knowledge workers and growing numbers of service workers to administer and care for the facilities. We also assumed that the computer and other office technology would have a dramatic negative effect on the number of clerical workers. Yet, as data-processing machinery has become a common part of any office, the number of knowledge and service workers in those offices has increased dramatically. As Drucker is fond of pointing out, economists have discovered that in these sectors 'capital cannot be substituted for labour (i.e. for people) in knowledge and service work' (1993, pp. 95–6).

In spite of this, there is little evidence that the productivity of knowledge and service workers has increased, at least in terms of a worker's capacity to increase productivity, real wealth and a competitive edge. One of the priorities of educational institutions must be to learn how to raise the productivity of knowledge and service work, and to learn how to communicate that to those who are destined to spend their lives working in these sectors. This is self evident with regard to middle and higher level workers, but it has not been so evident with regard to unskilled positions. The major growth in service work appears now to be at the unskilled level – those people who spend their lives standing behind the sales counter, ringing up sales at the cash register, making beds in hospitals, cleaning houses, mowing lawns, or washing windows; society must learn how to make these activities more interesting and more productive.

One of the curious phenomena of modern management is its failure to see that entry-level people, with almost no skills, require training as much as any other workers. There are some striking examples of firms that have come to recognize this shortcoming. Tom Peters (1987, pp. 4–5) has given striking accounts of the success of firms such as Federal Express and Disney, who devote considerable attention to those young people, who are usually with them for a short period of time. Disney, for example, provides young 17- and 18-year-olds, who will be little more than jungle boat drivers or street sweepers with as much training as many firms give to their skilled machinists. This training is primarily in human relations. Milliken provides 22 weeks of training for its shop towel salespersons. When Nissan started its auto assembly plant in Tennessee, it spent more than $30,000 per person training about

2000 workers, before the plant even opened. And it has continued to provide ongoing training to them since that time.

While many would question this type of investment in people, who are at the bottom end of the workforce, the firms just mentioned have a clear notion of what ensures success. Bill Wiggenhorn, the Director of Training at Motorola, claims that the return rate on training runs about thirty times the investment. Disney, Motorola and Milliken have recognized that superlative service pays. The customer does not see the owner, the administrative staff or the technical experts; they see the sales clerk, the janitor and the stock clerk. These people make the difference between a good reputation and a poor one, as has been demonstrated by firms such as Nordstrom, Federal Express, McDonald's, Disney and a few other successful firms. Tom Peters has outlined what he feels are the elements of a superior training programme:

1 Extensive entry-level training must focus on exactly the skills in which you wish to be distinctive.

2 All employees are treated as potential career employees, even though most of them may be temporary or part-time.

3 Regular ongoing training is required.

4 Both time and money are generously expended. Training is part of the work time.

5 On-the-job training counts, too.

6 There are no limits to the skills that can profitably be taught to everyone.

7 Training is used to herald a commitment to a new strategic thrust.

8 Training is emphasized at a time of crisis.

9 All training is line-driven. That is, those doing the work must be involved in the teaching.

10 Training is used to teach the organization's vision and values.

Peter Drucker (1992, p. 111), would undoubtedly agree with Peters about the importance of training. He has looked at a somewhat different set of firms, the multinationals, and has found that the productivity in the lower skills service positions in many multinationals have been increased by adopting a number of specific elements of operation.

1 The elements of the job must be specifically defined.

2 Performance levels must be specifically defined.

3 The worker must become a partner in productivity improvement. The worker is seen as a vital link in knowing what works best and what does not.

4 Learning, teaching and improving are continuous parts of the job definition.

The above insights have been applied to certain parts of the workplace but, unfortunately, they have not become a part of the schooling agenda. It is imperative that educators apply these principles to the schooling process itself. Otherwise, society will witness a greater and greater social class division, with the growing service workforce consisting of those poorly educated, unskilled masses, who become servants to the better educated. The only sound way to rectify this development is to find ways to increase the productivity of this part of the service sector. Of course, as the number of unskilled service workers increases, they will likely gain some clout through unionization, but raising wages without ensuring increased productivity is ultimately detrimental.

A number of steps can be taken to help schools to increase the productivity of the service worker and other types of expanding workplace positions. In the past, schools have been so isolated from the actual world that they have evolved an institutional framework that is not amenable to outside connections. This has been the case in both capitalist and socialist countries. In fact, recent evidence from certain countries of Eastern Europe indicates that, in spite of the polytechnical emphasis of the Soviet block, schooling may have been less connected with the work world than in Western Europe (Stanek, 1993).

In recent years, that has begun to change. In many countries, pupils are being given a chance to gain exposure to the work world around them. In the small village of Molkom, Sweden, for example, the local school has maintained a co-operative relationship with the local technical industries since 1986. Groups of four to six pupils spend time each week in local industries from the age of ten. At the same time, the school provides technical training related to regulations and safety, electronics, technical mathematics and computing, that are directly related to the workplaces in the community (Bergh, 1993). Such exposure is important, not only for the lower levels of the employment sector but at all levels.

In certain communities, students are able to spend time assisting scientists in their laboratories and working with other specialists (Waltner, 1992). In the US, for example, the National Alliance of Business has sponsored projects in a number of American cities which have created business-education partnerships in such firms as the Bank of America and Sears, Roebuck & Co. The employees of these firms become part of the instructional work force and monitor how students' education fits or does not fit into the workplace (National Alliance of Business, 1989).

In some countries, training programmes now exist as a part of the general education of all students. In Germany, the *Arbeits-lehreprogrammen* takes all young people in the seventh and eighth forms into special programmes that gives them exposure to themes such as technology, technical drawing, consumer studies, the money system, etc. Then, in the ninth and tenth years of schooling, they are exposed to the work world of Germany, training possibilities, regulations for apprenticeship, budgets, etc. All students, except those enrolled at the *Gymnasium* are taken out of regular school for a period of three weeks so that they can engage in a vocational activity.

One approach to resolving work-related problems is found in the UK where the conservative government has systematically moved the sponsorship of government schools away from the Department of Education and Science altogether. One of the major endeavours of the Conservative government has been to direct the 14- to 18-year-olds, mainly from the bottom 40 per cent, among whom are disproportionately high numbers from minority groups, the poor and families receiving welfare benefits, away from strictly academic studies toward educational programmes that will prepare them for various types of jobs. The government consequently, created a wide-ranging training programme known as the Technical and Vocational Education Initiative (TVEI), managed by the Manpower Commission, a central government body completely outside the DES, although the education authorities were expected to run the individual projects with TVEI funds and oversight (Jones, 1988). The expectations were that schools would adjust to the requirements imposed by TVEI in five explicit ways, by making sure that:

1 the curriculum uses every opportunity to relate education to the world of work, by using concrete/real examples;

2 young people acquire the knowledge and competencies and qualifications they need in a highly technological society;

3 young people themselves enjoy direct opportunities to learn about the nature of the economy and the world of work – through work experience, work shadowing, projects in the community, etc;

4 young people learn how to be effective people, solve problems, work in teams, be enterprising and creative through the way they are taught; and

5 young people have access to initial guidance and counselling, and then continuing education and training, and opportunities for progression throughout their lives (Jones, 1988, p. 11).

A major facet of education and training programmes is coming through compacts, partnership arrangements among employers, educators and the local community. Employers in the local community will provide jobs with training and training for jobs of those young people leaving full-time education, who have met targets set by the schools and the employer.

If schools are to become viable institutions in helping young people destined to the lower and unskilled positions to learn how to function, they must adopt a format that includes the workplace itself. Traditionally, a number of difficulties have prevented schools from thinking in such terms.

SCHOOLS IN THE SERVICE OF BEAUTY AND AESTHETICS

Whereas the modern educational world relegated art and aesthetics to the periphery of school programmes, the future will likely incorporate the arts and aesthetics into a central part of its agenda. Art and aesthetics are not only valuable but, if people are to make sense of the contemporary discourse on the social world and the role of education in that world, art and aesthetics have also to become a social imperative.

In the past, schools and universities have served as the custodians of high culture, and they have dictated how this high culture must serve popular culture. Of course, the tensions between the two may be cultural in itself. Americans, for example, have always taken pride in their democratic life, including democratic art as exemplified in figures such as Emerson and Whitman (Kroes, 1988, p. xii). Europe, on the other hand, has tended to see popular culture as subversive, or worse, reflecting a trend toward Americanization. It should be apparent that these issues are not confined to the developed world, although in the so-called developing world the issues are not so much between popular and high culture as they are between modern imperatives and traditional culture. The religion of modernism has attempted to impose itself on the traditional with little regard for what it is destroying. In the educational sphere, there undoubtedly remain many, who feel it a mark of success that modern schooling has been instrumental in helping to kill traditional cultures; but postmoderns see the world otherwise. They point out that modern schooling has usually been detrimental to most so-called traditional local and indigenous art. In Indonesia, for example, as young people's lives are consumed by formal schooling, which here means modern schooling, their whole cultural system begins to crumble, because children are no longer available to incorporate the aesthetics of life and art provided by traditional social experience. Educators must see the implications of political policies concerning schooling for culture, where the arts are not autonomous from other dimensions of traditional life.

The Training of Artists
As we noted in Chapter 2, there has been a great expansion of the arts industry. There could be a veritable renaissance of artistic workers – in the visual arts, poetry, dance, theatre and music – operating as actors, dancers, announcers, architects, authors, designers, artists, printmakers, photographers, musicians, composers, sculptors, etc. In employment terms, the number of people working as artists may be exponentially larger than at any time during the modern age. In the US, for example, the number of painters, authors and dancers almost doubled in the 1980s. This represented the single largest job growth sector so that there are now 1.5 million Americans working in art occupations (Naisbitt and Aburdene, 1990, p. 67). When the service sector maintaining these people and selling their products is added, a significant part of the economy may be based on the arts.

The implications of this for schooling ought to be apparent. The artist of the past was created in a largely elitist environment, where private tutors and multiple-year apprenticeships were the norm. Mass schooling could, at best, provide an outlet where the artist could demonstrate talent, or where artistic appreciation could be cultivated. The school of the future, with its specialized focus and its capacity to draw from the entire spectrum of the work world, will be capable of developing the unique skills of those wishing to commit themselves to an artistic career.

The Training of Boutique and Niche Workers
Another great workforce potential is to be found among those whose creative and artistic work satisfies specialized interests, but with a human touch. Technology and automation have done away with industrial standardization, so that every manufactured product can come in an endless variety of sizes, shapes, colours, etc. If one walks through the bread department of a supermarket, one can find literally hundreds of different types of bread. If one wishes to buy an automobile, that automobile can be so tailored that it is almost unique in that it can have a special paint job, engine size, seat fabric, blinker lights, cooling system, tyre design, bumper make, safety belt, etc. And all of this is possible through direct request so that the automobile is assembled by the highly automated process. However, all of this remains part of the mechanized production process.

Even though the assembly factory can now offer more than 25 million different versions of the same automobile, the customers do not appear to be satisfied with the machine products. A whole new industry is emerging, where individuals work directly with a car owner in giving that owner's car a special bent. It may be as simple as a special wax job, or a special windshield tint, but it may also be as complex as retooling the entire external surface of the automobile, to give it a special structure and design.

The day is past when technology appears to threaten individuality and takes away special cultural norms and tastes. A new type of worker will emerge, who adds to the already dizzying variety that automation can provide. That worker promises to go beyond the player-piano type of variety that automation promises and addresses the special tastes and nuances that only humans can provide. That worker will be a product of a school experience that has emphasized the creative aspects of life, the value of originality and the importance of individuality and cultural variety.

HUMAN AND COMMUNITY SERVICE

There are many cities in the Western world that have attempted to engage the public sector more actively in developing a new aspect of the economy: the human and community services. This would be a direct intervention in providing humans with the kind of helping services they require. Even while people are being put out of work there is a desperate need for human services around everyone. Cities are filthy, parks are no longer attractive places to spend a relaxing hour, libraries are closing or drastically cutting hours, schools are overcrowded, youth have no place to spend their free time, law-enforcement agencies are understaffed. In Los Angeles alone, 55,000 people are on welfare roles, who are employable. Already the county has been able to put one-third of these people into productive roles for eight or more days a month. They clean the beaches, the highways, police stations and patrol cars, work in hospitals, repair street lights, maintain public parks or help out in juvenile facilities (Adler, 1994, p. B9). The remarkable aspect of this programme is that it costs no more than the conventional welfare system, which demeans people by paying them for doing nothing.

A new employment opportunity could become a universal reality 'based on education, health services, care for the young, old and incapacitated, active recreation, repair and extension of the environment, and support of the arts' (Knight, 1993, pp. 6–7). It can be put into action to deal with some of the most critical human service needs of the future. And at the same time, it promises some prospect for employment of everyone in some important job that counts. The claim is that industrial and farming technology has brought humankind to the point that people no longer must work full-time for extended periods of time. It is now time to turn attention to an economy that gives priority to humans working with humans. Humankind must consider ways to give dignity to people, to help them feel they are making a contribution to themselves and the society where they live.

At the same time, people need to incorporate the educational institutions into this process. Certain American schools include service as a central part of the school curriculum. Students regularly spend part of their school time in the community engaged in service projects (McPherson, 1991). At one high school in America, students monitored a creek running through the city, removing trash and developing an environmental programme to improve the air, soil and water (Silcox, 1991). In Salt Lake City, primary pupils have been responsible in having a hazardous waste site cleaned up and they have taken initiatives that have led to the passage of environmental laws, the planting of hundreds of trees, and neighbourhood improvements (Nathan and Kielsmeier, 1991).

In some communities where native Americans live, community participation includes inducting the young into family service, community service and spiritual awareness. For example, the young worked on the restoration of a church that was several hundred years old and engaged at the same time in study of the role it had played in family and community cohesion (Hall, 1991). A Bronx regional high school engaged in the restoration of a building that would serve as housing for homeless people, including some of the students (Nathan and Kielsmeier, 1991).

Community Education

Since the progressive education period following World War I, both Great Britain and the US have maintained an active plan of community education. In these countries, many examples of a coupling between education and the local community can be found. In Custer, South Dakota, for example, the local secondary school has incorporated many of the community resources into its schooling programme. Students help the elderly find a reasonable loan at a savings and loan establishment, or they engage in a market analysis and then inform the local business firms about the products the local population would prefer to buy and what they ought to have in stock. They participate in collecting oral histories of people living in the area and support a local historical association that was begun by the school (Versteeg, 1993).

Local community education is beginning to be recognized in many countries not only for its educational potential but as an instrument for the development of the local environment. It involves people as partners, both within and outside the educational system and serves as a mechanism of empowerment for many people who have traditionally been marginalized because of helplessness, discrimination and racism.

Historically, community education has been seen as an attempt to develop the school into an institution that does more than collect students into a compact area to deliver instruction. It has helped schools to begin to open their doors to the community, to serve as a local centre for free-time activities, special hobbies, religious observance, sports and other activities. This tradition has continued to this day, but community education has also extended its own creative perspectives in that it now focuses on more general community development endeavours.

One finds a good example of community development in Berlin-Kreuzberg, Germany, which is located in West Berlin, near the wall that divided the two Berlins for four decades. Kreuzberg fell into a state of decay, with filth, trash and rubbish littering its streets. The capable members of the community eventually left for better parts of Germany, leaving only the poor, unemployed, old and helpless behind. Two types of people began to move into the empty spaces. On the one hand, the punks, skinheads and homeless began to occupy many buildings, while on the other hand a rising number of Turks living in Berlin as guest workers found refuge in the area. The district eventually became a time-bomb waiting to explode. Community education experts finally began to take some action and they began to work with the local inhabitants to develop a plan of restoration and renewal. They did not bring some foreign plan into the district but tried to help the local people themselves to begin to conceptualize what they would like to have. The result was far less demanding in time and money than anyone would have anticipated. The local people had rather simple interests. They wanted to improve their standard of living, to be safe and satisfy their basic needs. They did not want to change things so much that the well-off would begin to move back in and force them out. Community education specialists helped the residents to organize themselves in such a way that they could begin to satisfy their goals and they helped the people to find some economic resources to begin renewal. The school served as an integral part of the entire process. The curriculum became focused on local needs and interests, and teachers worked to help the people to improve their own sense of identity and to solve their own problems (Krüger and Buhren, 1992).

Learning by Participation

Schools themselves are prone to impose some external standards and conventionally do not include learners in the quality control process of education. This tradition must be reorganized so that internal quality control becomes a part of the ongoing process, which means that learning does not begin or end with the certificate or licence, it is a part of the job. Teaching must also be seen as being a part of learning. It must be a part of the process, rather than an isolated activity taking place in a school or training institution unconnected with real-life activities. If the lowest worker has knowledge that is critical, that person immediately becomes a potential teacher to all others, including supervisors and owners.

There are a number of projects that provide some insight into how young people might be drawn into participatory learning and teaching. IMTEC has sponsored a number of projects in recent years that led to publications entitled *Learning from Work and Community Experience* (Dalin et al., 1983) and *Læring ved Deltaking* (Dalin and Skrindo, 1981). The basic model evolving from these projects included the following components:

1 *Participation in society*: The student is expected to participate in challenging activities that are useful to others and intrinsically rewarding. They must take real responsibility in that they make decisions that affect others besides themselves, that they be held accountable for their actions.

2 *Critical reflection*: Students must be helped to reflect critically on the outcomes, significance and consequences of their behaviour.

3 *Theoretical knowledge*: Students must begin to relate their practical experience to theoretical knowledge.

4 *Integrative process*: Participation, reflection and theory must be integrated into a meaningful whole.

5 *Participation*: Students must participate in planning, developing, operating and evaluating the over-all programme

(Dalin et al., 1983, pp. 26–45).

More recently, a network has been established with somewhat similar aims, entitled the *International Network of Productive Schools in Europe* (Böhm and Schneider, 1993), which has gathered educators from twelve countries together to deal with increasing productivity among youth. The entire enterprise attempts to collect examples of youth putting their potential into practice in the real world rather than having them engage in passive learning or simulated learning in the classroom. *Productive learning* is:

> an educational process that promotes both the development of the individual with the community and the development of the community itself. The process is shaped by an 'educational method' based on product-oriented activities in real life situations organized within the educational context of a group supported by educationalists.

The network encourages the establishment of educational environments that put young people in situations where they focus on improving the situation they find themselves in. And so a group of young people in Spain are working on the improvement of tourism in their community. Teenagers in Manila are working in trash sites trying to figure out how they can collect and sell usable materials from the smoking rubbish. A young lady in a chemistry laboratory is given the task of helping to develop a rust-proofer. The thing they all have in common is that they are participating in real-life situations, and are attempting to improve the situation. The young people are functioning as partners in productivity improvement. They are recognized as a vital link in knowing what works best and what does not. The young people are functioning as partners in improving productivity.

The above process does not end with the termination of formal schooling but must continue throughout the working life. The Norwegians have been eminently successful in partnership arrangements that improve the workplace. Gulowsen (1984) describes a typical situation in an industrial setting where training was a part of the production process. In a formal workshop situation, half of each day was devoted to a training process where workers and supervisors participated as both teachers and students. The other half of the day was spend at the factory, where everyone was made familiar with the machinery, the processes, etc.

TRAINING FOR PERSONAL WORK

People have always assumed that a natural task of the school is to contribute to the preparation of youth for conventional work, and people have also at least tolerated the fact that school instruction might contribute to the local community. However, education for free-time and home life have seldom been seen as responsibilities of the school. In the following sections, we shall consider to what extent school systems have included free-time and family education. Then we will ask to what extent these ought to be included in schooling of the future. Finally, we shall ask to what extent constructive free-time and family living ought to be considered parts of work.

One of the consequences of industrial society is that young people have a great deal of free time. At the beginning of the modern age, conventional work took most of the time of workers, and free time was considered to be a period when they could rest and renew their strength. As the workday became shorter and shorter, free time came to be seen as a potentially useful commodity. In the process, a whole commercial industry developed that was dedicate to selling free time. Tourism exploded, the number of TVs and automobiles increased exponentially, many natural and scenic parks came into existence, swimming pools were constructed, hiking paths and camping places multiplied, etc. This development was a direct response to the growing belief that the free time available could contribute to personal interests, entertainment and amusement (Nahrstedt, 1990, p. 12).

However, a new perspective towards free time gradually came into view. There was a growing awareness that free time ought to be exploited for useful ends, and that it might contribute to the further development of human beings. Free time ought to be made more meaningful. Of course, this included the notion that free time could be used to contribute to society, as was noted above, but also that it can better satisfy the needs and development of the individual family. Unfortunately, free time has usually not been considered for its productive and educational potential, though that point of view appears to be changing. In Germany, the *Volkshochschule* has turned more and more of its attention to the free-time education of youth and adults. The Club of Rome recommends that free-time activities ought to be dedicated to the development of communication skills, greater creativity and an expanding of individual personalities. They recognize that free time ought to be combined with content learning so that both might be mixed with fun and enjoyment. Free-time pedagogues now advocate free-time cultural education, located in neighbourhoods and dedicated to development in creativity and communication. Free-time education was to serve as a motivational tool, helping youth to overcome passive consumer-style behaviours.

There is, of course, a force against the tendencies just noted. Some people argue that free time is free and it must remain free. It is a private matter and an autonomous area of life. This is especially the case in West Germany, where policy makers still wish to distance themselves from the old East Germany, where free time was taken over by the state and used for its own ideological and political purposes. While respecting the West German claim that free time is a private matter, it must be recognized that free time may already not be so private. The media and leisure-time industry have already invaded the home. Free time is now highly commercialized (Opaschowski, 1983, p. 144). Still another argument against invasion of free time comes from Janusz Korczak (1992), who claims that humankind must avoid an 'adult produced culture for children'. He feels that children are experts in their own world, and adults ought to respect the mystery and compulsions of youth, who are fully capable of organizing themselves for their unique purposes.

Nevertheless, free time must go beyond simple recreation and consumption. It must be appreciated for its potential as productive, creative and learning time.

It remains a point of dispute as to how much the state and schools ought to invade free time and the home in order to provide educational opportunities for the youth. In the former Soviet Union, there are multiple examples of misuse of the free and private spheres on the part of ideological fanatics, but one is also able to find examples where there was a healthy balance between the old system of invasive programmes and a healthy private interest in personal development. In Azerbaijan, for example, the old pioneer palace has been transformed into a Children's Creativity House where one finds activities for children related to drawing, sport, theatre, dance, natural science, technology and much, much more. In the process, the youth organization sponsoring these activities has dislodged itself from the strong ideological ties that were maintained in the former Soviet Union. The centre is now a quasi-public institution, relying on public assistance so that youth can participate with reasonable tuition fees. And the youth are learning about the world and their culture while they are using their free time in productive and creative ways.

In America, recommendations for balancing the public and private is coming from quite a different direction. There is a long tradition of free-time activities, but it has always been considered to be a task for the private sector. The Carnegie Corporation has recently recommended that the public sector join with the private sector in the US and commit to the extension of youth development institutions. Of course, these types of institutions have existed for some time, but they have rarely been given the attention Carnegie has shown them. The Boy Scouts, the American Camping Association, the YMCA, the Red Cross, etc. are tending to occupy increasing amounts of the youth's time and energies (Carnegie Corporation, 1992). However, these institutions are themselves highly specialized and attend to specific interests and values. They do not promise to provide a universal content and value orientation. As youth development institutions, they would be dedicated to a broader and more inclusive role.

Regardless of the way free-time and family education will become a more integral part of educational programmes, it remains an open question as to whether they will be recognized as legitimate parts of the work world of postmodern society. A large portion of the activities now defined as free-time and family oriented can easily be defined as genuine work. Activities that contribute to the development of the individual and society must eventually be defined as productive work. Some movement in that direction has already begun in America, at least in terms of their educational value. Because American education operates on a credit system, very many personal activities and private endeavours are already receiving credit within educational institutions. That is, even though they may not have learned something within the framework of a formal educational programme, people ought to be able to given recognition if they can demonstrate that they possess the competence necessary to do a specific task.

This is also becoming an educational imperative in the European Community. Because licences and certificates are being recognized on a reciprocity basis among countries of the European Community, the next logical step will likely be, to establish some form of certification process that allows people to demonstrate that they have skills and knowledge necessary to satisfy job requirements. That is already the case in some areas. In Norway, certified teachers are allowed to instruct their children in certain subjects if they are abroad for some reason. The Japanese have established a whole network of Japanese schools that function as free time or after-school programmes for the children who are living for extended periods of time abroad. Curiously, the Japanese do not even ask what the children are learning in the local schools of America, Germany or the UK. In other words, they do not give credit for learnings outside their own system, even when the child attends the regular public school. A logical consequence of such an orientation ought to be that centres be set up to evaluate what rather than where the child is learning.

A number of innovative practices exist related to health education (Carnegie Corporation, 1994) and family education (Rennie, 1993) raising questions about the role schools have and do not have in the broader society. It must find its place in a broad network of learning environments and build alliances with other educational activities going on outside the school. The final step in the movement toward recognition of free-time and family learning will be to give credit in the form of payments for personal, private work.

NEED FOR A COMPREHENSIVE APPROACH

At the beginning of this chapter, we noted that the approach taken by most advocates of change has been to focus on a single issue. For example, the four survival issues we have discussed – ecology, peace, health and poverty – have typically been seen as isolated issues and treated by educational advocates in a manner separate from the other issues. Those involved with environmental studies usually focus on the degradation of the environment and the need to become more sensitive to the world's delicate ecological balance. Those involved with peace studies usually focus on war and violence and the need for armaments control, conflict resolution skills and the humanitarian solutions to problems. Those involved in poverty studies usually focus on the imbalance of resource distribution and social injustice. They call for institutional arrangements that do not disadvantage certain groups and schooling schemes that will provide everyone with competence and the ability to thrive in the world. This discussion could be extended to issues such as multiculturalism and democratization. Those involved in multicultural studies usually focus on racism and prejudice and the need for greater social justice and appreciation of ethnic and cultural difference. As we look at these different issues, it becomes clear that the educational process being advocated for each of them has quite common strands and overlapping concerns. Most concern themselves with power relationships, justice, interdependence, resource allocation, human rights, environmental conditions, community development and appreciation of other peoples. The main thrusts of the future have enough in common that it is possible to develop a more comprehensive educational design which encompasses each of the special concerns. Derek Heater has suggested an encompassing set of educational objectives to which all special groups might easily subscribe:

1 knowing about the world and mankind as a whole – a global dimension to school subjects;

2 being aware of the interrelatedness of the contemporary world and viewing of problems on a global dimension, and understanding of the systemic nature of the contemporary world and the experiences that mankind has in common;

3 appreciating that people have rights and duties towards each other and that even the pursuit of self-interest necessitates co-operation;

4 being conscious that one's own perspective on world issues and other peoples is biased by one's own cultural background;

5 having empathy by viewing other societies from their own perspectives and one's own society from the perspective of others;

6 appreciating others, and having sympathy for the plight of the unfortunate and regard for the achievements of the creative;

7 having skills to understand a rapidly changing world and to make critical judgments from a mass of information;

8 having the ability to communicate with others across cultures both without prejudice in oneself and to combat prejudice in others; and

9 being ready to act in a responsible way to help to resolve world problems.

(Heater, 1984, p. 25)

All of this implies that education must begin to take a more holistic view of the world and it ought to have a social action component (Knight, 1987). Of course, various schools will stress different facets of the global concern. That is not only inevitable, but it is appropriate. The single issue that needs stressing is that educators must learn to see the interconnection of their special concerns with other social imperatives.

Chapter 8

What is a Good School?

One purpose of this book has been to provide a tentative answer to the question, at least in an abstract way: What is a good school? However, it is impossible to answer the question without some frame of reference as to the learning requirements of youth or what aims the school is expected to meet. The learning requirements of the young must take as a starting point, the requirements of contemporary society, but that cannot be the final context, because education ought always to be related to the future in which youth will live. Without a realistic picture of today and a vision for the future, it is impossible to define a good school.

Does society really need schools? There has always been criticism of schooling, of its organizational structure, its role and its effectiveness. That criticism is as strong today as it has ever been (Abbott, 1994). Is there some ground to think that humankind can enter a postmodern world, where learning requirements of youth and adolescents can be satisfied in some institutional form other than a school?

There are many components of a good school, and in this chapter we turn attention to certain learning processes, roles, relationships, climate factors and values of such a school. We will also outline certain characteristics of an ideal curriculum and educational system, of which the school is only a part.

A picture of a good school will be painted with broad brush-strokes, only. Some issues will not be addressed here, such as the distinction between primary and secondary schools (though there are great differences between the two) or between schools in different types of societies and political systems. Our school is assumed to be situated in a highly industrialized economic system. It is impossible to address in this book how to improve schooling and what good teaching is in the developing world, but we have struggled with this issue, elsewhere (Rust and Dalin, 1990; Dalin, 1994). This chapter summarizes the discussion in this book thus far and describes characteristics of a good school which prepares for the next century. An equally important question, of course, is how to manage the school reform process. That is the task of the second volume of this series.

WILL SCHOOLS BE NEEDED IN THE TWENTY-FIRST CENTURY?

The rapidly changing society humankind is experiencing will be no less dynamic in the next century. It can best be described as a learning society, because the key to its success will be knowledge. One of the major shifts in the future is that learning will no longer be focused mainly on youth, who are preparing for adulthood. Learning will characterize every age group and aspect of society. The notion of life-long learning is already a part of our consciousness, but that has usually been seen in connection with certain professions and roles. In the future society, we anticipate that all age groups, all social classes and worker categories will become a necessary part of the learning society.

The question, then, is what will best satisfy universal learning requirements? Can the school assume such a responsibility? Until now, it has been assumed that the school has such a task, but increasingly, it competes with other institutions, which are setting the agenda and defining the course of learning of major parts of society. A learning market is fast developing, fastest outside the formal school system, and informal learning activities are at least as important as the formal learning programmes

It is obvious that the mass media is assuming increasing importance as an educational institution, in both a positive and a negative sense. Free-time learning activities, such as travel and tourism, are critical in helping people to learn new ways of life, new languages, etc. The workplace is now teaching a curriculum that has long been housed mainly in the schools. In other words, the school may no longer be required to assume large parts of its former responsibilities. In addition, there are those who claim the school is filled with young people who are alienated from it and fail to benefit from its programme. Others claim the school is expensive and inefficient in doing its job (Coombs, 1968). If alternatives to the school can be found, they will likely be welcomed by large segments of the population. One thing is certain: the school will not assume the kind of autonomy and isolated role that it has had. Learning will be more differentiated and dispersed through many institutions. Schooling will, consequently, be characterized by more flexibility and diversity than has been the case in the twentieth century. In recent years, debates have been carried out that place the role of schooling at two extremes: on the one hand, there have been those who have argued for a deschooled society; on the other hand, there are those who have argued for a schooled society, in which schooling comes to dominate life.

A DESCHOOLED SOCIETY?

Some years ago there was a general discussion in various societies concerning the possibility that schools may have outlived their usefulness. In Norway, Niels Christie (1971) asked a fundamental question: What would Norwegians do to satisfy the learning needs of society and the individual if the school did not exist? That book appeared about the time Ivan Illich (1970) came out with his recommendation that we deschool society. His basic thesis was that too many institutions in society have become manipulative and destructive. He wanted simply to deinstitutionalize environments that are manipulative and rely more seriously on the development of what he called convivial institutions. These are distinguished by spontaneous and self-initiated use and included museums, libraries, parks, and even sidewalks; Illich recommended that schooling take on the character of a convivial institution.

Illich objected to a learning process that had been defined by the state and its representatives, including school officials and teachers. The learning process had become almost completely prescriptive in nature. He wished to restrict the role of the state to that of defining parameters within which the school might work but allowing it complete freedom within those parameters. His desire was that prescription be replaced by proscription, something similar to the role of parent and child. In that case, a mother usually tells the child it may not go across the street, may not climb over the neighbour's fence, may not do this or that, but the child is then free to do what it wants in the context of the boundaries set by the mother.

While Illich remained rather abstract in what he meant by a deschooled society, his colleague, Everett Reimer (1971) developed a more concrete model of the type of learning environment they envisioned. Schools would not disappear but would represent one of many alternatives learners had available.

Both Illich and Reimer were more intrigued by learning materials than by instruction. The focus of both authors was on audio-visual materials, which today would be related to what is known as information technology, resource outlets in communities, and other pupils as learning partners. Their lowest priority was given to teachers, 'who by virtue of experience, can facilitate the use of the more essential learning resources' (Reimer, 1971, p. 94–5).

The deschooled society is not a reality. In fact, during the modern age, the school increasingly established its position in society. However, that position has recently again been called into question. The school will probably not die away, but its role in the postmodern society will certain not be the same as in the late modern world.

John Abbott, who leads the organization *Education 2000* in the UK, says:

> Learning and schooling are not synonymous. If you want to improve education, don't start by trying – yet again – to fix the schools; rather reconsider how learning takes place . . . and then think how all the resources of the community could be harnessed to create a new Model of Learning.
>
> (Abbott, 1994)

Abbott argues strongly that modern society needs a redesigned learning system. He illustrates this by contrasting what it takes to achieve conventional academic success with commercial success: Academic success requires largely solitary study, generally uninterrupted work, concentration on a single subject, much written work and an analytical ability. Commercial success involves working with others, having the ability to cope with constant distractions, competence in different disciplines, as well as verbal, problem-solving and decision-making skills.

Abbott argues also for a different process of learning. Taking into account what specialists know about how the brain functions (see Chapter 6), he argues for schools to concentrate by doing fewer things, in greater depth.

The theme *restructuring* is key to this debate. Albert Shanker, in a speech prepared for *Education 2000* quotes Jack Bowsher, the former Director of Education at IBM, as saying:

> If IBM were producing results comparable to those of many American schools – that is, if 25 per cent of their computers were falling off the assembly line before they reached the end, and if 90 per cent of the completed ones didn't work properly for 80 per cent of the time – the last thing in the world the company would do would be to run that same old assembly line an additional hour each day for an extra month each year. Instead, IBM would re-think the entire production system.
>
> (Abbott, 1994)

The deschooling debate is more real today than it was in the early 1970s. The main reasons are that the pressure for renewal is much stronger and that the media and other learning resources are becoming real alternatives to schools.

SCHOOLING FROM CRADLE TO GRAVE

A schooled society would be one where schooling is given the charge of satisfying a large share of educational requirements throughout life. The European Cultural Foundation has been one group to establish a programme for a schooled society as it worked on a project entitled Education for the Twenty-First Century (Schwartz, 1974). In its programme, the European Cultural Foundation anticipates that by the beginning of the twenty-first century education will be organized into four main phases.

1 Nursery schools and pre-schools will occupy the lives of children until they are five years old. They still will not replace the family and parents, but will serve as a strong complement to family education.

2 The basic school will provide formal education for children until they are sixteen years of age. It will consist of two cycles. The first will last six years and will stimulate pupil awareness of the technical and social environment, give pupils competence in mathematics, oral expression in foreign languages, the mother tongue, and the ability to engage in artistic and physical activities, and provide cultural and sporting outlets. The second cycle will last five years and pupils will explore the key concepts of the major fields of study. The educational process will be individualized and based on personal contracts, and the examinations will be recognized in all European countries.

3 The third level will also be compulsory and will consist of a college and a vocational stream. The European Cultural Foundation does not draw a sharp distinction between the two streams but finds value in distinguishing between the two. If students do not attend college they will be obliged to attend a vocational programme for at least two years.

4 The final phase of education will consist of university study and/or adult education. Attendance will not be compulsory, but every person will have certain rights to access educational institutions. The European Cultural Foundation is committed to lifelong education and expects most people to be engaged in some form of education at the final phase for the remainder of their lives.

In order for the European Cultural Foundation to realize its aims, it maintains that school buildings will play a dominant role but that non-school institutions, such as libraries, museums, cinemas, laboratories, auditoriums, office buildings, etc. will also become major players in the educational process. It also anticipates that TV and computer terminals will play an increasingly large role in education.

THE ESTABLISHED TRUTHS

Before we take a position regarding the form the school will have in the next century, there are some questions to be answered.

What and Who is a Student?

A student is today typically a young person between the ages of six and twenty-five years, but such a definition is becoming increasingly blurred. In the future the youngest babies will receive extensive inputs related to their developmental needs. Of course, most of this will come in connection with parents and families, but that informal learning will be recognized for what it is. We will also find students in the older age groups. It will be taken for granted that some form of learning and continuing education will take place to the end of life, but that learning will likely be quite different from that which takes place in today's schools. Teachers will also, through their whole career, be tied to resource networks and colleges, developing their profession, thus they will be eternal students.

The important message is that the learner must be put at the centre. Increasingly, the individual student will be able to choose from a variety of learning opportunities and learning modes. Only those learning options which build on the child's natural learning skills and the uniqueness of each child will be in the learning market.

What and Who is a Teacher?

The traditional teacher will continue to be important; however, the distinction between student and teacher will become blurred. Students with extensive resources will engage in teacher roles, and teachers also will be students, in that they will engage in lifelong education and training. Teachers and students will engage in mutual learning activities, in activities such as co-operative learning. Parents will serve extensively as resource persons to lower schooling in their communities. They will share their expertise by voluntary contributions to the learning community. Of course, teachers will serve as role models in the school where understanding will be more important than knowledge (see Chapter 5), where personality development will be essential and where the whole person will stand in the centre. Teachers will likely encounter difficulty, not only because of a continuing need for them to change but also because teachers will be expected to function in several roles outside their subject fields. The teaching profession will consist of many people who function as full-time professionals and be active their entire working life. The probability is great that many who do not identify with the teaching profession will function in some way as teachers although their career focus will be quite different.

The message to teachers is that the 'answer' is no longer the key in the learning process. The key is the 'question'. Teachers will no longer be expected to have the one and only right answer. They will be expected to stimulate the curiosity of each child, to focus on the basic issues and to help each child to discover and to work systematically.

What is a Curriculum?

It will be increasingly difficult to define a comprehensive curriculum, both because the knowledge revolution will bring new and important knowledge into the school arena, and because the student's needs will constantly be changing. In all likelihood, educational officials will likely move away from detailed teaching plans and focus more on general and thematic goals. They will attempt to define what is fundamental and exemplary. At times, officials will try to operationalize the goals, but these will certainly only be temporary and fleeting. The real instructional plans will be defined at the local level by individual institutions, and the task of more central officials will be to provide some framework and values within which these plans will be defined. There will be great latitude given to the individual teachers as they work with students and local institutions.

The message is that a detailed outline of the content of the curriculum will no longer be the primary issue. Rather, the task will be to identify the few basic areas that need deep knowledge and to connect the student to these important areas of study.

What is a Textbook?

The information society gives each person access to an enormous well of information in nearly any area of society. Through computers, CD-ROMs and other learning media, everyone will have access to the entire spectrum of knowledge. Already today, teachers can create their own teaching books for a particular subject, and it is filled with the most current information. This access will make possible school-based and individualized teaching plans and lead to the development of whole new ideas of what a school book is. It may be that a form of basic information will remain within the two covers, but more often tailored books will play a greater role. In fact, students will have access to the same sources of current information that teachers will have, so the teaching book may be something that is continually revised and updated by teachers and students alike.

The message is that all textbooks are outdated. That does not mean they are not useful. The best textbooks give students basic knowledge and overviews and help them explore the many facets of a field.

What is a Classroom?

The school was created in a time when a gathering place was a necessary condition for organized learning. The content to be learned was generally known, the curriculum was in the lesson books, and the teacher played a central role as transmitter of information and concepts. Even now, most knowledge and information is found somewhere other than in the school. They are in computers, in libraries, in the local community, in media outlets and in the workplace. Contemporary society has reached a point that the walls of the school act as a barrier, a restriction and no longer provide an opportunity to gain access to the world of learning. The classroom in the next century has no walls. It is without limits, and like knowledge, it has no boundaries.

The community will become the expanded classroom. The more authentic learning tasks are explored, the more the community will be a resource. Increasingly, electronic networks are becoming a type of community without walls. They give students and teachers, alike, new possibilities to expand the classroom.

The message is not only that the school will learn from a wider community, but also that it will contribute to the local and the world community. This give and take between school and community will lead to a more useful and expanded classroom.

What is Well-organized Instruction?

In the past, instruction from a podium has been the dominant method. Gradually this mode has been transformed, especially in the primary school, in that more student-active methods have come to dominate. Even so, the instructional method has remained one of presenting information. The model instructional process remains one of a teacher presenting a specific subject to a group of learners in a self-contained classroom. Many have recognized difficulty with this organization model, and schools themselves have begun to take some initiative in reforming their instructional organization. In the years ahead, new forms will come into being, dictated, in part, by economic imperatives. For example, large groups of learners could be the norm, with team-teaching and use of students as teachers' helpers. More extensive use will be made of the library, computers, individualized projects and lengthened study periods. Older students will develop contracts that release them from traditional instruction while they engage in their own research activities. The schools that will survive the competitive atmosphere will be those that are more flexible with the way instruction is organized.

These are not new ideas, they are at least as old as John Dewey. However, only a small percentage of schools are using alternative methods of instruction. Schools need to overhaul their learning organization.

Who Owns the School?

Schools were originally owned or sponsored by the church or some private organization. Since the middle of the last century, schools in the developed world have become the property of the state, except perhaps in the Netherlands where more than 70 per cent of the schools still remain private. The public sector in OECD countries is in crisis, and the public sector must limit itself and concentrate itself with the central assignments for the state. In the West, there is already a tendency toward private and market models with a sharing of ownership (Reichard, 1992). In many respects, the issue of sponsorship is becoming increasingly unimportant. It does not matter whether the state or some private agency owns a school. The critical factor is, increasingly, who pays for the education taking place in the institution. In the Netherlands, for example, the church owns the most schools, but the state pays 100 per cent of the financial costs. In Norway, the state pays 85 per cent of the costs of private schooling. A number of new owner combinations and financing models will likely come into existence, that combine economic financial commitments, local public, private philanthropy, business companies, religious communities and parents/students. Sponsorship will fall under a large umbrella of groups and include home schools and private schools.

Schools need to take advantage of all available learning resources. One of the most important learning resources is commitment and empowerment that is released when people feel that they have real responsibility, when they have a sense of ownership of the school where their children attend. The message is to open up to the environment.

Who Controls the School?

While sponsorship and financial arrangements are essential, the actual control of schooling will likely fall increasingly under alliances of groups, who will act as interested partners of schooling. One of the problems of the public monopoly of schooling has been that clients (parents and children) have been marginalized and distanced from the decision-making process of schools. Public schooling has become a large enterprise, and schooling has been largely taken over by a bureaucracy. Students and parents have largely been treated as objects. One of the imperatives of the future will be that parents and young people become directly involved in the schooling process. Of course, the professionals (principal and teachers) will play a strong role in terms of pedagogic leadership, but the clients will have an active role and responsibility in schooling. This model is already rather active in countries such as New Zealand and The Netherlands.

The message is: professionals will have to redefine their role, and so will the users, if public organizations, in this case the schools, become effective institutions.

Which Values will Rule?

In a decentralized society the principle of local control applies, but that does not eliminate existing conflicts. This is especially the case in multicultural societies with their different lifestyles, customs and values, that strain many local societies. It is no longer easy to define national values, because no society has a uniform set of values. A central issue in tomorrow's school is how to learn to live with, respect and value others' values. Knowledge of and understanding for others' values also set personal values in perspective. A meeting between cultures and other values can include conflicts that must be solved in every community.

This value conflict is an opportunity for schools. One of the most valuable skills in future societies will be the ability to confront and work with conflicts. Students need to learn how to solve problems and conflicts.

The message is: each school needs to develop its own process of conflict resolution and to develop its own school-specific norms and values.

Can the School Learn?

Our conclusion is that the school, as an organization, can learn. Will schools continue to have strength and the creativity to master the big assignment that the world will face in the years ahead? An essential part of the school's assignment is to live with change and master the necessary problem solving and conflict solving that follows (Dalin and Rolff, 1993).

This should already give response to one question: do we believe in a deschooled society or a school from cradle to grave? We maintain that schools as they exist today, will not survive into the next century, though some form of creative institutional structure, known as a school, will surely exist and meet many of the challenges society will face. That institution will not be static but continually changing and learning in order to meet the challenges of its day.

CAN SCHOOLS MEET THE STUDENT'S NEEDS?

In Chapter 5, we discussed three learning needs of children and youth that must be met in the twenty-first century. The needs we have defined are all related to the ten visions we see as central for postmodern society (see Chapter 4). Is it possible to find organizations and forms of learning that can meet these needs? We will consider some examples.

The Ability to Communicate

Fundamental knowledge and competencies include the ability to learn to learn, to understand subject fields, to master problem solving and to communicate. In Chapter 6, we discussed the importance of all students to work toward high professional standards. In particular, students must learn systematic ways of studying, to develop problem-solving skills and creativity.

Communication will be a basic and essential skill, both in spoken and written form in the mother language, two foreign languages, as well as mastering communication through text, pictures and computer. Communication between people is the accomplishment that becomes most important, as society functions more horizontally.

The future will have new and important learning resources at its disposal. First and foremost is the school as society, the ability to work seriously with interpersonal communication. Schools with immigrant children will have an important resource because understanding other cultures and commanding a language can have new possibilities in a multicultural environment.

Equally important, is the development in our vision of partnership between men and women, between boys and girls. The future school must think through all sides of its activity so that it can have equal participation and at the same time make sure boys and girls receive opportunities for development. Again, it is the school as society that will stand in the centre of development.

Knowledge and Understanding

We see two equally important goals for the future school: to help learners to engage in deep learning, which requires the ability to put together the pieces, and to extract meaning out of complicated material; and, at the same time, to develop insight, empathy and understanding (see Chapter 6).

These goals can best be achieved by helping youth engage in activities that require them to act responsibly and be accountable or, in other words, giving them adult-like responsibilities. They should be provided with authentic learning assignments comparable to those related to learning by participation and similar programmes.

Equally important is to help youth to gain a sense of independence, while at the same time satisfying their need for love and affection. If students are to develop empathy for other people and other cultures, we must begin with the small, with the class, the school society and local environment. Solidarity with the weak in the society and an active commitment to children in developing countries can be examples of assignments that have a great potential for learning and for developing understanding.

These attitudes and behaviours toward the welfare of others do not come by themselves. Children and youth need adults as role models. Here the parents play the decisive role for children but as young people mature, teachers and others become important role models. In fact, all committed adults who are associated in some meaningful way with education and youth can serve as role models.

Young people have the tendency to turn to their peer group as role models, but the fundamental conflict is not between the adult role models and teen idols. The difference is between the 'I-culture' and the 'we-culture', between those who are, on the one hand, concerned only with their own success and advantage and those, on the other hand, who have sympathy and understanding for others. Youth who struggle to accept themselves, who have a poor sense of self-esteem, are under great temptation to move in directions that lead away from a broad social consciousness.

No patent exists that can provide a formula for the way adults ought to behave, but parents and care-takers of children must work caringly and diligently to help them to develop self-confidence and a belief that they count. Educational institutions must work in co-operation with the home to ensure that each student will develop empathy and solidarity with others.

The Consumer and the Producer

In Chapter 5, we distinguished between the consumer role and the producer role. The producer role is dependent on creativity and often problem-solving skills. If one becomes more than a consumer and becomes a producer, then creative accomplishments stand in the centre, either in terms of the ability to solve complex problems or the power to make the world a more beautiful place through artistic creation.

Everyone is a consumer, and it is imperative that everyone become a well-informed and conscious consumer. North America and Europe are consumer societies but if consumers do not give anything back to their respective society, it becomes unbalanced and eventually is unable to regenerate and restore that which has been taken from it. The pattern of consumption must change, as has been argued in Chapters 3 and 4, and the school has an important assignment, as it helps learners to understand the consequences of excessive consumption. It must help to show the way toward economic balance, health and sharing of goods. Many undertakings that help the students to engage in joint activities with those less fortunate than themselves are available, that help them to see the interdependence of consumption and health, and then youth can, in certain respects, serve as role models for those of the older generation, who have lost sight of the relationship between consumption and production.

Few people are producers. Too much that happens in the school is simply reproduction. Students write down what is written on the blackboard, they memorize formulae, and try to guess what answer the teacher may have in mind. Students even try to guess what kinds of question the teacher thinks they should ask. All of this places learners in the position of being consumers. The dialogue is formal and predictable. Students learn to consume what is being delivered, and they are delighted when they have the right answer or pass the test (Educational Leadership, 1994).

The future schools must, to a much greater degree than exists today, encourage the creative side of the students. The artistic side must be a part of daily work. Students must be encouraged to participate as creators. They must engage in projects that bring students out of the routine, that lead them toward the incomplete and unknown. It is not only important in relation to tomorrow's work market. All fields of endeavour need our creative abilities. Human creativity must become an important value of life.

THE CURRICULUM FOR THE FUTURE SCHOOL

In this section, we will discuss what we see as some of the most important principles in the school curriculum of the future, especially those aspects that will likely differ from today's schools. What we shall discuss is the general dimensions of the curriculum and their interrelations. More detailed aspects of didactics will not be discussed here; see, for example, Gundem (1989) and Hameyer (1991).

There are certain basic principles that should guide any decision concerning the future curriculum. We consider them under the following headings:

1 Less is better than more

2 Everything ties together

3 The disciplinary and the interdisciplinary

4 School learning and everyday learning

5 Individual and group learning

6 The school and society

7 Personal development

8 Social development

9 The teacher that learns

10 The learning school

Less is Better than More

Most curriculum plans are overloaded. There is seldom place for discussion, for reflection, to go deeper into the subject and to really understand. The decision must be made to determine the core and exemplary facts and concepts, that together create a solid base for further learning.

Everything Ties Together

Research has long determined that everything is interconnected. It is counter-productive to change one part of the curriculum without thinking about the rest. Further, it is senseless to think only of general frameworks without considering how those things shall be implemented. Overall objectives and a strategy for implementation are essential – to relate the various components together and to link the plan with its actual use.

Purely cognitive knowledge and proficiency cannot be isolated from personal development, just as personal development of each child must be considered in the context of cognitive knowledge. Instructional plans must be so conceived that they integrate the two.

The Disciplinary and the Interdisciplinary

In Chapter 6, we argued for a solid, core programme of studies. This will become increasingly imperative in the future school. If individual fields of study have merit, they must address the problems students face in their daily lives. Fields of study must be seen in the school as problem oriented, allowing the student to gain insight into the perspective that this field has toward these problems. Further, an understanding that different fields of study have different perspectives and some understanding of the totality of perspectives is necessary, if an instructional plan is to satisfy its fullest potential.

School Learning and Everyday Learning

The learning process in school has its own autonomous nature, but must ultimately relate to the everyday learning and to the maturity level of students. It is too often the internal logic of a field of studies that dictates the curriculum. However, traditional subject-matter programmes represent but a part of what students learn.

Therefore, it is important that school learning be harmonized in some manner with the learning that utilizes everyday activities and insights. Students learn, when they are motivated to learn, when they understand why and they can relate what they learn to something else in their experience.

Individual and Group Learning

Students in the compulsory phase of schooling typically work with a common curriculum, a curriculum that gives training in basic knowledge and proficiency and that, above all, helps students to develop an understanding of the basic structure of fields of study. Students in a class need to have some common reference point, that forms the framework for further educational development. School learning is cumulative and students who do not have a foundation, a solid grounding, are truly disadvantaged. The so-called learning gap between those who gain this foundation and those who do not quickly develops and it becomes increasingly difficult to hold the group together in such a way that everyone benefits from instruction. There are ways to overcome this tendency, so that group solidarity can be maintained; see, for example, Stevenson and Stigler, 1992.

The School and the Society

Students are exposed to the problems of today and the tasks of the future in their practical life through the mass media and other avenues. The school's assignment must be to describe, analyse and reflect over the challenges that have decisive meaning for the student's life, to put information in context, and to develop knowledge and understanding. These challenges can be:

- to develop and live in a multicultural society;
- to develop a practical and living partnership between genders;
- to develop and take responsibility for local surroundings;
- to take responsibility for the physical environment and understand the consequences of an ecological perspective in daily life;
- to understand possibilities and dangers related with an advanced economic/technological society;
- to work for peace and prevent war;
- to live and take responsibility for a multigenerational society;
- to understand media language, and how to cope with the flood of information confronting humankind;
- to understand differences in conditions of life, and work for a fair and just world;
- to understand the internationalizing tendencies and learn to take responsibility to live and function in an international society;
- to understand the dynamics in work and industry, to learn to create an active relationship to work life and the challenges that wait when a major focus of life is work; and
- to take advantage of a boundless learning market, and become capable of developing an individual instructional plan, which incorporates co-

operation between student, home and teacher, and t... electronic market.

Personal Development

It is important for all students that they experience the thrill of real something. An important dimension of personal development is for people to know their strengths and weaknesses. Equally important is that all students find place and room to credit themselves with genuine achievement. That talent can find expression through discourse, dialogue and written form, but it can also come through music, pictures, athletics and play.

Social Development

One of the main features of social development is the movement away from hierarchical structure toward a more horizontal structure. The major reason for a greater mastery of communication and problem-solving skills is that they are a necessity in a horizontal society. Students must learn to function productively in situations where all participate in the decision-making process. They must all become involved in dealing with the major problems confronting society. Those problem solutions cannot be left to those at the peak of the social pyramid. Whereas modern schooling was almost completely oriented toward individual competence and performance, the school of the future must focus more and more on communal competence and performance. Of course, this does not negate individual expression but it must be balanced with common interests and concerns.

The Teacher that Learns

The teacher has the key to the school's future. Without a continuously motivated and qualified teaching staff, all thoughts of the future schools are only day-dreams. Therefore, a central point of educational reform is that the teacher become a central player. The teacher must have an ongoing opportunity to develop further and receive support from colleagues and other resource persons. In other words, if teachers are to help others to learn, they themselves must continuously be engaged in learning. The teacher, in co-operation with other colleagues, must be in a much greater position than is the case today to modify, form and deepen the instructional plan.

The Learning School

The curriculum assumes that teachers, students and others, often must work with assignments where there is no known answer or with an approach where the solution is not fully known. The curriculum assumes that the school develop itself toward a learning organization, where the standard is that the entire staff participates in investigations, does research, works together and creates results together. If such a learning climate exists, the school is able to develop itself into an organization that is continually growing and evolving. It is a learning school.

Fields of Study

In the last few years, the tendency in OECD countries has been to move away from a one-sided theoretical curriculum to a wide spectrum. Even so, it remains difficult, if not impossible, to find some common topology that defines the main structure of

...ulum. Lawton (1983) has, for example, used a form for cultural analysis ...h results in no less than eight curriculum systems dictating the instructional ...an for British secondary schools:

- the social-political
- the economic
- communication
- rationality
- technology
- morality
- faith/belief
- aesthetics.

In the UK, in recent years the tendency has been to locate instructional plans at the local school level, although these plans must now conform, for the first time in modern history, with highly centralized curriculum plans. In this design, the inspector plays a central role in overseeing that consistency exists with regard to specific areas of experience (DES, 1985):

- aesthetics and creativity
- the human and social
- linguistics and literature
- mathematics
- natural sciences
- morality
- physical health
- spiritual development
- technology.

This list is contradictory and is reminiscent of Scandinavian attempts to develop spheres of experience to be found in all school curricula. The tendency is that such lists become quite long and comprehensive, and the elements demanding. Therefore, it is important for planners as well as teachers to ask the critical question, why a given field is included in the curriculum. Any future attempts at general instructional guidelines must include important areas of choice on the part of the teacher. Any school instructional plan must coincide with the specific pedagogical profile that the school has defined for itself.

Many examples are available that demonstrate curriculum plans that are formulated as part of a national framework but which also rely on the individual school to develop its own instructional plan within the context of its own institutional profile. One such example comes from New Zealand (1993), which has developed just such a curriculum framework.

Figure 8.1 is a visual picture from the instructional plan. This plan is based on the following principles:

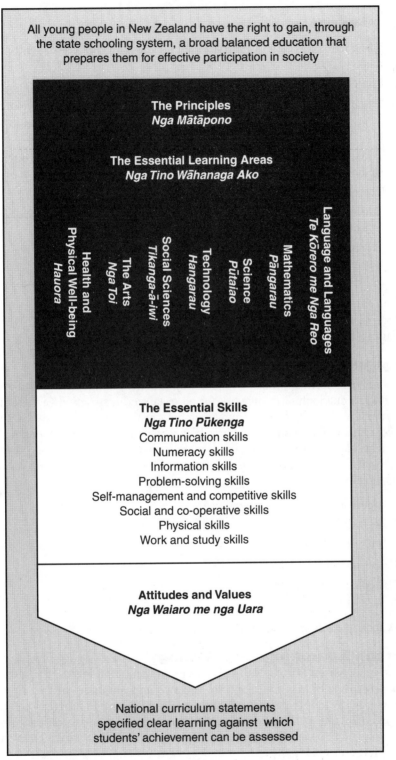

All young people in New Zealand have the right to gain, through the state schooling system, a broad balanced education that prepares them for effective participation in society

The Principles
Nga Mātāpono

The Essential Learning Areas
Nga Tino Wāhanaga Ako

Language and Languages
Te Kōrero me Nga Reo

Mathematics
Pāngarau

Science
Pūtaiao

Technology
Hangarau

Social Sciences
Tikanga-ā-iwi

The Arts
Nga Toi

Health and Physical Well-being
Hauora

The Essential Skills
Nga Tino Pūkenga
Communication skills
Numeracy skills
Information skills
Problem-solving skills
Self-management and competitive skills
Social and co-operative skills
Physical skills
Work and study skills

Attitudes and Values
Nga Waiaro me nga Uara

National curriculum statements specified clear learning against which students' achievement can be assessed

Figure 8.1 *The New Zealand Curriculum Framework, Te Anga Marautanga o Aotearoa*
Source: New Zealand Curriculum Framework (1993)

1 The curriculum establishes direction for learning and assessment in New Zealand schools.

2 The curriculum fosters achievement and success for all students.

3 The instructional plan gives large flexibility to the individual school to develop programmes that address their students, e.g. the allocation of time for specific units is left entirely up to the individual school.

4 The curriculum ensures that learning progresses coherently throughout schooling.

5 The curriculum ensures equality of educational opportunity.

6 The curriculum recognizes the significance of minority cultures and reflects the multicultural nature of New Zealand society.

7 The instructional plan is open-ended and ties New Zealand to the international society

(The New Zealand Curriculum Framework, 1993).

Such a curriculum assumes professional teachers, a close co-operation with parents and industrial society, proficiency in conflict solving, and work with many cultures

THE NORWEGIAN CURRICULUM FRAMEWORK

By introducing Reform 94, the Norwegian Department of Education has taken steps to introduce a curriculum framework for all organized instruction (general part of the curriculum). There are many new elements in this plan. For the first time, all types of educational institutions are being included. As a consequence, the Department has tried to describe the principle direction of instruction, formulated in a way that encourages dialogue and debate. The Department has six main goals for schooling:

1 a person searching for meaning

2 a creative person

3 a working person

4 an enlightened person

5 a co-operating person

6 an environmentally sensitive person.

We now look at each of these in turn.

A Person Searching for Meaning

The plan emphasizes Norway's Christian and humanitarian legacy, the meaning of tolerance (especially in a multicultural society) and emphasis of the democratic state governed by law. It stresses the importance of scientific progress and the scientific process itself. The plan stresses the importance of a moral contract in society and on people as moral beings with their 'ability to seek for that which is true and do that which is right' (KUF, n.d., p. 9).

KUF attempts to find a bridge between the established Christian and humanitarian values of Norway and the cultural legacy, religions and values of others. It does not deal with the possible conflicts that can arise, but it stresses the school's role in facing the conflicts and developing the ability of students to work together.

A Creative Person

The plan emphasizes the need to meet new challenges with expectations and a real desire to overcome contradictions. Schools must build on children's natural desire to learn and must help them utilize their creative ability to the greatest possible degree. Of course, factual knowledge is deemed important because it can stimulate 'dream, fantasy and play' (KUF, undated, p. 12).

In this context, the plan stresses an active student and the scholarly way of work, giving weight to the ability to wonder, to find possible explanations and to help to define ultimate explanations. Concerning education, the plan claims: 'Education must find the difficult balance between respect for established knowledge and the critical attitude that is necessary for developing new knowledge' (KUF, undated, p. 15). It also indicates the existence of ethical questions related to the development of new knowledge and the moral judgments that must be made concerning the use of new knowledge.

A Working Person

The curriculum places great weight on technological developments and the impact new technology has had on the historical epochs of the country. The Norwegian plan claims that 'technology, in its broadest sense, has replaced chance and coincidence with predictability and security' (KUF, undated, p. 17). The plan also recognizes that technology has brought about a tremendous capacity for war and destruction. The task of the school is to clarify the possibilities and dangers of technology, to help students to move from the unfamiliar to the familiar, to develop the capacity to change, to adjust to technological advances and to develop a well-rounded personality. The future demands that formal education be focused on active learning, that the teacher is a central guiding figure, based on 'respect for the integrity of students, sensitivity to their differences, and to their need to test the boundaries and discover new land' (KUF, undated p. 22). It also stresses that learning is teamwork and that the teacher is the team leader.

An Enlightened Person

The curriculum plan demands that Norwegians strive to create an educational programme that contributes to a broad, general enlightenment of the people. This is defined in the follow way:

- concrete knowledge about people, society and nature which ensures a broad overview and perspective;
- experience and maturity to meet life – practically, socially, and personally;
- characteristics and values that facilitate co-operation between people and demonstrate the value and excitement of living together (KUF, n.d., p. 23).

Knowledge that ought to be pursued is enlightened knowledge (*Bildung*); the curriculum plan aims to draw away from the past tendency towards greater and greater specialization and focus on a broad, common understanding. If this is to be achieved, Norway cannot isolate itself from the world, but it must be oriented toward the world and internationalism.

A Cooperating Person

The plan makes plain that the contemporary youth culture is, to a large degree, not involved in the work world. This has contributed to an 'indirect education at the expense of the direct' (KUF, undated, p. 30). The plan emphasizes the obligation and responsibility students must exercise with regard to practical work. The school society itself must function in harmony with other aspects of society. It encourages the establishment of a broad learning environment where students, parents and local society participate.

An Environmentally Sensitive Person

The plan emphasizes the study of nature, ecology and ethics, where real consequences of the Western lifestyle are discussed and debated. 'Our mode of living has deep and threatening consequences for the environment.' The plan emphasizes the need for 'responsible development'. The school's role would be to impart a broad understanding of 'natural sciences and ecological knowledge'.

The Integrated Person

Towards the end of this curriculum document, the concept of the integrated person is discussed, where the various components of the six elements are seen in context. The list of good intentions is becoming fairly long and, towards the end, it says:

> Training must balance dual aims. The schools must provide for a
> comprehensive development of abilities and uniqueness that facilitate moral
> behaviour, creativity and work, and help people learn to function in harmony
> with nature. The training promises to contribute to a character education
> that gives individuals power to take control of their own lives, committed to
> the community life and empathy for the environment.
>
> (KUF, n.d., p. 40)

This instructional plan is an unusually well-shaped and important document for the Norwegian school. Policy makers have chiselled out a vision and a programme that, to a large degree, goes beyond the current sentiments of the Norwegian people.

It is unclear which data the Norwegian Ministry of Education has used to come to the learning needs of the children and youth learning needs. Even though it is possible for us to interpret it, we do not find clear visions for the future of Norway, and we also find little discussion about what forces could hinder and what forces would facilitate a change in the direction of the curriculum framework.

It is likely that consensus can be arrived at with regard to the various subjects of study, but it remains today a centralized plan and a general instructional plan demands thorough planning and wide participation. A vision is something that must be owned by those expected to put the plan into reality.

What this instructional plan does not do, is prioritize the many values and desires that are outlined. The plan is comprehensive and has a number of built-in areas of conflict (including time and resource problems). The curriculum plan does not spell this out, but the only way to resolve the in-built conflicts in the curriculum is to leave room for manœuvring with the individual school.

EDUCATION 2000 CURRICULUM

We shall briefly outline the thinking behind the curriculum renewal that the comprehensive development project *Education 2000* represents (Abbott, 1994). It is stressed that the curriculum incorporates both content and process, and should consider the following six dimensions:

1 *Constantly pursue understanding*: The curriculum must encourage students to think independently. It must induce active engagement, reduce coverage and increase depth. It must help students to understand their own learning.

2 *Select knowledge content*: The curriculum must demonstrate why knowledge is organized into subjects and disciplines, cultivate the use of various symbols, constantly search for connections, confront misconceptions, match the intellectual maturity and capability of the learner, create interest and enjoyment, and learn how to learn.

3 *Educate for the future, not for the past*: The curriculum must include content that anticipates change, demonstrates the changing nature of knowledge, projects present-day concerns into the future and uses modern media.

4 *Emphasize images*: The curriculum must be oriented toward human beings as learners and thinkers, stressing the unique role of human beings as thinkers, celebrating people as the makers, designers, creators and symbolizers, illustrating how people construct understandings by social collaboration and discourse, how people share common problems, and how learning changes the world.

5 *Lifelong orientation*: The curriculum must stress that learners prepare themselves for lifelong learning in a rapidly changing world; they need to become independent and responsible for their own learning. Students face profound moral, ethical and political choices; they need the confidence to choose and the will to act in the absence of certainty and stability.

6 *Technology*: The curriculum must stress that all written knowledge is now available through the enormous power of information technologies, and the purpose of the curriculum shifts to learning how to learn.

We have included these three examples of forward looking curricula, and we can observe major common objectives and fields of study. We will take a step further and propose an outline for a future curriculum framework:

A SKETCH OF A CURRICULUM FRAMEWORK

An illustrative curriculum framework of the future using a simplified model suggests the more important elements that must be considered. It consists of four main areas: nature, culture, myself and others.

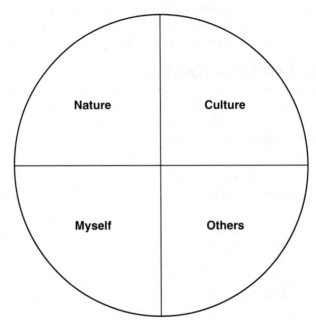

Figure 8.2 *The four areas of a curriculum framework*

Nature

Knowledge, insight and understanding of nature's qualities must be included along with emphasis on ecological understanding. Students must gain a basic insight into the laws of nature, how people must live in harmony with nature, and what can be done to maintain balance in nature. Throughout history, nature has had different meanings for people, and there are also different ways to understand nature. We maintain an understanding of nature demands basic knowledge of natural sciences facts, concepts and procedures, but must also include a foundation for responsible administration of natural resources.

The study of the natural sciences must receive a central place, provided that ecological priorities are included, because people's relationship with nature has created the ecological crisis being experienced today, which will probably become even more difficult in the next century. Insight about the complex interdependence in nature will demand considerable time to learn the basic concepts and laws. Subjects such as biology will have a more central place in the postmodern school. It will emphasize co-operation and conflict in relation to humankind and nature, and the individual student will, to a much greater degree than today, experience nature as part of their learning processes. To the extent possible, natural sciences must include practical relationships with nature and outdoor life and, to a lesser degree, the cultivation of sports.

Culture

Knowledge, insight and understanding of people's history and cultural development must be a standard part of the plan. A review of previous plans indicates that cultural studies have dominated these instructional plans, if we include the study of the community, the humanities and aesthetics. However, we must include the ways cultures have attempted to control and exploit nature and use natural resources for the benefit of cultures. All essential sides of economic and technological culture must be set in focus.

As the world moves toward truly multicultural societies, it is important to understand and assess each individual culture, beginning with the immediate culture in which each person is located. Educational programmes must support efforts for peace, for a responsible solidarity with the world's poor in the broadest sense.

Historical studies will likely place increasing importance on cultural history, history of art, local and foreign religions and languages, provided that the school prioritizes work with a multicultural society. This will not only be important in large urban areas but in rural areas as well. The individual student will have the opportunity to live in a multicultural society and participate either directly in multicultural classes or as part of a travel programme. The instructional plan will emphasize how different cultures throughout history have interacted with nature.

Myself

Knowledge, insight and understanding of 'who I am, how I react and function, and what I must do to work with my own development', is another central area of the instructional plan. The purpose with this part of curriculum is to ensure the development of a sound self-esteem, to gain insight in personal strengths and weaknesses, and to develop positive attitudes toward work and learning (gaining social capital). It is within this part of the curriculum that the student develops attitudes and proficiency in communication skills. Students must be given room to discover themselves, develop artistic and aesthetic abilities, and become proficient at taking care of their own body.

Self-development, proficient study techniques and communication skills, and development of social capital, are a necessary part of the curriculum, because these form the foundation of general school learning. It will be necessary to give high priority to these proficiencies when students come from homes that provide little or no social capital and fail to stimulate and support the learning process. If this does not occur at home, then the school must create the conditions necessary to ensure they occur in formal education. Self-development can best take place where there is cooperation with others and where these become a systematic part of the regular subjects of study. The goal would be to help the students to identify with the subjects of study in such a way that students are motivated and disciplined as they engage in formal learning.

Others

Knowledge, insight and understanding must be gained about how others exist, what motivates other people and how each individual relates with others. This part of the curriculum must be tied to close interpersonal relationships, such as the class, the school and the local environment. It is also important to work with understanding the relationship to other cultures, religions and languages. Part of this aspect of the programme can take place within conventional school walls, but it can be facilitated if the school co-operates with volunteer organizations, organizes travel and uses electronic networks. In this area of the instructional plan, it is clear that the school must be open to the surrounding environment. Without practical co-operation with the neighbourhood and use of electronic networks, the learning resources will be too limited.

THE INTEGRATED INSTRUCTIONAL PLAN

The school instructional plan, until now, has been connected mainly to two sectors: culture and nature. These two sectors have been the focus of the essential school resources in the form of qualified teachers, lesson plans, school books, materials and equipment. These areas of curriculum will continue to be central, but they will also be related to two other sectors: myself and others. The school's integrated instructional plan will attempt to maintain a balance in all four sectors. The school's basic values should steer toward a balance both within each sector and between the sectors. The school's values must leaven the instructional plan and help the school, the teacher and the student to make appropriate choices. Therefore, the instructional process must contribute to a clarification of the values that are central to each school. In fact, the school's values form the core of the school instructional plan, as illustrated in Figure 8.3.

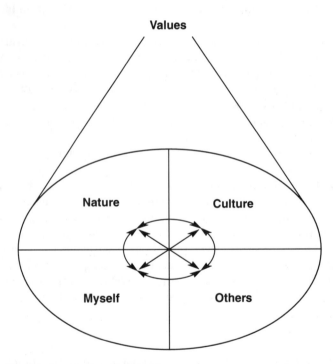

Figure 8.3 *An integrated curriculum framework.*

What are the basic values of a school? In Chapter 4, we have described what we see to be superior societal values that should guide the daily practice of schooling. The school must be founded on healthy democratic values and ethical and moral values supported by the public. In European and North America these values are typically derived from Judeo-Christian and humanitarian traditions. In the coming century, it is imperative that these traditions enter into a dialogue with other religious communities so that the multicultural school can embrace a more comprehensive value and religious tradition.

Even if it attempts to create a common value system, if the past is at all instructive, the school will make provision for different values, though these may best be reflected in the private system. The right to private schools is an important personal right and should not be disadvantaged through bureaucratic and economic sanctions. Everyone must have the right and opportunity to choose an appropriate school, whether it be a home school or an alternative private school.

THE SCHOOL PROFILE

All schools must develop an instructional plan based on a common set of principles that steers the school, the teachers and its leaders. Older students should be active in helping to form the school profile. In the lower schools, parents should be active in discussions of these basic principles. In developing the school instructional plan, the school ought to be able to exercise a certain freedom, but the choices available ought to be consistent with the more general national values, standards and goals. It will be the school's responsibility to demonstrate to the state that its school profile, organization of learning, learning resources and instructional approach contribute to national and international goals, even while it contributes to the development of the local culture.

A school could, for example, prioritize its work by emphasizing communication and co-operation between different cultures, because it sees this as the best preparation for a conflict-filled future and because the local society creates tension between different cultures. Because interpersonal proficiency will, to an increasing degree, stand as an important characteristic of the future, the school could stress co-operative learning. That happens best in small groups, such as small classroom groups, which would expand to the class, and school in general and then to the larger community, and to other cultures.

Central principles ought to be imbedded in local school aims. While its profile reflects the more general priorities, each school profile would be largely defined by the school itself. This must occur through a participatory process where all participants take part in the work to create a common foundation of values for the school and the neighbourhood that carries the responsibility for it.

In addition, the individual teacher must be able to exercise freedom to tailor a learning contract with individual students. Such a contract should not be so designed that all students are expected to conform to the same profile, time, place and content included. The student and the teacher are responsible for designing a programme that stretches the individual student and provides opportunities for each to develop their unique and individual talents. This necessitates special assignments working in the field, working together with other students, using the electronic network and exploiting media options.

A school may be conscious of central imperatives, but the school must also address the needs of the individual student and be in touch with local environmental imperatives. It assumes a professional teacher has great freedom to define how to use resources and freedom to create individualized learning programmes where it is necessary. A student will work as a responsible participant in regard to common goals but also work actively to satisfy individual learning goals.

The individual school has great responsibility with regards to outcomes. Real, interesting contradictions must somehow be solved in the individual school and the local environment. The resolutions have consequences for students, teachers and leaders. The school, in practice, must develop itself in such a way that it is continually a learning organization.

We have in another context pointed to the meaning of the organization of learning for the future students (Dalin and Rolff, 1993). The students that have insight in other people's values, that have taught themselves to listen, that have education with constructive problem solving and conflict solving, will stand much stronger than those that have prepared for a standard test or have been overly influenced by their peer group. If the school is to master this, the students must become active participants in the school continuing to develop. A good school for the twenty-first century is, above all, a learning organization where the learner is in the centre.

How schools ought to develop themselves toward learning organizations is a complex question. That is the theme for the next volume in this series.

Bibliography

Abbott, J. (1987) IMTEC Schoolyear 2020 MAP no. 220.

Abbott, J. (1994) Learning makes sense; recreating education for a changing future, *Education 2000*, Hertfordshire.

Aburdene, P. and Naisbitt, J. (1992) *Megatrends for Women: From Liberation to Leadership*, New York: Random House.

ACOT (1993) *Apple Classroom of Tomorrow Project*, IMTEC Schoolyear 2020 MAP no. 501.

Adams, B.S, Pardo, W. E. and Schneidewind, N. (1992) Changing the way things are done around here, *Educational Leadership*, **49** (4), 37–42.

Adler, J.N. (1994) The importance of a real job, *Los Angeles Times*, 4 January, p. B9.

Adorno, T.W. and Horkheimer, M. (1947) *Dialektik der Aufklärung*, Amsterdam.

Aftenposten (1994) Interview with A. Toffler and E. Morin, 19 January.

Aho, E. (1987) *Education and Communications*, IMTEC Schoolyear 2020 MAP no. 361.

Allerbeck, K.R. and Hoag, W.J. (1985) *Jugend ohne Zukunft*, München/Zürich: Piper.

Allis, S. (1993) Angels among us, *Time*, 27 December, 56–65.

Altman, L.K. (1991) WHO says 40 million will be infected with AIDS virus by 2000, *New York Times*, 18 June.

Anderson, J.R. (ed.) (1981) *Cognitive Skills and their Acquisition*, Hillsdale, NJ: L. Earlbaum Associates.

Anderson, J. (1983) *The Architecture of Cognition*, Cambridge, MA: Harvard University Press.

Anderson, J. (1993) *Integrating Action Research in Washington's Schools*, IMTEC Schoolyear 2020 MAP no. 442.

Anderson, R.H. (1993) *A Total School District Restructuring Effort*, IMTEC Schoolyear 2020 MAP no. 443.

Arac, J. (1986) Introduction, *Postmodernism and Politics*, Minneapolis: University of Minnesota Press.

Aries, P. (1975) *Centuries of Childhood*, New York: Vintage.

Baethge, M., Hantsche, B., Pelull, W. and Voskamp, V. (1989) *Jugend: Arbeit und Identität*, Leske: Opladen.

Bailey, T. (1991) Jobs of the future and the education they will require: evidence from occupational forecasts, *Educational Researcher*, **20** (2) AERA, March.

Bane, M.J. (1976) *Here to Stay: American Families in the Twentieth Century*, New York: Basic Books.

Banks, J.A. (1988) *Multiethnic Education: Theory and Practice*, Boston: Allyn & Bacon.

Banks, J.A. (1993) Multicultural education as an academic discipline. *Multicultural Education*, **1** (3), 12–14.

Baptiste, H.P. Jr and Hughes, K.R. (1993) *Education in a Multicultural Society*, IMTEC Schoolyear 2020 Map no. 490.

Barton, P. (1982) *Worklife Transitions: The Adult Learning Connection*, New York: McGraw Hill.

Bell, D. (1973) *The Coming Post-Industrial Society*, New York: Basic Books.

Bell, D. (1976) *The Cultural Contradictions of Capitalism*, London: Heineman.

Bellah, R.N., Madsen, R., Sullivan, W.M., Swidler, A., and Tipton, S.M. (1985) *Habits of the Heart*, New York: Harper & Row.

Bergh, L. (1993) *Technique-Industry-Future: What Role Can our School Play?* IMTEC Schoolyear 2020 MAP no. 422.

Bergsten, C.F. (1988) *America in the World Economy: A Strategy for the 1990s*, Washington, DC.

Berman, P. and McLaughlin, M. W. (1977) *Federal Programs Supporting Educational Change. IV: The Findings in Review*, Santa Monica, CA: Rand Corporation.

Bernbaum, G. (1993) *From School to Work: A Critical Discussion*, IMTEC Schoolyear 2020 MAP no. 300.

Bernstein, H. (1994) It's a fine line between profit and greed, *Los Angeles Times*, 2 January, p. M5.

Berntsen, T. (1994) Bærekraftig forbruk, *Aftenposten*, 30 January.

Bjørkvold, J.R. (1993) *Det musiske menneske*, Oslo: Freidig Forlag.

Bjorn-Andersen, N. (ed.) (1982) *Information Society: For Richer, for Poorer.* New York: Oxford.

Bjørndal, L. (1988) Skole for Os, *Arbeiderbladet*, 14 May.

Blatt, R. (1987) *Open Education and the Apple Vivarium Project: Multi-Sensory Learning Now and in the Future*, IMTEC Schoolyear 2020 MAP no. 225.

Bloom, A. (1987) *The Closing of the American Mind*, New York: Simon & Schuster.

Bluestone, B. and Harrison, B. (1989) Changing occupational and reward structures, in D.S. Eitzen and M.B. Zinn (eds), *The Reshaping of America*, Englewood Cliffs, NJ: Prentice Hall, pp. 103–07.

Bobbitt, F. (1912) The elimination of waste in education, *Elementary School Journal*, **1 2**.

Böhm, I. and Schneider, J. (1993) *Schools and the World of Work*, IMTEC Schoolyear 2020 MAP no. 430.

Bolam, R. (1987) *The Garth Hill School, England.* IMTEC Schoolyear 2020 MAP no. 221.

Botvin, G.J. and Eng, A. (1982) The efficacy of a multicomponent approach to the prevention of cigarette smoking, *Preventive Medicine*, **1 1**, 199–211.

Bouvier, L.F. and Grant, L. (1994) *How many Americans: Population, Immigration and the Environment*, San Francisco: Sierra Club Books.

Brandenburg Ministry (1993) *Pedagogical Principles of Orientation for the Elementary Schools of Brandenburg*, IMTEC Schoolyear 2020 MAP no. 455.

Brandt, R. (1994) Helping professional dreams come true, *Educational Leadership*, **5 1** (7), p. 3.

Briggs, J. and Peat, F.O. (1989) *Turbulent Mirror: An Illustrated Guide to Chaos*

Theory and the Science of Wholeness, New York: Harper and Row.

Brisco, J. (1991) PennSERVE: The Governor's Office of Citizen Service, *Phi Delta Kappan*, **72** (10), 758–60.

Brock-Utne, B. (1985) *Educating for Peace: A Feminist Perspective*, New York: Pergamon.

Brophy, J. (1982) *Classroom Organization and Management*, Washington DC: National Institute of Education.

Brown vs Board of Education of Topeka (Kansas) (1954) 347 US 483, 74 Sup. Ct. 691.

Brown, A.L. (1980) Megacognitive development and reading, in R.J. Spiro, B.C. Bruce and W.F. Brewer (eds), *Theoretical Issues in Reading Comprehension*, Hillsdale, NJ: L. Earlbaum Associates.

Brown, D., Deardorff, A., and Stern, R. (1992) A North American free trade agreement: analytical issues and a computational assessment, *The World Economy*, **15** (1), 11–30.

Brown, L.R. (ed.) (1984) *State of the World*, New York: W. W. Norton.

Brown, S. (1993) Earning and learn: apprenticeship program pays students to stay in school, *Vocational Education Journal*, **68** (4), 34–5.

Brzezinski, Z. (1970) *Between Two Ages: America's Role in the Technetronic Era*, New York: Viking Press.

Budd, S.A. and Jones, A. (1990) *The European Community: A Guide to the Maze*, 3rd edn, London: Kogan Page.

Canter, L. (1976) *Assertive Discipline*, Santa Monica, CA: Canter and Associates.

Capra, F. (1983) *The Turning Point*, Toronto: Bantam Books.

Carnegie Corporation (1992) A matter of time: risk and opportunity in the nonschool hours. Report of the Task Force on Youth Development and Community Programs, New York: Carnegie Council on Adolescent Development.

Carnegie Corporation (1994) *Frontiers in the Education of Young Adolescents*. Report of conference at Marbach Castle, Germany, 3–5 November.

Carnegie Forum on Education and the Economy (1986) *A Nation Prepared: Teachers for the 21st Century*, Washington, DC: Task Force on Teaching as a Profession.

Carnevale, A.P. and Gainer, L.J. (1989) *The Learning Enterprise*, Washington, DC: US Dept of Labor.

Cawelti, G. (1993) *The National Study of High School Restructuring*, IMTEC Schoolyear 2020 MAP no. 446.

Christensen, K. (1989) The new social organization of work, in D.S. Eitzen and M.B. Zinn (eds), *The Reshaping of America*, Englewood Cliffs, NJ: Prentice Hall.

Christie, N. (1971) *Hvis skolen ikke fantes*, Oslo: Universitetsforlaget.

Cipolla, C.M. (1978) *The Economic History of World Population*, 7th edn, Harmondsworth.

Clark, H. and Sloan, H. (1958) *Classrooms in the Factories*, Rutherford, NJ: Dickinson College.

Clendon, M.M. (1993) Model environmental education summer camp and business plan. Unpublished Master's thesis, Department of Social Ecology, University of California, Irvine.

Coleman, J.S. (1987) Families and schools, *Educational Researcher*, August–

September.

Coleman, J.S. (1988) *Future Schools: Relations to Family and Student*. IMTEC Schoolyear 2020 MAP no. 379.

Coleman J.S. and Hoffer, T. (1987) *Public and Private High Schools: The Impact of Communities*, New York: Basic Books.

Collis, B. and De Vries, P. (1994) New technolgies and learning in the European Community, *THE Journal*, **21** (8), 83–7.

Conrad, D. and Hedin, D. (1981) National Assessment of Experimental Education: Summary and Implications, Center for Youth Development and Research, University of Minnesota.

Conrad, D. and Hedin, D. (1982) The impact of experimental education on adolescent development, *Child and Youth Services*, **4** (3–4), 57–76.

Coombs, P. H. (1968) *The World Educational Crisis*, New York: Oxford University Press.

Council on Environmental Quality (1982) *Global 2000: A Report to the President: Entering the Twenty-first Century*, Washington, DC: US Government Printing Office.

Crane, K., Asch, B. J., Heilbrunn, J.Z. and Cullinanc, D.C. (1990) *The Effect of Employer Sanctions on the Flow of Undocumented Immigrants to the United States*, Santa Monica, CA: Rand Corporation.

Curtin, P., Cochrine, L., Avila, L. and Adams, L. (1994) A quiet revolution in teacher training, *Educational Leadership*, **51** (7), 77–80.

Dalin, Å. (1993) *Kompetanseutvikling i arbeidslivet, Veier til den lærende organisasjon*, Oslo: Cappelen.

Dalin, P. (1987) *Evaluation of the Norwegian Educational Computer Program: Process and Outcomes*, IMTEC Schoolyear 2020 MAP no. 353.

Dalin, P. (1991a) 'Å lære å tenke', *Norsk Skoleblad*, 24–5; 26; 27; 28.

Dalin, P. (1991b) Field notes, Sochi, Russia, 11 September.

Dalin, P. (1994) *How Schools Improve: An International Report*, London: Cassell.

Dalin, P. and Rolff, H.G. (1993) *Changing the School Culture*, London: Cassell.

Dalin, P. and Skrindo, M. (1981) *Læring ved Deltaking*, Oslo: Universitetsforlaget.

Dalin, P., Dollar, B., Rust, V. D., Van den Bosch, L., Kershaw, N., and Skrindo, M. (1983) *Learning from Work and Community Experience*, Windsor: NFER-Nelson Publishing.

Darby, K. (1993) A tale of two cities: school/housing partnership revitalizes arizona towns, *Vocational Education Journal*, **61** (6) 40–1.

de Bono, G. (1994) *De Bono's Thinking Course*, New York: Facts on File.

de Jouvenel, H. (1988) Europe at the dawn of the third millennium: a synthesis of the main trends, *Futures*, **20** (5).

Deakin, N. (1987) *The Politics of Welfare*, London: Methuen.

Department of Education and Science (DES) (1985) *The Curriculum from 5 to 16*, London: HMSO.

Der Spiegel (1993) Intervju med Jürgen Mittelstraß, 18 October.

Derr, B. (1986) *Managing the New Careerists*, London: Jossey-Bass Inc. Publishers.

Deutsch, K. (1961) Social mobilization and political development, *American Political Science Review*, **15** (September), 493–514.

Dewey, J. (1899) *School and Society*, Chicago: University of Chicago Press.

Dewey, J. (1916) *Democracy and Education,* New York: Macmillan Co.

Dixon, R. G. (1994) Future schools and how to get there from here, *Phi Delta Kappan,* **7 5** (5) .

Domini, M. (1993) *Education in a Multicultural Society*, IMTEC Schoolyear 2020 MAP no. 414.

Drucker, P.F. (1989) Changing occupational and reward structures, in D.S. Citzen and M.B. Zinn (eds), *The Reshaping of America*, Englewood Cliffs, NJ: Prentice Hall, 81–84..

Drucker, P.F. (1993) *Managing for the Future: The 1990s and Beyond*. New York: Truman Talley Books.

Dwyer, D. (1994) Apple classrooms of tomorrow: what we've learned, *Educational Leadership,* **5 1** (7), 4–10.

Dyrli, O.E. (1993) The Internet, *Technology & Learning,* **1 4** (2), 50–8.

Economist (1989) *AIDS in Africa*, 25 November 16.

Edelman, G. M. (1992) *Bright Air, Brilliant Fire: On the Matter of the Mind*, New York: Basic Books.

Eder, K. (1982) A new social movement? *Telos*, no. 52 (Summer), 5–20.

Educational Leadership (1994) *Teaching for Understanding*, **5 1** (5), ASCD, VA, USA.

Eisler, R. (1987) *The Chalice and the Blade, Our History, Our Future*, San Francisco: Harper.

Ellul, J. (1981) *Perspectives on Our Age*, New York: Seabury.

Enkenberg, J. (1987) *Information Technology as a Medium of Developing the Municipality and its Educational System*, IMTEC Schoolyear 2020 MAP

Etzioni, A. (1968) *The Active Society: A Theory of Societal and Political Processes*, New York: Free Press.

Everett R. (1971) *School is Dead: Alternatives in Education*, Garden City, NY: Doubleday.

Feinberg, W. (1993) *Japan and the Pursuit of a New American Identity*, New York: Routledge.

Ferrell, D. (1993) Battling the Demons of City Life, *Los Angeles Times*, 22 December, A1; A6–7.

Fortune 500 (1992; 1993) *Fortune* (20 April); (19 April).

Foucault, M. (1984) What is Enlightenment? in Paul Rabinow (ed.), *Foucault Reader*, New York: Pantheon.

Fullan, M. (1984) *External Professional Development Programme*, IMTEC Schoolyear 2020 MAP no. 3.

Galtung, J. (1975) *Peace Education: Problems and Conflicts, in Education for Peace*, Builford: IPC Science and Technology Press.

Gardner, A. B. (1984) *Cultural Pluralism and Other Major Issues in American Education*, IMTEC Schoolyear 2020 MAP no. 308.

Gardner, H. (1993) On teaching for understanding, *Educational Leadership*, **7**, ASCD: Association for Supervision and Curriculum Development.

Gazman, O. (1991) Reform of school organization and management in Russia. Unpublished document on file at IMTEC, Oslo.

Gibbs, N. R. (1993) Angels among us, *Time*, 27 December, 56–62.

Glass, K. H. (1982) Peace – in and out of our homes: A report on a workshop, *Teachers College Record*, **84** (1), 232–9.

Glasser, W. (1981) *Station of the Mind*, New York: Harper & Row.

Godler, Z. (1993) *Education in a Multicultural Society*, IMTEC Schoolyear 2020 MAP no. 415.

Goeudevert, D. (1992) *The Wolfsburger Manifesto - Today*, Wolfsburg: IPI.

Golik, D. (1993) *Development of Humanitarian Education in Ukraine*, IMTEC Schoolyear 2020 MAP no. 453.

Goodchild, S. (1994) Coombes Infant School, an information sheet of the Berkshire Department of Education, Reading, England, 26 July.

Goodlad, J. I. (1975) Transition toward alternatives, in John I. Goodland, G.D. Feustermacher, R. Skager, C. Weinberg, T. J. La Belle and V. D. Rust, *The Conventional and the Alternative in Education*, Berkeley, CA: McCutchan Publishing Corp, 241–68.

Gordon, H. and Demarest, J. (1982) Buberian learning groups: the quest for responsibility in education for peace, *Teachers College Record*, **84** (1), 210–25.

Gore, A. (1993) *Earth in the Balance: Ecology and the Human Spirit*, New York: Plume Book.

Gottschall, D. and Schulte, B. (1991) Mit dem Chaos Leben, *Manager Magazin*, **8**, 138–55.

Gray, D.B. (1985) *Ecological Beliefs and Behaviors*, Westport, CN: Greenwood Press.

Gray, P. (1993) Teach your children well, *Time* (special issue), 69–71.

Greenberg, P. (1992) How to institute some simple democratic practices pertaining to the respect, rights, roots, and responsibilities in any classroom, *Young Children*, July, 10–17.

Greenberger, E. and Steinberg, L. D. (1986) *When Teenagers Work: The Psychological and Social Costs of Adolescent Employment*, New York: Basic Books.

Griffin, D. (1989) Joint ventures: a new agenda for education, *Vocational Journal*, **64** (3).

Grünfeld, B. (1993) Sykdomsbehandling uten noen grense, *Aftenposten*, kronikk, 16 March.

Guardian (1989) Schools which became grant maintained from 1 September 1989, 29 August, 23.

Gulowsen, J. (1984) *Heavy Trends in the World of Work*, IMTEC Schoolyear 2020 MAP no. 311.

Gundem, B. B. (1989) *Skolens oppgave og innhold. En studiebok i didaktikk*, Oslo: Universitetsforlaget.

Gunleiksrud, P. (1990) Med skjegget i postmodernismen, *Norsk Pedagogisk Tidsskrift*, February.

Gutmann, A. (1987) *Democratic Education*, Princeton, NJ: Princeton University Press.

Haavelsrud, M. (1981) *Approaching Disarmament Education*, Guildford, Surrey: Westbury House.

Habermas, J. (1983) Modernity: an incomplete project, 315, in H. Foster (ed.), *The AntiAesthetic: Essays on Postmodern Culture*, Seattle, WA: Bay Press, 3–15.

Habermas, J. (1989) *The New Conservatism*, translated by Shierry Weber Nicholsen, Cambridge, MA: MIT Press.

Haines, C. (1993) *Flexible Change: Managing Learning*, IMTEC Schoolyear 2020 MAP no. 454.

Hall, M. (1991) Gadugi: a model of service learning for Native American communities, *Phi Delta Kappan*, **7 2** (10) 754–7.

Hamburg, B.A. (1994) Education for health futures: health promotion and life skills training. Paper prepared for the Carnegie Corporation's *Frontiers in the Education of Young Adolescents* conference, Marbach Castle, Germany, 3–5 November.

Hameyer, U. (1991) Curriculum theory, in A. Lewy (ed.) *International Encyclopedia of Curriculum*, Oxford/New York: Pergamon.

Hamilton, S.F. (1992) Contrasting vocational education in the United States and West Germany: what a difference a system makes, in V. D. Rust, H. Silberman, and M. Weiner (eds), *Vocational Education: Germany and the United States*, Berlekey, CA: National Center for the Study of Vocational Education.

Hamilton, S.F. and Hamilton, M.A. (1992) A progress report on apprenticeships, *Educational Leadership*, **4 9** (6) , 44–7.

Harding, S. (1991) *Whose Science? Whose Knowledge?*, Ithica, NY: Cornell University Press.

Hassan, I. (1975) Joyce, Beckett, and the postmodern imagination, *Tri Quarterly*, **2 4,** Fall.

Hassan, I. (1982) T*oward a Concept of Postmodernism: The Dismemberment of Orpheus*, Madison: University of Wisconsin Press, 259–71.

Haugen, H. (1988) *Entering Phase 2 of the Norwegian Policy for Information Technology in Education*, IMTEC Schoolyear 2020 MAP no. 397.

Heater, D. (1984) *Peace through Education*, London: Falmer Press.

Hechinger, F. M. (1992) *Fateful Choices: Healthy Youth for the 21st Century*, New York: Carnegie Council on Adolescent Development.

Heller, H. C. and Kiely, M.L. (1994) Hum Bio: Stanford University's human biology curriculum for the middle grades. Paper prepared for the Carnegie Corporation's *Frontiers in the Education of Young Adolescents* conference, Marbach Castle, Germany, 3–5 November.

Helm, L. (1994) Talk is cheap, and now Bells future is rich, *Los Angeles Times*, A1; A26.

Hepburn, M.A. (ed.) (1983) *Education in Democratic Schools and Classrooms*. Washington, DC: National Council for the Social Studies.

Herbert, N. (1987) *Quantum Reality: Beyond the New Physics*, New York: Anchor Books.

Hernes, G. and Knudsen, K. (1976) *Utdanning og Ulikhet*, Oslo: Universitetsforlaget.

Hesse, J.J. and Zöpel, C. (1987) *Zukunft und staatliche Verantwortung*, Baden-Baden: Forum Zukunft, Nomus Verlagsgesellschaft.

Hewton, E. (1986) *Education in Recession*, London: George Allen & Unwin.

Hoachlander, G. (1987) Californias High Schools: Preparing for 2010. Unpublished paper prepared for the California Economic Development Corporation, 24 August.

Hockheimer, M. and Adorno, T.W. (1947) *Dialektik der Aufklärung*

Philosophische Fragmente, Amsterdam: Querido.

Hollin, T. (1993) *A Systematic Change for a School*, IMTEC Schoolyear 2020 MAP no. 458.

Holmes, B. (1983) *International Guide to Educational Systems*, Paris: UNESCO.

Hopkins, A.G. (1987) *Promotion of Experimental Learning through Peer Group Seminars*, IMTEC Schoolyear 2020 MAP no. 157.

Horsfjord, V. and Dalin, P. (1988) Læreren og naturfagsundervisningen, Rapport no. 2, SISS-prosjektet, Oslo: Universitetsforlaget.

Hostrop, R. W. (ed.) (1973) *Foundations of Futurology in Education*, Homewood, IL: ETC Publications.

Hostrop, R. W. (ed.) (1975) *Education beyond Tomorrow*, Homewood, IL: ETC Publications, Foreword.

Howe, I. (1959) Mass society and postmodern fiction, *Partisan Review,* **26** Summer.

Hungerford, H. R. and Volk, T. L. (1990) Changing learner behavior through environmental education, *Journal of Environmental Education,* **21** (3), 8–23.

Hunter, M. (1984) Knowing, teaching and supervising, in I. P. Hosford (ed.), *Using What We Know about Teaching*, Alexandra, VA: Association for Supervision and Curriculum Development.

Hurrelman, K. and Engel, V. (1989) *The Social World of Adolescence, International Perspectives*. Berlin/New York: Walter de Gruyter.

Husen, T. (1972) *Social Background and Educational Career*, Paris: OECD.

Hutchins, C. L. (1987) *Restructuring as the Third Wave Strategy for School Reform*, IMTEC Schoolyear 2020 MAP no. 350.

Hutchins, C. L. (1988) *Design as the Missing Piece in Education*, IMTEC Schoolyear 2020 MAP no. 358.

Huyssen, A. (1986) Mapping the postmodern, in A. Huyssen (ed.), *After the Great Divide: Modernism, Mass Culture, Postmodernism*. Bloomington, IN: Indiana University Press, 3–15.

Hyseni, A. (1993) Education in Multinational Kosova. IMTEC Schoolyear 2020 MAP no. 416.

Illich, Ivan (1970) *Deschooling Society*, New York: Harper & Row.

Inkles, A. and Smith, D. H. (1974) *Becoming Modern*, Cambridge: Harvard University Press.

Jameson, F. (1983) Postmodernism and consumer society, in H. Foster (ed.), *The AntiAesthetic: Essays on Postmodern Culture*, Seattle, Washington: Bay Press, 111–125.

Jameson, F. (1984) Postmodernism, or the cultural logic of late capitalism, *New Left Review,* **146** July/August, 55.

Jencks, C. (1987) *What is PostModernism?* New York: St Martins Press.

Jennings, M. K. and Niemi, R. G. (eds) (1974) *The Political Character of Adolescence: The Influence of Families and Schools*, Princeton, NJ: Princeton University Press.

Johnson, D. W., Johnson, R. T. and Holübec, E. (1991) *Cooperation in the Classroom*, 3rd edn, Edina, MN: Interaction Book.

Johnston, W. J. and Packard, A. E. (1987) *Workforce 2000: Work and Workers for the Twentyfirst Century*, Indianapolis. IN: Hudson Institute.

Johnstone, B. (1988) Fading of the miracle, *Far East Economic Review*, 1 January.

Jones, A. (1988) *Schooling and the World of Work*, IMTEC Schoolyear MAP no. 368.

Jordan, S. (1993) *The Impact of EC Programmes on Educational Transformation in East Germany*, IMTEC Schoolyear 2020 MAP no. 426.

Joyce, B., Rolheiser-Bennett, C. and Showers, B. (1987) *Students Growth and Models of Teaching*, IMTEC Schoolyear 2020 MAP no. 358.

Junne, G. and Birman, J. (1989) The impact of biotechnology on European agriculture, in E. Yoxen and V. Di Martino (eds), *Biotechnology in Future Society*, Aldershot: Gower.

Kagen, J. (1994) Interview, *Newsweek*, 7 February.

Kahn, H. and Wiener, A. J. (1967) *The Year 2000: A Framework for Speculation on the Next ThirtyThree Years*, New York: Free Press.

Kanning, R. G. (1994) What multimedia can do in our classrooms, *Educational Leadership*, **51** (7), 40–44.

Kennedy, P. (1993) *Preparing for the Twenty-first Century*, New York: Random House.

Kern, H. and Schumann, M. (1986) *Das Ende der Arbeitsteilung? Rationalisierung in der Industriellen Production*, Munich: R. Piper & Co.

Kiuru, S. (1988) *The Role of Broadcasting*, IMTEC Schoolyear MAP no. 369.

Klausmeier, H. J. and Goodwin, W. (1971) *Learning and Human Abilities: Educational Psychology*, New York: Harper & Row.

Knight, B. (1988) *Flexible School Day Patterns for the Future*, IMTEC Schoolyear 2020 MAP no. 375.

Knight, T. (1987) *Education for Democratic Future*, IMTEC Schoolyear 2020 MAP no. 355.

Knight, T (1988) *A Democratic Apprenticeship in Primary School*, IMTEC Schoolyear 2020 MAP no. 222.

Knight, T. (1993) *A Human Service Society: Renewing the Relationship between Education, Work, and Schooling*, IMTEC Schoolyear 2020 Map no. 425.

Kohonen, V. (1988) *Towards Experimental Learning in Elementary Language Education*, IMTEC Schoolyear MAP no. 233.

Konttinen, R. (1987) *Integrating the Computer as a Tool in the School Work*, IMTEC Schoolyear 2020 MAP no. 219.

Korczak, J. (1992) Hur man älskar et barn, Stockholm: HLS Publishers.

Kreitzberg, P. (1993) *Democratic vs. Scientific and Expert Legitimation*, IMTEC Schoolyear 2020 MAP no. 482.

Kroes, R. (1988) *High Brow Meets Low Brow: American Culture as an Intellectual Concern*, Amsterdam: Free University Press.

Krüger, A. (1993) Local communities and urban regeneration: the contribution of community education, *Community Development Journal*, **28** (4), 342–54.

Krüger, A., and Buhren, C.G. (1992) *Community Education in Germany: Development, Concept, Practice*, Essen: COMED, e.V.

Krylova, N. B. (1993) *Sociocultural Conditions for Educational Democracy in Russia*, IMTEC Schoolyear 2020 MAP no. 478.

KUF (n.d.) Læreplan for grunnskole, videregående opplæring, voksenopplæring – Generell del, Oslo.

Küng, H. (1990) *Etikk for verdens fremtid*, Oslo: Gyldendal forlag.

Kupchan, C.A. (1994) What Ukraine especially needs now is a little more nationalism, *Los Angeles Times*, 27 November, M2.

Kurtakko, K. (1988) *Environment Centered Education and Instruction in School: The OKO Project and New Approaches to Education*, IMTEC Schoolyear 2020 MAP no. 223.

Kwiecinska, A. and Gokas, K. (1993) *How to Develop A Democratic Culture of School in the Changing Polish Society?* IMTEC Schoolyear 2020 MAP no. 401.

Laaksonen, T. (1987) *Nokia Information Systems*, IMTEC Schoolyear 2020 MAP no. 370.

LaBelle, T. J. (1981) An introduction to the nonformal education of children and youth, *Comparative Education Review*, **25** (3), 315–29.

Lasch, C. (1978) *Culture of Narcissism*, New York: Norton.

Lasch, S. (1990) *Sociology of Postmodernism*, London: Routledge.

LAUSD (Los Angeles Unifed School District) (1993) *Humanities Approach to Culture: Hands Across the Campus Program*, Draft Copy, Los Angeles: Los Angeles Unified School District.

Lawton, D. (1983) *An Introduction to Curriculum Research and Development*, London: Heinemann.

Leino, J. (1987) *New Technology and Teachers Knowledge Accessing Modes*, IMTEC Schoolyear 2020 MAP no. 356.

Lemke, H. (1984) *Development of New Occupational Training Structure for the Industrial Metal Working and Electrical Enngineering Occupations in the Federal Republic of Germany*, IMTEC Schoolyear 2020 MAP no. 158.

Leonard, G.B. (1974) How we will change? *Intellectual Digest,* June.

Lerner, D. (1958) *The Passing of Traditional Society*, New York: Free Press.

Levin, H. (1969) What was modernism? *Massachusetts Review,* **1**, August.

Levin, H. (1976) Educational Opportuntiy and social inequality in Western Europe. *Social Problems,* **24** (2), pp. 148–72.

Levin, H. (1993) Education for democracy: Western Europe and the US State of the Art. Paper prepared for the IMTEC Fourth International School Year 2020 Conference, Bogensee, Germany, 5 September.

Lewis, D. and Greene, J. (1990) *Thinking Better*, New York: Holt, Rinehart & Winston.

Liegle, L. (1990) Vorschulerziehung, in O. Anweiler, W. Mitter, H. Peisert, H.P. Schäfer and W. Stratenwerth (eds), *Vergleich von Bildung und Erziehung in der Bundesrepublik Deutschland und in der Deutschen Demo-kratischen Republik*, Köln: Verlag Wissenschaft und Politik.

Liket, T. (1991) Dutch experience with school choice: implications for american education. Unpublished paper.

Lobocki, M. (1993) *Altruism as an Urgent Educational Task*, IMTEC Schoolyear 2020 MAP no. 480.

Lockhead, M.E. (1986) Teaching analytic reasoning skills through pair problem solving, in J.W. Segal, S.F. Chipman and R. Glaser (eds), *Thinking and Learning Skills*, 1, Hillsdale, NJ: Erlbaum.

Lockhead, M.E. and Verspoor, A.M. (1991) *Improving Primary Education in Developing Countries*, Washington DC: Oxford Press.

Lorand, F. (1993) Contradictions in the Democratization process of public education in Hungary, IMTEC Schoolyear 2020 MAP.

Los Angeles Times (1990) For the strong, a new dynamic of power. A World Report Special Edition: Seeking a New World, 11 December.

Lowell Elementary School (1984) *Lowell Elementary Sparkle Proposal Schools of the 21st Century Project for Washington State Legislature*, IMTEC Schoolyear 2020 MAP no. 226.

Lyotard, J.-F. (1984) *The Postmodern Condition: A Report on Knowledge*, G. Bennington and B. Massumi (trans. of original (1979) French edn), Minneapolis: University of Minnesota Press.

McCune, S., Jesse, D., Brown, J. and McFairland, K. (1988) *Educational Restructuring and an Agenda for the 21st Century*, IMTEC Schoolyear 2020 MAP no. 378.

Machlup, F. (1962) *The Production and Distribution of Knowledge in the United States*. Princeton: Princeton University Press.

McPherson, K. (1991) Project service leadership, *Phi Delta Kappan,* **72** (10), 750–3.

Malthus, T. R. (1798) *An Essay on the Principle of Population as It Affects the Future Improvement of Society*, London; printed and reviewed (1965), J. Bonar, New York.

Mannheim, K. (1936) *Ideology and Utopia,* L. Wirth and E. Shils (trans.), New York: Harcourt, Brace & World.

Marcuse, H. (1966) *Eros and Civilization*, Boston: Beacon Press.

Marton, F., Hounsell, D. and Entwistle, N. (1984) *The Experience of Learning*, Edinburgh: Scottish Academic Press.

Marzano, R. and Dole, J. (1983) *Teaching relationships and pattern of information*, Denver: Mid-Continent Regional Educational Laboratory.

Maslow, A. H. (1971) *The Farther Reaches of Human Nature,* New York: Viking Press.

Mathismoen, O. (1993) Sårbart matfat, *Aftenposten,* 15 October.

Max-Neef, M.A. (1992) *From the Outside Looking In: Experiences in 'Barefoot Economics'*, London: Atlantic Highlands.

Mayeas, D. (1978) About women: the post-divorce poly-family, *Los Angeles Times,* 7 May.

Meadows, B. V. (1972) World III, *Limits to Growth.*

Meadows, B. V. (1993) Through the eyes of parents, *Educational Leadership,* **51** (2), 31–4.

Meadows, D. H. (1974) *The Limits to Growth: A Report for the Club of Rome's Project on the Predicament of Mankind*, New York: Universe Books.

Meyer-Dohm, P. (1988) Neue Technologien: Herausforderung fuer die Qualifikation der Mitarbeiter im Betrieb, in S. Bachmann, M. Bohnet and K. Lompe (eds), *Industriegesellschaft im Wandel: Chancen und Risiken heutiger Modernisierungsprozesse*, Hildesheim: Olms Weidmann, 169–88.

Mittelstraß, J. (1993) Thesen zum Begriff schulischer Bildung, Internt Skrift. Unpublished paper.

Moi, T. (1988) Feminism, Postmodernism, and Style: Recent Feminist Criticism in the United States, *Cultural Critique,* **9** (Spring), 3–22.

Moynihan, D.P. (1993) *Pandemonium: Ethnicity in International Politics*. New York: Oxford University Press.

Nahrstedt, W. (1990) *Die Enstehung der Freizeit,* Göttingen: Vandenhocck & Ruprecht.

Naisbitt, J. and Aburdene, P. (1990) *Megatrends 2000: Ten New Directions for the 1990s,* New York: Avon Books.

Nathan, J. and Kielsmeier, J. (1991) The sleeping giant of school reform, *Phi Delta Kappan,* **7 2** (10), 739–42.

National Alliance of Business (1989) *The Compact Project: School-Business Partnerships for Improving Education,* Washington, DC: National Alliance of Business.

National Commission on Secondary Vocational Education (1984) The unfinished agenda: the role of vocational education in the High School, Columbus, OH: The National Center for Research in Vocational Education, Ohio State University.

National Education Association (NEA) (1984) *Action Plan for Restructuring Schools: The Learning Laboratories,* IMTEC Schoolyear 2020 MAP no. 231.

NCEE (National Center on Education and the Economy) (1990) *America's Choice: High Skills or Low Wages,* Rochester, New York: National Center on Education and the Economy.

Newmann, F.M. and Wehlage, G. C. (1993) Five standards of authentic instruction, *Educational Leadership,* ASCD, **5 0** (7).

New York Times (1991) A Latin American ecological alliance (paid announcement), 22 July.

New Zealand Curriculum Framework (1993). Wellington: Ministry of Education.

Newton, E. (1986) *Education in Recession,* London: George Allen & Unwin.

Newton, E. (1988) *Implementation of a Provincial School Improvement Program; Problems and Possibilities for 2020,* IMTEC Schoolyear 2020 MAP no. 390.

Nicholson, C. (1989) Postmodernism, feminism, and education: the need for solidarity, *Educational Theory,* **3 9**, 197–205.

Nickerson, R. (1984) Kinds of thinking taught in current programs, *Educational Leadership,* **4 2** (1), 26–37.

Niemonzynski, A., Dorczak, R., Stepski, M., Kwiecinska, A. and Gokas, K. (1993) *How to Develop a Democratic Culture of School in the Changing Polish Society,* IMTEC Schoolyear 2020 MAP no. 401.

Noewle, T. (1993) Growing up responsible, *Educational Leadership,* **5 1** (3).

Nonaka, I. (1988) Creating organizational order out of chaos: self-renewal in Japanese firms, *California Management Review (*Spring), 57–73.

Odmark, T. (1993) *From Detailed State Regulation to Municipal Wisdom: A Change of Paradigm in Swedish School Politics: The Uppsala Project,* IMTEC Schoolyear 2020 MAP.

OECD (Organisation for Economic Co-operation and Development) (1989) *Schools and Quality. An International Report,* Paris: OECD

Opasschowski, H.W. (1983) *Arbeit, Freizeit, Lebenssinn?* Leverkusen: Lelske.

Orr, D.W. (1992) *Ecological Literacy: Education and the Transition to a Postmodern World,* Albany: SUNY Press.

Owen, J.D. (1986) *Working Lives: The American Work Force since 1920,*

Lexington, MA: Lexington Books.

Owens, C. (1983) The discourse of others: feminists and postmodernism, in H. Foster (ed.). *The Anti-Aesthetic: Essays on Postmodern Culture*, Seattle: Bay Press.

Papadakis, E. and Taylor-Goodby, P. (1987) *The Private Provision of Public Welfare*, Brighton: Wheatsheaf.

Paul, R. (1984) Critical thinking: fundamental to education for a free society, *Educational Leadership*, **42**, (1).

Paulston, R.G. (1976) *Conflicting Theories of Social and Educational Change*, Pittsburgh: University Center for International Studies, University of Pittsburgh.

Pentz, M.A., Dwyer, J.H., Mackinnon,, D.P., Flay, B.R., Hansen, W.B., Wang, E.Y.I. and Johnson, A. (1989) A multi-community trial for primary prevention of adolescent drug abuse: effects on drug use prevalence, *Journal of American Medical Education*, **261**, 3259–3266.

Perelman, L. J. (1990) *Further Education and Training of the Labour Force: Country Reports: United States*, Paris: Organisation for Economic Cooperation and Development (OECD).

Peters, T. (1987) *In Search of Excellence*, New York: Harper Collins.

Pickover, C. (1990) *Computers, Pattern, Chaos, and Beauty*, New York: St Martin's Press.

Pirsig, R. M. (1974) *Zen and the Art of Motorcycle Maintenance*, New York: Bantam.

Population Today (1988), **16** (1).

Postman, N. (1987) *Will the New Technologies of Communication Weaken or Destroy What is Most Worth Preserving in Education and Culture?* IMTEC Schoolyear 2020 MAP no. 360.

Purkey, S.C. and Smith, M.S. (1983) Effective schools: a review, *The Elementary School Journal*, **83**, no. 4.

Raaen, F.D. (1984) *The School in its Local Environment*, IMTEC Schoolyear 2020 MAP no. 142.

Ragsdale, R. (1987) *Computers in the School of the Future*, IMTEC Schoolyear 2020 MAP no. 362.

Ragsdale, R.G. and Durell, B. (1994) Final Report: Happy Valley Computer Project, presented to the Rural County Board of Education, January.

Reimer, E. (1971) *School is Dead, An Essay on Alternatives in Education*, Garden City, NY: Doubleday.

Reitan, T. (1984) *Open Schools in Norway*. IMTEC Schoolyear 2020 MAP no. 215.

Rennie, J. (1993) School and the community: a state art. Paper on Community Education, IMTEC Schoolyear 2020 MAP.

Resnick, L. (1983) Toward a cognitive theory of instruction, in S. Paris, G. Olson and H.W. Stevenson (eds), *Learning and Motivation in the Classroom*, Hillsdale, NY: Erlbaum.

Reynolds, D. (1988) *Effective Schools Research in Great Britain: The End of the Beginning*, IMTEC Schoolyear 2020 MAP no. 373.

Richert, G. (1988) *InterAgency Collaboration for Schools of the 21st Century*, IMTEC Schoolyear 2020 MAP no. 394.

Ricoeur, P. (1965) *History and Truth*, Evanston, IL: Northwestern University Press.

Riedl, R. and Carroll, S. (1993) Impact North Carolina: 21st century education, *THE Journal*, **21** (3) October, 85–9.

Rogel, J. (1984) *Action Research on Cooperative Learning*, IMTEC Schoolyear 2020 MAP no. 228.

Röhrs, H. (1983) Frieden-Eine Pädagogische Aufgabe. Idee und Realität der Friedenspädagogik, Agenter Pedersen: Westermann.

Röhrs, H. (1994) *The Pedagogy of Peace as a Central Element in Peace Studies: A Critical Review and an Outlook on the Future,* pamphlet No. 63 of Peace Education Miniprints, Malmö, Sweden.

Rolff, H.-G. (1988) *Preparing for the Information Society*, IMTEC Schoolyear 2020 MAP no. 380.

Rolph, E.S. (1992) *Immigration Policies: Legacy from the 1980s and Issues for the 1990s*, Santa Monica, CA: Rand Corporation.

Roosens, E. (1994) Education for living in pluriethnic societies. Paper prepared for the Carnegie Corporation's *Frontiers in the Education of Young Adolescents* conference, Marbach Castle, Germany, 3–5 November.

Rorty, R. (1979) *Philosophy and the Mirror of Nature*, Princeton: Princeton University Press.

Rorty, R. (1990) The dangers of over-philosophication–reply to Arcilla and Nicholson, *Educational Theory,* **40** Winter 41–5.

Rust, V. D. (1978/79) An educational interpretation of Marcusian thought, *Philosophy of Education: Proceedings of the Far West Philosophy of Education Society,* **12**.

Rust, V. D. (1989) *The Democratic Tradition and the Evolution of Schooling in Norway*, Westport, CN: Greenwood Press.

Rust, V. D. (1993) *The Transformation of East German Education: The Case of Blenheim Street School in Berlin,* IMTEC Schoolyear 2020 MAP.

Rust, V. D. and Dalin, P. (1985) Computer education Norwegian style: a comprehensive approach, *Educational Technology,* **25** (6), 17–20.

Rust, V. D. and Dalin, P. (eds) (1990) *Teachers and Teaching in the Developing World,* New York: Garland Press.

Rust, V. D. and Schofield, T. (1978) The West German sports club system: a model for lifelong learning, *Phi Delta Kappan*, April, 54–36.

Rust, V. D., Knost, P. and Wichmann, J. (eds) (1994) *Education and the Values Crisis in Cental and Eastern Europe,* Frankfurt am Main: Peter Lang.

Sandvand, J.E. (1994) Vi ler ikke lenger av 'Ola Dunk', *Aftenposten,* 19 February.

Sayer, J. (1993) *Education for Democracy*, IMTEC Schoolyear 2020 MAP no. 482.

SCANS (The Secretary's Commission on Achieving Necessary Skills) (1992) *Learning a Living. A Blueprint for High Performance*, Washington: US Dept of Labour.

Scherer, M. (1992) School snapshot: focus on African–American culture, *Educational Leadership,* **49** (4), 17–19.

Schierbeck, O. (1994) *Ondskapens automatikk*, København: Politiken, 19 February.

Schlechty, P.C. (1991) *Schools for the 21st Century*, San Francisco: Jossey-Bass.

Schlesinger Jr., A.M. (1995) The disuniting of America: reflections on a multicultural society, in J.A. Shapiro and A. Shapiro (eds), *Campus Wars: Multiculturalism and the Politics of Difference,* Boulder: Westview Press, 226–34.

Schmidt, H. (1983) Technological change, employment and occupational qualifications, *Vocational Training Bulletin,* **11**, June.

Schmidt, H. (1992) German vocational education and the dignity of work, in *Vocational Education: Germany and the United States,* V. D. Rust, H. Silberman and M. Weiner (eds) Berkeley, CA: National Center for the Study of Vocational Education.

Schumann, M. and Wittemann, K. P. (1985) Entwisklungstendenzen der Arbeit im Productionsbereich, in E. Altvater, M. Baethge, and others (eds), *Arbeit 2000: Über die Zukunft der Arbeitsgesellschaft,* Hamburg: VSE Verlag, 32–50.

Schwann, G. (1986) Das deutsche Amerikabild seit der Weimarer Republik. *Aus Politik und Zeitgeschichte,* 31–5.

Scott Paper Company and Lowell Elementary School (1988), IMTEC Schoolyear 2020 MAP no. 227.

Scott, P. (1990) Reaching beyond enlightenment, T*imes Higher Education Supplement,* 24 August, 28.

Senge, P.M. (1990) *The Fifth Discipline, The Art and Practice of the Learning Organisation,* New York: Doubleday Currency.

Shanker, A. (1987) *The Role of the Teacher in Year 2020.* Presentation at the School Year 2020 Conference, Finland. IMTEC 1987.

Silcox, H. (1991) Abraham Lincoln High School: community service in action, *Phi Delta Kappan,* **72** (10), 758–9.

Sills, D. and Merton, R.K. (eds) (1991) *International Encyclopedia of Social Science,* vol. 19, 70.

Simmons, J. (1974) Economic development and educational reform: a research proposal, Washington, DC: World Bank.

Sivard, R.L. (1987) W*orld Military and Social Expenditures 1987–88,* Washington, DC: World Priorities.

Sleeter, C.E. (ed.) (1991) *Empowerment through Multicultural Education,* Albany, NY: State University of New York Press.

Sloan, D. (1982) Toward an education for a living world, *Teachers College Record,* **84** (1), 1–14.

Smith, S.L. (1980) *Schooling: More or Less,* Auckland, NZ: Jacaranda Press.

Smolowe, J. (1993) Intermarried ... with children, *Time* (special issue), Fall, 64.

Soja, E.W. (1989) *Postmodern Geographics: The Reassertion of Space in Critical Social Theory,* London: Verso.

Solmon, L. (1992) An economics perspective of vocational education, in V. D. Rust, H. Silberman, and M. Weiner (eds), *Vocational Education: Germany and the United States,* Berkeley, CA: National Center for the Study of Vocational Education.

Southeimer, M. (1990) Die Erde ist voll, *Die Zeit,* **52** (21 December), 15–17.

SSB (1978) *Historisk statistikk,*Oslo.

SSB (1992) *Utdanningsstatistikk, videregående skole,* Oslo

Stammer, L.B. (1993) Astonishing religious revival abloom in Russia: study finds, *Los Angeles Times* (25 December), B6.

Stanek, M. (1993) *Demands of the Labour Market and Education in the Czech Republic,* IMTEC Schoolyear 2020 MAP no. 431.

Stevenson, H. and Stigler, J. (1992) *The Learning Gap*, New York: Summit Books.

Svingby, G. (1993) Effektive kunnskaper, *Bedre skole*, **2**.

Sykorova, A. (1993) *The Position of a Teacher in the Process of Social Change*, IMTEC Schoolyear 2020 MAP no. 477.

Sylvester, R. (1985) Research on memory: major discoveries, major educational challenges, *Educational Leadership*, **42** (7), 69–75.

Task Force on Economic Adjustment and Worker Dislocation (1986) *Economic Adjustment and Worker Dislocation in a Competitive Society*, Washington, DC: US Department of Labor.

Taylor, F. (1911) *The Principles of Scientific Management*, New York: Harper and Row.

Technology in Education Act of 1993–S. 1040 (1994) *THE Journal*, **21** (1), 8.

Tella, S. (1994) New information and communication technology as a change agent of an open learning environment, Pt 2, Department of Teacher Education, University of Helsinki, Research Report 133.

Thomas, D.C. and Klare, M.T. (1989) *Peace and World Order Studies*, Boulder, CO: Westview Press.

Toffler, A. (1970) *Future Shock*, New York: Bantam.

Toffler, A. (1980) *The Third Wave*, New York: Bantam Books.

Toffler, A. (1983) *Previews and Premises*, New York: Bantam Books.

Toffler, A. (1990) *Powershift: Knowledge, Wealth, and Violence at the Edge of the 21st Century*, New York: Bantam Books.

Totten, S. (1982) Activist educators, *Teachers College Record*, **84** (1), 199–209.

Toynbee, A. (1954) *A Study of History*, IX, London: Oxford University Press.

Tyler, R. (1985) *Basic Principles of Curriculum and Instruction*, Chicago: University of Chicago Press.

Udgaard, M. (1992) Valuta som politisk seismograf, *Aftenposten*, 11 September.

UNICEF (1988) *The State of the World's Children*, New York: Oxford University Press.

US News and World Report (1993)Outlook.

van Daele, H. (1991) Education and Changing Social Realities in Europe. Paper presented at the Comparative and International Education conference, Pittsburgh, 14–17 March.

Versteeg, D. (1993) The rural high school as community resource, *Educational Leadership*, **50** (7), 54–5.

Vilarmau, J. M. (1993) *The Feabe Scheme (EC and Catalonia)*, IMTEC Schoolyear 2020 MAP no. 421B.

Vision: California 2010 (1988) A Special Report to the Governor, Sacramento: California Economic Development Corporation.

von Reichard, C. (1992) Kommunales Management im internationalen Vergleich, *Der Städtetag*, 12 January.

von Weizsacker, E.U. (1992) *Why the North Must Act First*, Geneva: International Academy for the Environment.

Voutuilainen, T. (1987) *Developing Effective Thinking Skills*, IMTEC Schoolyear 2020 MAP no. 357.

Wald, S. (1992) Biotechnology, agriculture and food, *OECD Observer*, no. 177.

Wallis, C. (1994) A class of their own, *Time*, 31 October, 52–61.

Waltner, J.C. (1992) Learning from scientists at work, *Educational Leadership,* **49** (6), 48–52.

Weiler, H.N. (1983) Legalization, expertise, and participation: strategies of compensatory legitimation ineducational policy, *Comparative Education Review,* **27**, 259–77.

Wertheimer, M. (1945) *Productive Thinking,* New York: Harper & Row.

Weugelers, W. (1988) *The modular approach in The Netherlands: a technical Rationality in the Relationship between Education and Labor,* IMTEC Schoolyear 2020 MAP no. 160.

White, A. (1988) *Education in the Information Age,* IMTEC Schoolyear 2020 MAP no. 376.

Williams, R. and Heritage, M. (1988) Increasing lay power in school site management: comparing and contrasting England and Chicago, IMTEC Schoolycar 2020 MAP no. 383.

World Population Prospects (1988) United Nations Population Division, New York.

World Resources, 1990-1991 (1990) World Resources Institute and International Institute for Environment and Development, New York/Oxford.

Your Resource Guide to Environmental Organizations (1991), Irvine, CA: Smiling Dolphin Press.

Index